World Food

PORTUGAL

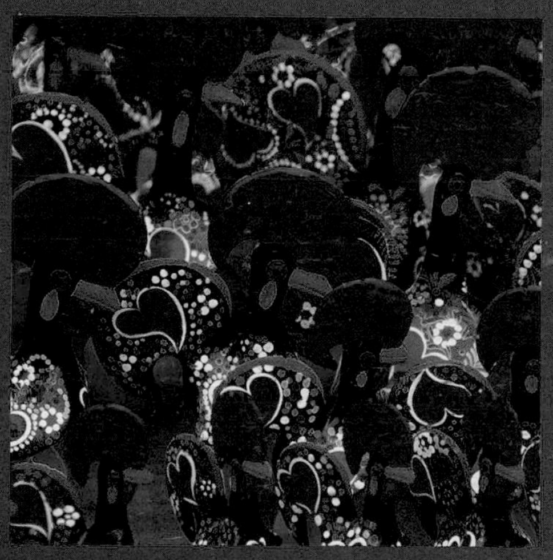

Lynelle Scott-Aitken
Clara Vitorino

WORLD FOOD Portugal
1st edition – August 2002

Published by Lonely Planet Publications Pty Ltd ABN 36 005 607 983

Lonely Planet Offices
Australia Locked Bag 1, Footscray, Victoria 3011
USA 150 Linden Street, Oakland CA 94607
UK 10a Spring Place, London NW5 3BH
France 1 rue du Dahomey, 75011 Paris

Publishing manager Peter D'Onghia
Series editor Lyndal Hall
Series design & layout Brendan Dempsey
Editor Joanne Newell
Mapping Natasha Velleley
Photography Carl Clemens Gros

Photography
Many of the photographs in this book are available for licensing from Lonely Planet Images: www.lonelyplanetimages.com

Front cover – Egg pastries with sweet egg shreds, Portalegre, Alentejo
Back cover – Uncorking the local white wine, Monsaraz, Évora, Alentejo

ISBN 1 86450 111 1

Printed by The Bookmaker International Ltd
Printed in China

10 9 8 7 6 5 4 3 2 1

MAP KEY

Place to Eat & Drink	Place to Eat & Drink
Building	Building
Mall	Mall
Plaza Square	Plaza Square
Urban	Urban
Park, Garden	Park, Garden
Sports Ground	Sports Ground

- International Border
- Regional Border
- Freeway
- Primary Road
- Secondary Road
- Tertiary Road
- Wall
- Railway, Station

- National Capital
- Town
- Mountain
- Church
- Fort
- Museum
- Ruins
- E1 Route Number

About the Authors

Lynelle Scott-Aitken spent an idyllic childhood in Tasmania supping on the spoils of her crayfisherman father, foraging for food in the organic family garden and reading books. She left home at 15 to learn how to cook properly and, via a two year detour in Paris, ended up in Sydney, a qualified chef with a degree in religion and literature. She persuaded *Vogue Entertaining* to publish her unruly comments on food and produce, and she has since spent substantial time as food editor of *Australian Country Style* and editor of the only fashionable magazine for herbivores, *GourmetVeg* (and www.gourmetveg.com.au). She's also found time to start (and finish) a Masters in journalism. She's happiest trotting the globe in search of food and wine epiphanies, and her spiral of addiction led her to Lonely Planet, and the enviable task of eating, drinking and writing about it for the World Food series. She likes to call it work.

Lynelle wishes to thank Cristina Salsinha at the Lisbon office of the national tourist organisation, ICEP, for her extraordinary work in putting together an itinerary that had us visiting every nook and cranny of the country armed with daunting lists of local contacts. Her surname means 'Little Parsley', and this inspired us to look for food-related family names (which then made their way into the manuscript). She was our anchor. Thanks to all the people too numerous and generous to list who shared the secrets of their beloved regions and tables, and fed us to bursting point. Final thanks go to Robert Leys, without whose unerring support before, during and after, and masterful driving in treacherous conditions, this book would have remained an imaginative figment.

Clara Vitorino is a Portuguese literature teacher and has also worked as a translator. She gained a Masters degree in modern French literature and she is currently undertaking research towards a PhD on 17th century Spanish and Portuguese literature. Clara works in consultation with AmeriConsulta, Lda, a Lisbon-based company that provides educational, translating and editing services to clients worldwide. It's owned and managed by Audrey Un and Paula Fassman – Americans who have lived in Portugal for many years.

Clara wishes to thank Cláudio Silva, Kyle Oliveira, Dionisio Martínez and Wendy Graça for their first-hand knowledge and unflagging moral support. And a special thanks to Anne and António Parada, Fernando and Helena Afonso, Candida and Hugo Coelho, Ana Maria Rodrigues, Paulo Parada and António Silvano.

About the Photographer

Carl Gros was born in Germany. He studied photography in London, then kicked up his heels in the world of fashion photography, with a studio in

New York and several years working in Paris. He was most recently based in Sydney, where he photographed for Australia's top food magazines. His only interest has ever been to photograph people, places and objects of beauty, and he especially enjoys the edible perks of food and travel work.

Carl would especially like to thank Cristina Salsinha from the Lisbon office of ICEP, whose highly professional assistance enabled him to get under the surface of life in Portugal. Her guidance was exceptional.

From the Publisher

This first edition of *World Food Portugal* was edited by Joanne Newell and designed by Brendan Dempsey. Natasha Velleley mapped, Shelley Muir proofed and Lyndal Hall oversaw the book's production and indexed, while Peter D'Onghia, manager, dealt with big picture issues. Thanks to Lonely Planet Images for coordinating the supply of photographs, and for captioning, cataloguing and pre-press work. A big thank you to Mark Germanchis in the Melbourne office for production advice. Thanks also to Fernando Goncalves of Sagres restaurant in Elwood, Australia, and to Roberto Burdese of the Slow Food association in Bra (Italy). And finally, thanks must go to photographer Greg Elms for providing us with a selection of extra images.

WARNING & REQUEST

Things change – prices go up, schedules change, good places go bad and bad places go bankrupt – nothing stays the same. So, if you find things better or worse, recently opened or long since closed, please tell us and help make the next edition even more accurate and useful. We genuinely value all the feedback we receive. A well-travelled team reads and acknowledges every letter, postcard and email and ensures that every morsel of information finds its way to the appropriate authors, editors and cartographers for verification.

Everyone who writes to us will find their name listed in the next edition of the appropriate guidebook. They will also receive the latest issue of Planet Talk, our quarterly printed newsletter, or Comet, our monthly email newsletter. Subscriptions to both newsletters are free. The very best contributions will be rewarded with a free guidebook. We may edit, reproduce and incorporate your comments in all Lonely Planet products, such as guidebooks, Web sites and digital products, so let us know if you don't want your comments reproduced or your name acknowledged.

Send all correspondence to the Lonely Planet office closest to you:

Australia Locked Bag 1, Footscray, Victoria 3011
USA 150 Linden St, Oakland, CA 94607
UK 10a Spring Place, London NW5 3BH
France 1 rue du Dahomey, 75011 Paris

Or email us at: **talk2us@lonelyplanet.com.au**

For news, views and updates see our Web site: **www.lonelyplanet.com**

Contents

PORTUGAL

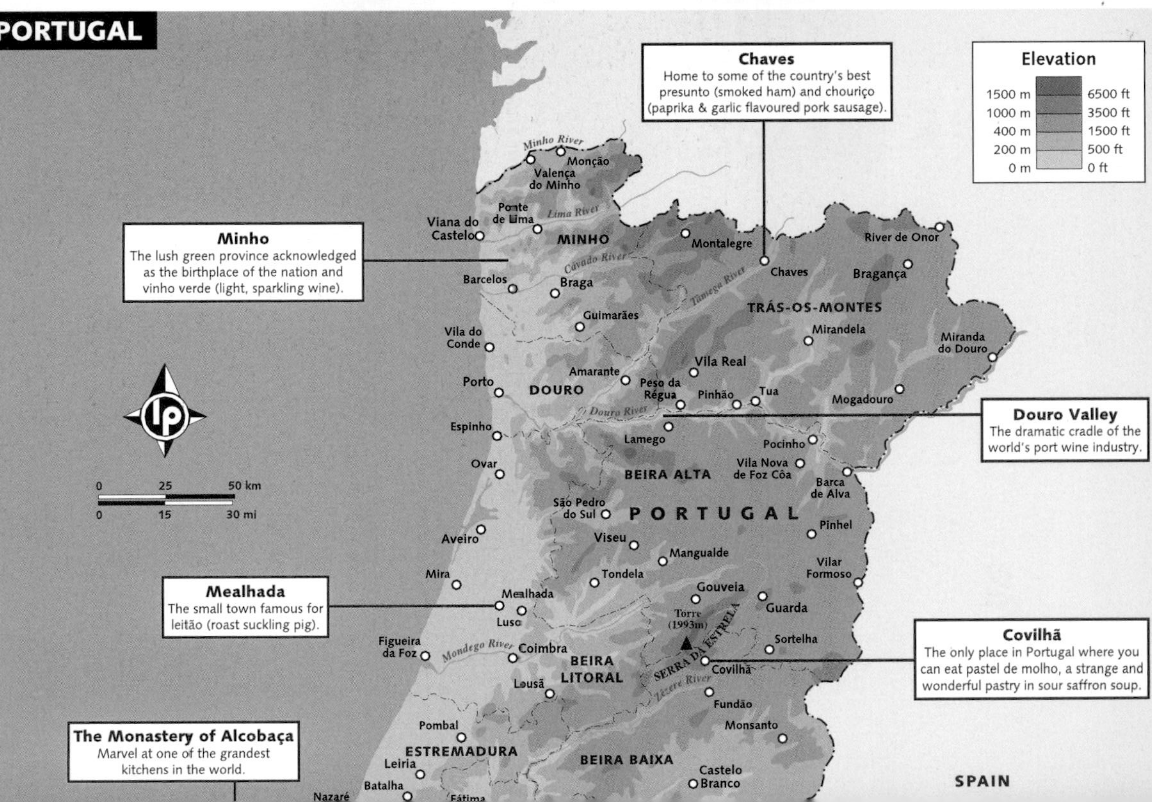

Chaves
Home to some of the country's best presunto (smoked ham) and chouriço (paprika & garlic flavoured pork sausage).
Elevation
1500 m
1000 m
400 m
200 m
0 m
6500 ft
3500 ft
1500 ft
500 ft
0 ft
Minho
The lush green province acknowledged as the birthplace of the nation and vinho verde (light, sparkling wine).
Douro Valley
The dramatic cradle of the world's port wine industry.
Mealhada
The small town famous for leitão (roast suckling pig).
Covilhã
The only place in Portugal where you can eat pastel de molho, a strange and wonderful pastry in sour saffron soup.
The Monastery of Alcobaça
Marvel at one of the grandest kitchens in the world.
0
25
50 km
0
15
30 mi
Minho River
Monção
Valença do Minho
Ponte de Lima
Lima River
Viana do Castelo
MINHO
Cávado River
Barcelos
Braga
Guimarães
Vila do Conde
Porto
DOURO
Amarante
Montalegre
Chaves
Tâmega River
River de Onor
Bragança
TRÁS-OS-MONTES
Mirandela
Miranda do Douro
Vila Real
Peso da Régua
Pinhão
Tua
Mogadouro
Douro River
Espinho
Lamego
Pocinho
Vila Nova de Foz Côa
Barca de Alva
Ovar
BEIRA ALTA
São Pedro do Sul
PORTUGAL
Pinhel
Aveiro
Viseu
Mangualde
Vilar Formoso
Mira
Tondela
Mealhada
Luso
Gouveia
Guarda
Torre (1993m)
SERRA DA ESTRELA
Sortelha
Figueira da Foz
Mondego River
Coimbra
BEIRA LITORAL
Covilhã
Lousã
Zêzere River
Fundão
Pombal
Monsanto
ESTREMADURA
BEIRA BAIXA
Leiria
Castelo Branco
Batalha
SPAIN
Nazaré
Fátima

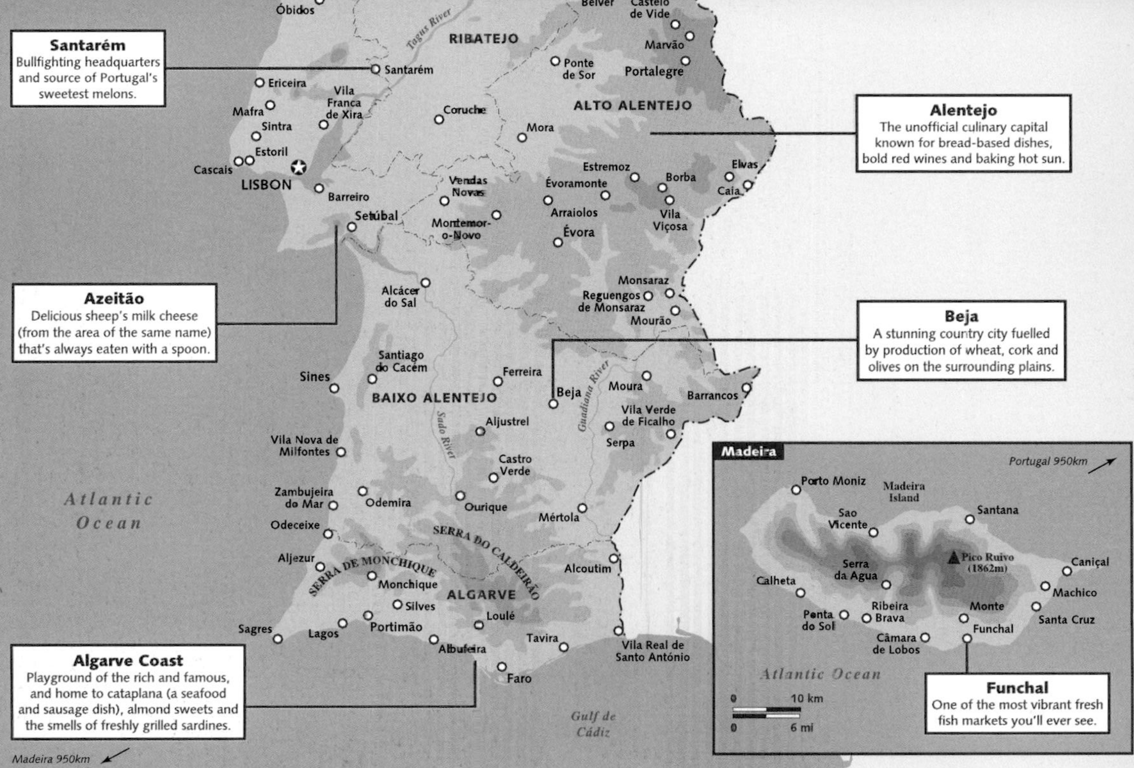

Santarém
Bullfighting headquarters and source of Portugal's sweetest melons.
Azeitão
Delicious sheep's milk cheese (from the area of the same name) that's always eaten with a spoon.
Algarve Coast
Playground of the rich and famous, and home to cataplana (a seafood and sausage dish), almond sweets and the smells of freshly grilled sardines.
Alentejo
The unofficial culinary capital known for bread-based dishes, bold red wines and baking hot sun.
Beja
A stunning country city fuelled by production of wheat, cork and olives on the surrounding plains.
Funchal
One of the most vibrant fresh fish markets you'll ever see.
Óbidos
Belver
Castelo de Vide
Marvão
Portalegre
Ponte de Sor
RIBATEJO
Tagus River
Santarém
Ericeira
Vila Franca de Xira
Mafra
Sintra
Estoril
Cascais
LISBON
Barreiro
Setúbal
Coruche
Mora
ALTO ALENTEJO
Estremoz
Évoramonte
Borba
Elvas
Caia
Vila Viçosa
Arraiolos
Évora
Vendas Novas
Montemor-o-Novo
Alcácer do Sal
Monsaraz
Reguengos de Monsaraz
Mourão
Santiago do Cacém
Sines
Ferreira
Beja
Guadiana River
Moura
Barrancos
BAIXO ALENTEJO
Vila Verde de Ficalho
Serpa
Aljustrel
Sado River
Vila Nova de Milfontes
Castro Verde
Zambujeira do Mar
Odemira
Ourique
Mértola
Odeceixe
SERRA DO CALDEIRÃO
Aljezur
SERRA DE MONCHIQUE
Monchique
Alcoutim
ALGARVE
Silves
Sagres
Lagos
Portimão
Loulé
Albufeira
Tavira
Vila Real de Santo António
Faro
Atlantic Ocean
Gulf de Cádiz
Madeira 950km
Madeira
Portugal 950km
Porto Moniz
Madeira Island
Santana
Sao Vicente
Pico Ruivo (1862m)
Caniçal
Serra da Agua
Calheta
Machico
Monte
Ribeira Brava
Ponta do Sol
Santa Cruz
Funchal
Câmara de Lobos
Atlantic Ocean
0
10 km
0
6 mi

Present day Portugal is a cosmopolitan banquet of the foods and moods of her near neighbours and far colonial ports – from char-grilled sardines to bacalhau and beer, this small country of roughly 10 million has made its mark on the culinary globe.

Portugal is perched on the south-western edge of Europe and up until 500 years ago was awash with the influence of the Moors from the south, Spanish to the east and British and Flemish to the north. The fearless Portuguese then took to the high seas in search of trade routes and profit from the bounty of the Orient. So you'll find plenty of seafood dishes along with the spoils of its outposts – spice and rice from the Indies, tea and silks from the Orient and corn from the Americas. Acorn-fed pork, eel stew, golden Madeira, sweet pastries from the convents and tawny port all colour the pantry picture.

Portugal is divided into seven (or eight or nine, depending on who you ask) mainland regions, broadly referred to as the North, Central and South, and two Atlantic archipelagos, Madeira and the Azores. Regional cuisines reflect the changing landscape as its major rivers, the Tagus and the Douro, wend their way from Spain and across Portugal to the ocean through verdant pastures and wine growing areas to the fish-rich sea.

Cabbage and spicy sausage soup in Minho, slippery tripe in Porto, cured ham from Chaves, roast suckling pig in Bairrada, wines from Colares, muscatel from Setubal, silky Serra cheese in the Beiras, almond sweets from the Algarve and egg sweets from Aveiro: in these pages you'll discover the pleasures of the Portuguese table as experienced by those who enjoy them every day – from families and local restaurants to late night bars and market sellers. Its flavours will melt you, its generosity will supplicate you and its honesty will make you want to pack up and relocate. In Portugal, food is family, vitality, health and happiness and whether your visit is actual or anticipated, we promise to stuff you with local lore and whip your appetite into a frenzy. "Bom apetite!"

the culture of portuguese cuisine

Patriotism can be said to spring from a passionate attachment to all good things tasted in childhood, and Portuguese people are passionately attached to protecting and perpetuating their heritage through family and traditional food and drink.

"He who doesn't work,
doesn't drink
and he who doesn't work,
doesn't eat."

History

When you say Portugal, where do you mean? That skinny strip of land between Spain and the Atlantic at what was once the nether edge of the known world? It's only been known as Portugal since the 11th century, and only independent since the 12th. Before that the land had a rich and busy history that goes back to the Phoenicians who had trading posts along the coast in the 3rd century BC. The Celts settled here in the north; the ancient Lusitanians came under Roman rule here in the 2nd century BC; the Germanic Suevi tribes established the settlement that later gave the country its name (at Porto, called Portucale); the Visigoths brought Christianisation in the 6th century; the Muslim Moors conquered the country in the 8th; and Viking raids during the 9th century paved the way for Christian reconquest and independence. Phew.

Temple of Diana, Évora, Alentejo

All of this invasion mishmash was, with the benefit of hindsight, about the best thing that happened to the area that became Portugal. Many of the traditions that define its food and wine culture can be traced back to the influence of invaders, and Portugal can be grateful to two groups in particular: the Romans, who brought a love of wine, good agricultural practices and the base of a language that is now the fifth most common in the world; and the Moors, who stamped their style on the Algarve and instilled a love for an impossible amount of sugar and the cultivation of almonds.

But this wasn't enough for the plucky Portuguese. Unlikely to have much luck expanding into the territory of their neighbour, Spain, they struck a deal to divvy up the rest of the globe between them. They then sailed out of sight of the coast, where it was said you'd fall off. By the early 16th century, Portugal was a major maritime power, with outposts of its plump empire in Africa, the Far East, India and the Americas. Its sailors discovered Newfoundland's Great Banks of fresh cod, sparking a fathomless fishy love affair that endures to this day. The Portuguese now eat more fish and rice than any other European country. They became experts at trading in new and exotic ingredients, including spices. They got fat and sassy.

Cellar worker, Viseu, Beiras

A SPLASH OF COLOUR

Espinho, Beiras

Portugal's fishing boats are small but plentiful and their bright colours are one of the most distinguishable features of the coastline. Bobbing on moorings, hauled up onto the sand, or low in the water and heading back to port with a catch, they all look festive. For the bigger trawlers that head way offshore, the tradition of bright colours dates back to the Phoenicians, and it was the invention of the speedy and seaworthy caravels in the 15th and 16th centuries that put the Portuguese ahead in dominating the spice trade.

While spices had long been available to the European middle classes (including the wealthy monasteries and nunneries, which may explain the dominance of spices in conventual sweets), it wasn't until Vasco da Gama made his sea route to India in 1498 that Lisbon became the spice queen. Established in Goa and on Sri Lanka, the Portuguese exploited cinnamon over the next couple of hundred years to such an extent that almost every sweet in Portugal is still flavoured with cinnamon. Some places even give you a quill of it instead of a spoon to stir your coffee. While spices have been used throughout Asia, the Near East and the Mediterranean for thousands of years, and while Portugal dominated the scene for a couple of hundred years, the spices were traded and used well before the Portuguese and their fast boats and short cuts came along.

Portugal's good times soon ended. The royal line ended in 1580, and the Spanish swooped. The Spanish may have had sherry, but they did not have good financial advice and lost a lot of what Portugal had gained in wars. After spending some time testing the waters of absolutism, Portugal remained a backwater for all of the 18th century before reluctantly hosting the French – while their own royals were sipping cocktails in the Brazilian sunshine – and sliding towards destitution. It was a case of riches to rags. Assassinations and insurrections were happening everywhere, and the Portuguese wanted some peace. It came in the form of the dictatorial António de Oliveira Salazar, who kept Portugal quiet (and in the dark) for a large part of the 20th century. His restrictions on knowledge and cultural expression encouraged subsistence farming and self-reliance. This is great if you want to raise good chickens, but not so great if you want an education. Portugal looked to the new colonies of Africa and Brazil rather than to the intellectual developments around it in Europe.

Now in between all of this is the influence wielded by staunch Catholicism and adherence to its rituals. From the Middle Ages on, the Catholic Church was a wealthy landowner and its nuns and monks were strategically placed in some of the warmest, lushest parts of the country amid fertile land. Since they were collecting payments from agricultural properties that were tenants on Church land, the nunneries and monasteries could maintain a very wealthy lifestyle and had plenty of time to play with wine and food. This resulted in some of Portugal's best wines, most traditional dishes, and famous conventual sweets (sweets made by nuns) that define certain regions to this day. That is, until the Marquês de Pombal came along in the 18th century, took away their wealth and closed them down. (See the boxed text Is that a Yolk in Your Pocket? in the Staples chapter.)

After the millennia of turmoil it's amazing Portugal made it at all. But make it it did, and arguably a strong sense of nationhood was part of the recipe. That, and codfish and **aguardente** (a brandy-like spirit).

Dancing with passion, Loule, Algarve

SEALING THE QUALITY

Portuguese traditional products and production methods are protected by a system of certification that guarantees consumers of their quality. The system in part protects consumers and genuine producers from a kind of fraud that sees a non-genuine food being sold as genuine. For example, a cheese from Rabaçal can be labelled clearly with the word Rabaçal, but it may not necessarily be the lush and wonderful cheese officially *called* Rabaçal. And yes, there definitely are attempts to cash in on famous products.

So there's the DOP and IGP standards, which both meet EU regulations for certifying products, but are administered by Portugal's Direcção Geral de Desenvolvimento Rural (General Direction of Rural Development). DOP refers to Protected Origin Denomination, which means there must be an irrefutable connection between the product's quality and the region of origin (the method of production, the raw materials used etc). IGP, meaning Protected Geographical Indication, covers a product that originates in a specific place or region and whose characteristics can be associated with that place or region.

Rabaçal cheese, Rabaçal, Beiras

Hungry visitors can use these product markings as a guide. The rating can cover a fresh fruit, a sausage, a particular meat, or even a potato. It's the equivalent of the wine world's DOC system, and in the case of food is an excellent way to make sure that what you're eating is the real thing. This is especially true if you've crossed the globe to try a high quality product from a traditional region, prepared in the traditional manner. It's in the interest of most parties to acknowledge what is probably already known on a local level by formalising the system. Producers want you to buy a brand name. But hey, why not? Other EU countries are doing it, and in this case, both the genuine producer and the consumer win.

Detail of footpath, Funchal, Madeira

Geography

Why do so many northern Europeans head to Portugal? Because it gets plenty of sun during the long, hot summers. And while the sun is good for slouching around on the beach, it can be even better for growing lots of fresh produce. Along with the tourists, tomatoes love the sunny Mediterranean climate of the southern Algarve region. Citrus and almonds also flourish, along with a vibrant fishing industry that stretches from the Algarve right up the coast to Spain and nourishes the national obsession with the fruits of the sea.

North of the Algarve stretch the vast, hot plains of the Alentejo, host to cork and olive trees (and where livestock graze in abundance). Adjoining it to the west are the fertile flood plains of the Ribatejo region, home of rice, horses and fighting bulls. The flooding comes from the Tagus river. The Tagus and Douro rivers both characterise the northern regions, making their journey from Spain and across Portugal to the Atlantic coast through spectacular scenery. Cold, harsh winters in Trás-os-Montes make for a harder life than that experienced by the coastal cousins, but this is countered by rich meat dishes and an inward focus. The upper Douro valley is the cradle of port production, a vibrant element of Portugal's economy and culture for centuries.

Portugal may be small but its borders have remained the same for eight centuries. The diversity of its landscape has resulted in stark regional cultural differences that remain, with some exceptions, firmly entrenched. The dilution of tradition is most evident, and most tragic, in the Algarve, which has been gutted by hordes of tourists and rapacious developers.

DON'T CALL US SPANISH

Portugal has always had a fraught relationship with Spain. The two countries often single out the way the other cooks as proof of their own superiority. A popular Portuguese saying is 'From Spain neither good marriage nor good wind'. It's important to get this very clear. Portugal is not Spain. It never has been, and never will be. Lumping them together under the heading of Iberia has perhaps been convenient but both parties are at pains to point out that each country is not interchangeable. They do not eat and drink, or prepare food and drink, in the same way. Most crucially, they do not speak the same language and the wise traveller will know that to speak Spanish to a Portuguese is an affront. Even if they can speak Spanish, they may not answer. If you want to leave here well fed and with new friendships, treat Portugal as if Spain doesn't exist, and never did. Don't compare the two countries, even secretly. Just let the wonder of Portugal nourish your bones.

In stark contrast the remote north remains relatively free from outside invasion, and traditional lifestyles are unaffected by modernity. It's only in the last 20 years that the transport networks have been upgraded, so that it's possible to drive to Porto from Lisbon in an hour instead of requiring a whole day. Lisbon itself is a small and charming capital that offers, like most capitals, a taste of everything, but even it has food traditions linked to its location (see Lisbon Coast in the Regional Variations chapter).

Take the mountainous road less travelled, between Covilhã and Viseu, Beiras

How Portuguese Eat

With gusto. The best of Portuguese food is prepared with simple cooking methods, and strongly reflects its region and proud past. It is fiercely independent of fashions and international trends, and alone the Portuguese have defended their right to reject an intellectual or superior approach to eating and drinking. The produce of the land and the ways it is prepared are part of a strong culture and heritage. Richly satisfying dishes should be ingested at intervals of a few short hours, for maximum enjoyment. Portuguese food eschews airs and graces and must be shared with family, friends and anyone who looks remotely like they could do with some fortitude, regardless of rank, race or rancour.

The effect of poor transport and communication on local food and wine culture, right up until the last decades of the 20th century, cannot be underestimated. The regionality developed over centuries is so geographically specific that even within one small region traditional sweets made in one town will be made differently only 10km away. Sausages can also be made with slight but very specific differences from year to year, based on an abundance or scarcity of an ingredient, or some local preference. The result is that, even now, Portuguese families will travel not just to a region but to a particular town or part of a region to taste a traditional dish, prepared as it has been done for centuries.

AUTHENTIC PORTUGUESE FOOD

In *Os Gatos (The Cats)*, writer Fialho de Almeida defines traditional Portuguese food as:

> *... a culinary creation which resents being written down in manuals; it is characteristic, incapable of being expressed in amounts of ingredients, fractions of time and the quick or slow action of cold, heat, water, ice, the use of a strainer, a food-mill, a knife or spoon ... Like a national legend, a national dish is the product of collective genius: no one in particular invented it – it has been invented by all.*
>
> (quoted in Edite Vieira's *The Taste of Portugal*)

And could we gild the lily by mentioning that apart from being invented by all, Portuguese cuisine also belongs to all? At one of the most important meals on the calendar, Christmas Eve dinner (see the Celebrating chapter), families across all socioeconomic groups tuck into the very same dishes of **bacalhau** (dried salt cod). There's no such thing in Portugal as a distinction between dishes for the poor and dishes for the wealthy.

Wine making azulejos (tiles), Douro

This brings us to the important question of who's actually at the stoves. You won't see fancy hospitality schools offering to teach the next generation of cooks how to prepare local specialities. Restaurants tend to be family run, and when they are (and have developed a reputation for their dishes), they keep their recipes secret and only pass them on to the next generation of family. There are few definitive written recipes, because these aren't the kind of secrets that can be written down. Everyone will prepare the food differently when they learn a recipe, and it's only over time and with practice that they make it the correct family way. The official handover of the reins takes many years, and the reins are only reluctantly relinquished. This specificity also means that in a particular town (such as Mealhada, famous for roast suckling pig), the locals' knowledge of – and definite preference for – the way that one restaurant prepares it over another is common. But you'll find this regard for specific tastes is not as important in the cities and tourist areas. That's why, to experience the real food of Portugal, you have to get off the beaten track and be prepared to sniff out local treasures.

Breakfast usually consists of coffee, and white breadrolls and butter, or perhaps breadrolls with cheese or ham. In agricultural areas, you may receive a more substantial breakfast of soup and bread. A richer start to the day would also require a glass of wine or even something stronger. Mid-morning

Restaurant Casa de Hospedes, Viseu, Beiras

could see another coffee and one of a myriad of fresh pastries, maybe with an aguardente or a beer with red vermouth. But the really serious start of the eating day is lunch. It would be near impossible to get through three courses in an hour, so it is usual in the cities and towns to take 90 minutes for lunch. At least.

Lunch may occasionally start with a slab of cheese and olives, with bread and perhaps soup. This is followed by a meat or fish dish (usually with potatoes and often rice), finishing with a sweet cream or rice dessert and coffee. All of this would require plenty of wine along the way, usually by the carafe and not the bottle, and then finish with a hefty shot of aguardente: some splashed into the coffee, and the rest to scorch the throat. So hang onto the kilojoule counter because dinner will be more of the same, with salty meat or fish snacks in between. At a small restaurant there will also be plenty of banter, with colleagues and old friends or new. At weekends, restaurants are full of extended families and their children, who are coaxed into a full appreciation of their culinary heritage. A plate of **ameijoas** (steamed fresh clams) scattered with coriander here, a heady garlic **açorda** (a bread-based thick soup) there, a slice of crisply fried pig's **morcela** (blood sausage), or a sweet invented by the local nuns hundreds of years ago and still prepared by the caretaker of the tradition: this is what Portuguese people get to eat. The bounty of the land is prepared in a simple way by people who grew up with it and carefully passed preparation traditions on to the next generation. Salad rarely appears: your vegetables are in the soup. Fish, bread, rice, potatoes, meat, **caldo verde** (Galician kale and potato soup), egg yolks, sugar, wine and aguardente. These are major food groups, and variations upon them are what distinguishes one family, town or region from the next.

Etiquette

Portuguese people are polite, some say more so than the people of any other European country. You will not encounter confusion about what utensil goes with which dish. One knife and fork will be with you for the meal (what do you think the bread is for if not to wipe your knife for the next course?). You will not have to dither over which glass goes with which wine. More than likely you'll stay with the same glass for the meal, until it's time for a shot of spirits, and a glass for water if you ask for it. It is acceptable to ask for a **meia dose** (half serve), or to ask whether the dish you're interested in will serve two. It probably will, and it's not cheap of you to share. It will save your girth from growing unchecked.

Salt and pepper will not be routinely on tables, even in restaurants, and if it is then you're probably in a tourist trap. The reason is that the cook will season the food as she or he thinks it should be seasoned, and apart from adding a bit of **piri piri** (red hot chilli pepper sauce), the diner shouldn't tamper with it. It's borderline rude to ask for salt and pepper, and you'll only get finely ground white pepper anyway, so give in and let the cook do the deciding. Most food will be well salted and only subtly peppered. You will, however, be expected to do your own drizzling: vinegar and olive oil cruets will sometimes be put out with boiled or steamed dishes for you to dress yourself, and a salad will also come without dressing.

Curiously, it is not impolite to clear your throat of any constriction, in the popular Asian manner, as loudly as you can, and gathering as much of your own moisture as you possibly can. It is also not impolite to wave your knife and fork around, and to speak loudly and consistently with a mouth brimming with food. Men and women will both do this, so don't be offended if you see it happen. And it is not impolite to light up a cigarette and puff continuously in the direction of your nearest neighbour, who may or may not wish to eat a meal laced with nicotine. It is impolite, in a **tasca** (cheap eatery) or simple restaurant, to come in off the street and not wash your hands at the small sink in the corner of the room before eating. It's there as a service for manual labourers, and you will gain brownie points for using it. And if you're not a fan of football, or locally produced soapies, ignore the television – despite the seeming impossibility of this, as it will be angled so that most patrons can get a good view. Television will be your constant dining companion in most restaurants, so get used to it.

Sometimes in simpler restaurants people who are already seated and eating may ask a new arrival – friend or stranger – "E servido?" (Have you been served?), meaning, "Would you like some of ours?". The newcomer is obliged to return with, "Nao, muito obrigado. Bom proveito." (No, thank you very much. May it profit you.). This is a trick question. Do not, under any circumstances, think the invitation means you should sit down and scoff this polite person's food. It doesn't. It's a roundabout way of saying they hope you enjoy your meal.

Less expensive eateries rely on turnover to make a profit, so try not to hang around after finishing your meal if you can clearly see there are others waiting. While you probably wouldn't be asked to leave, it's impolite not to. Also, there is no such thing as BYO (bring your own) in Portugal; never turn up to a restaurant with your own wine. And unless you want to crawl under the table with embarassment, remember to ask in advance whether a restaurant takes credit cards ("Aceita cartões de crédito?"), because often they won't. Memorise the word for "hello" ("Olá"), smile at your hosts and bring your appetite. It's Portugal. You'll be spending some time at the table.

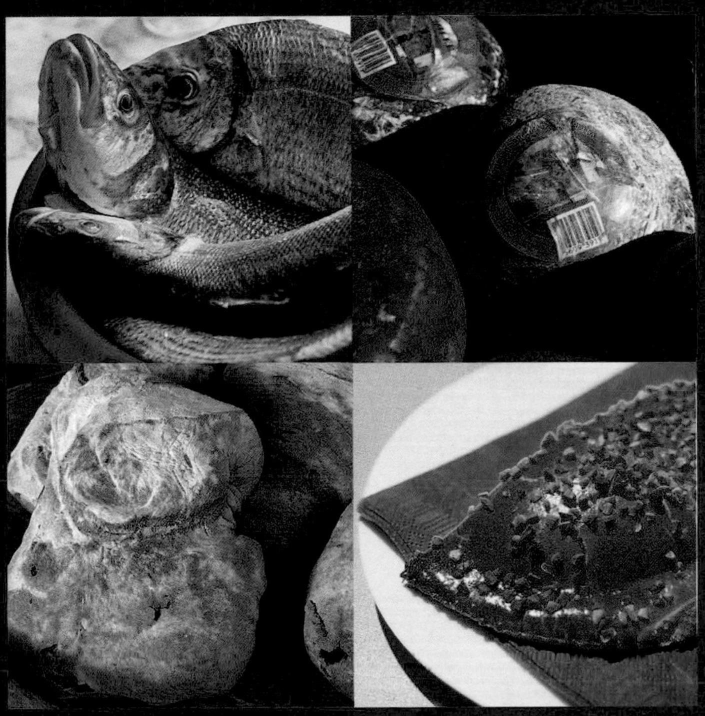

staples & specialities

In the Portuguese pantry you'll find terminology, textures and tastes all tossed up in the air and assembled at random. Soup is dry. Vegetables are made into jam. Chicken is a dessert. Pies are made with bread dough. Cakes are savoury. Bread can be a biscuit. But it all tastes delicious.

Bacalhau (Dried Salt Cod)

You will not understand Portugal unless you partake of **bacalhau**, and unless you fall instantly and irretrievably in love with it you can never say you've truly been there. It's bound up with myth, history and mealtimes, including everyday meals and the most important celebrations on the calendar. It's the sixth food group, and so much more than the sum of its parts. To say that the Portuguese came across the great cod fishing grounds of Newfoundland then used simple salting methods to preserve the fish is not enough. This will not help you understand how important it is in daily life and how many ways there are to cook it (see the Understanding the Menu chapter). It will not prepare you for how often you'll eat it, and how much you'll crave it once converted.

It used to be that Portuguese fishermen caught the cod and brought it back to be salted and dried by women in towns all along the coast. Now the fish are bought from other countries, with the best and most expensive catch from Norway and Iceland and others from Newfoundland, Canada, Denmark and Nova Scotia. The fish are split open, gutted and beheaded, then layered in salt. They are then delivered to a Portuguese drying factory for processing, where they are washed, stacked on massive pallets to drain, and then layered on racks in a temperature controlled drying room. This is a far cry from the more poetic open-air traditional version, which, especially over the past few years, has begun to slow, almost to a halt. While everyone agrees that cod dried in the open air is superior, it's a fiddly process. It can only be performed from March to June and from September to November when there is not too much humidity and when the temperature is likely to be between 18° and 20°C, so the cod can dry. The work is backbreakingly hard. It's traditionally done by women, who don't want to do it any more. And processors prefer the more predictable conditions of modern methods. However, if you're lurking about in the towns of Viana do Castelo or Aveiro at the right time, you may see what the whole coast of Portugal used to look like with different types of splayed, salted fish set in the sun to dry. The obsession goes so deep that even in Madeira, where no fresh cod is sent for salting and drying, they catch a similar local fish, prepare it in the same way and call it false bacalhau.

False bacalhau drying in the sun, Madeira

Peixes & Mariscos (Fish & Seafood)

Portugal and seafood are like Ginger and Fred, Marilyn and peroxide: it's almost impossible to imagine them apart. Nor can you think about eating in Portugal without the bounty of the ocean and rivers. So grab a plate and take a tour.

Sardines are probably the most favoured fish (remembering that **bacalhau** – dried salt cod – which would topple them, is in a class of its own). You will see sardines grilling in the streets, on restaurant menus, and on family dining tables. They will be barely scaled, full of their own guts, and heads left on (for the remedy see the boxed text How to Grill Sardines). Grill, squeeze some lemon over, salt and eat with your fingers. If you hear anyone saying – or selling – 'sardinhas do nosso mar' around the town of Viana do Castelo, it means 'sardines from our sea'. This concept is very important to the Portuguese, as they like to think of everything they eat as being local, including the fish. Eating fish from 'our sea' – meaning that stretch of ocean closest to home – supports local fishermen. Curiously, this is irrelevant when it comes to bacalhau, for which demand is so great that they'll take it from anywhere.

HOW TO GRILL SARDINES

You may be surprised to find that the freshly grilled sardines in Portugal are frequently not even scaled, let alone gutted. This may offend your sensibilities, and if it does, here's how to prepare sardines the neat way once you get home:

Scrape the entire body of each sardine (from tail to head) with the back of a knife held at a gentle angle. Do this on both sides, and give the fish a rinse to get rid of the scales. Then stick the point of a sharp knife in the hole under the gills and run it back to the tail. Open up the fish and rinse out its guts. Pat the fish dry. Have your assistant jack up the fire and prepare a double metal fish grill by brushing the bars with olive oil. Give the fish a little sprinkle of salt, and sandwich each one between the bars of the oiled grill. Cook the sardines over a fierce heat so that by the time the sardines are cooked (which should only take a few minutes, turning once) the edges are starting to catch and burn, which will taste delicious. Serve with plenty of fresh bread, **açorda** (bread soup) or **gaspacho** (cold tomato and onion soup), or steaming hot potatoes. Sardines are at peak quality in summer.

Tuna steaks sold at Mercado dos Lavradores, Funchal, Madeira

Fresh **bifes de atum** (tuna steaks) along the Algarve coast and on the islands, especially on Madeira (see the Regional Variations chapter), are popular but tend to be overcooked and quite dry (as is the case with meat). Squid, cuttlefish and octopus are all over the country, including inland. You haven't lived until you've eaten finger-thick tentacles of freshly caught, deep-fried octopus. Look for them around the town of Tavira, where they're caught in clay pots by local fishermen.

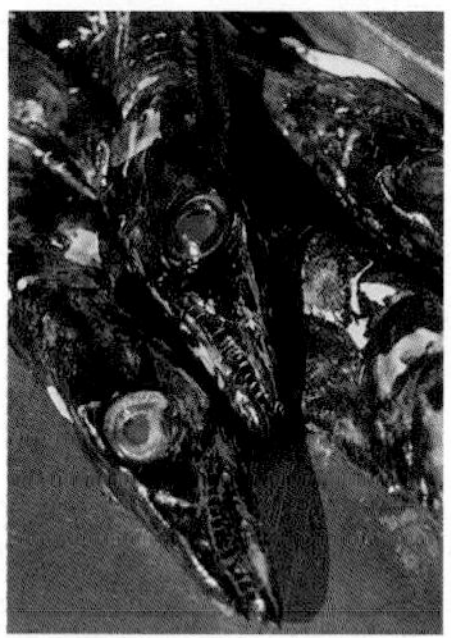

Scabbard fish, Mercado dos Lavradores, Funchal, Madeira

The Setúbal area is renowned for the quality of its fish, and in particular red mullet. **Peixe espada** (scabbard fish) is a permanent fixture at the markets of Funchal and can also be caught off Sesimbra. It sounds like, but is completely different from, **espadarte** (swordfish). Make sure you wear your glasses while reading menus or you'll take a wrong turn. Sea perch is inexpensive and available all over. Look out for fish that aren't necessarily caught out to sea any more, such as bream and bass, which may be the product of aquaculture and, some say, much inferior to the wild ones. Prawns and lobster are just as expensive in Portugal as in other countries, but surely it's better to have a small amount of something extravagant than lots of what you usually eat? Some of the best shellfish are the tiny clams, simply steamed in **vinho verde** (light sparkling wine) and scattered with coriander; garlic butter grilled limpets in Funchal; and – oddest of all – the strange-looking tiny barnacles that have an overwhelmingly marine flavour. Inland areas have always had a steady supply of fish too – either freshwater, or regular dried or salted deliveries from the coast. Enjoy **sopa de cação** (dogfish bread soup) in Alentejo, trout in Minho, and fresh eel or elvers (young eels) in the Beiras. Whichever way you look at it, you'll be stocking up on Omega-3s.

STAPLES

CARACÓIS (SNAILS)

They may not be flesh (well, not as in beast), nor fish, nor fowl, but the Portuguese do like their snails, and you should try them too. There's only really one way to cook them and that's to wash them thoroughly (you'll be using farmed snails that don't need the elaborate cleaning required for wild snails), then boil in their shells in a broth of onion, garlic, bay leaves, chilli, pepper and oregano with either water, stock or lots of white **vinho verde** (light sparkling wine) and some olive oil. They take an hour or two to cook, and their tenderness can be checked with a pin or toothpick. Simply follow the signs for 'Há Caracóis!' ('Here Snails!') and order up a cold plateful with a lovely icy beer. This is a common snack in the Algarve in the lead-up to summer. By the way, when you were at the market, what did you think all those 5kg nets of small, slimy creatures in shells were? If you'd looked closely, you might have seen a small illustration of a happy snail on the outside ...

Sopa de cação (dogfish bread soup), O Aqueduto Restaurant, Évora, Alentejo

Carnes (Meats)

Haven't you heard? "Peixe não puxa carroça" (Fish does not pull a cart) means that you can't fuel a mule on fish. Energy and sustenance, according to the Portuguese, can only come from meat. Of course, this is total bollocks from a scientific point of view. But it's obvious the Portuguese have a love affair with meat. It may be present at every meal, and is a reminder that life is good. In the old days only the wealthy could afford it and if recent per capita consumption of meat is any measure, Portugal would hover around the highest GDP in the western world. Roasted, grilled, baked, boiled, stewed, smoked, braised: it even turns up in dessert.

Pork is among the most favoured flesh, and in particular the wild boar of Alentejo, which is twice the price of the garden variety because of higher fat content (which you really need ...) and better flavour. Wild boar feed on the fallen acorns of cork oak groves, and the flesh is said to be exquisite because of it. Their younger northern cousin, the suckling pig, is the highly prized regular type in Bairrada (see Beiras in the Regional Variations chapter) that is roasted whole. There are strict limits on the dimensions and age of the piglet, and if the way its flesh melts in the mouth is any indication, it generally has a short and coddled life on mother's milk. There's pork in so many dishes, including the lard that crops up as a popular cooking fat, and slow cooked **bucho de porco** (pig's stomach) for the brave offal eaters out there. Equally unusual for some will be the **carne de porco à Alentejana**, or Alentejo-style pork with clams (see the recipe in the Regional Variations chapter). Portuguese cooks have also mastered the preserving technique of smoking, and the favourite subject for such treatment is the pig (see the following Presunto & Enchidos/Chouriços section).

Beef, veal, and calf's liver are all popular meats, either as the confusing **bife** (steak), which is a term that also applies to 'steaks' of other meats and even poultry, **costeletas** (cutlets), or freshly grilled. On Madeira the best way to have beef is definitely on the skewer, or **espetada**, of which a single serve offers more prime beef than any individual has a right to in a week, let alone a single meal. Tripe from the stomach lining is especially enjoyed in Porto, and the brave should try it for its luscious texture.

Lamb is popular but it is kid (baby goat) that makes the punters go crazy. Usually just a month old, it is small enough to fit whole into a domestic oven, and once roasted is brought to the centre of the family table for everyone to feast on. You will see 'cabrito à moda da' (kid in the style of) in restaurants, as well as 'cabrito assado' (roast kid). Tiny lambs, should they be available, also get the same trip to the oven. Both dishes are associated with celebrations, but some restaurants specialise in cooking them throughout the season of their availability.

Arroz de linguiça (sausages with rice), Évora, Alentejo

Rabbit and hare are also common on restaurant menus – hare is more likely to be a rich dish, and if a family prepares it nothing will be wasted, not even the blood. It will be kept and mixed with a splash of vinegar to prevent it from coagulating, then stirred through the dish for the last few minutes of cooking. But those who prefer their meat bloody or rare, beware: Portuguese like their meat, including tuna steaks, well cooked. Ask for 'mal passado' for medium rare or 'muito mal passado' for rare, but bear in mind most people will find this very strange.

Presunto & Enchidos/Chouriços (Smoked Ham & Sausages)

The Portuguese love a pig and every part of the beast finds its way to the table. In some parts of the country, workers start the day with soup or slices of smoked sausage. King among the smoked pork products is **presunto** (smoked ham), every bit an equal to Italy's prosciutto, France's Bayonne, Germany's Westphalia and Spain's Serrano. The whole legs are brushed with a paste that varies from region to region but always includes salt, garlic, paprika and wine. The meat is left for several weeks between layers of salt, then the salt is rubbed off and the hams are suspended in the **fumeiro** (smokehouse) for up to two months. Once the ham is smoked it is brushed with olive oil and sprinkled with paprika and borax (acting as a preservative), then hung to age for at least a year. Presunto is delicious as a thinly sliced snack, in sandwiches, sliced thickly and panfried as a steak, or cut up and added to other dishes for flavour. The best presunto comes from the Chaves and Lamego sub-regions of Trás-os-Montes, and Monchique in the Algarve, but it is available all over the country. The wild black pig of Alentejo's hills, **javali**, is also made into presunto. **Fiambre** is a pale, lightly smoked boiled ham used more as a sliced snack or sandwich filling than for cooking.

Intensive pig farming also means sausages, and lots of them. The most common are **chouriços**, which are 2cm to 3cm across and made in two lengths: 15cm, or double that and looped. Lean and fat pork meats are used in the sausages, which are highly seasoned with garlic, red pepper paste and herbs, then given a good smoking. Good quality chouriços are delicious raw as a snack, or finely sliced to season and enrich a dish (during cooking or added at the table). Different producers dry the chouriços for varying amounts of time. This is the sausage most likely to grace your steaming bowl of **caldo verde** (Galician kale and potato soup). **Linguiças** are a longer, thinner version of chouriço and the word itself is used as a generic term for sausages, so look out for some confusion. **Paio** and **salpicão** sausages are much thicker than chouriço but in terms of flavour are not so different. Better cuts of the pig may be used to make them and different spices will vary the flavour. Thin slices make a good snack while

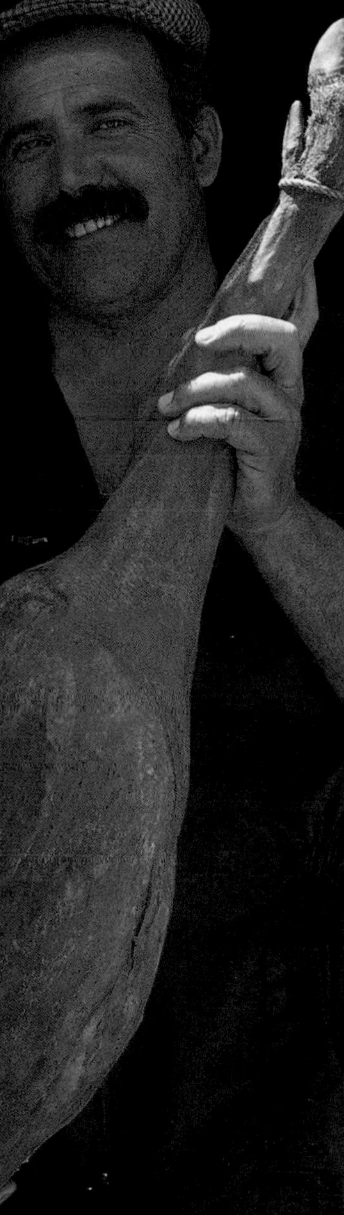

thicker slices can be used in cooked dishes. Paio may have more meat and less fat, tasting more pickled than smoked. But let's face it, it's still a sausage and fat is what makes it taste so good.

Fat-o-phobes should steer well clear of **farinheiras**, which are sausages made with flour, pork fat, spices and wine. The richness of spiced flour with as much pork fat as it can absorb, grilled in a sausage skin, is difficult to describe, and even more difficult to digest if you're not used to it. If you manage to acquire a taste at least try to disperse a few of the globules with red wine. Small farinheiras may be served as an **acepipe** (hors d'oeuvre) while larger ones often go into a stew. **Alheiras**, on the other hand, are among the lightest members of the sausage family because they are made from lighter meats, such as poultry or game, along with bread, plenty of seasoning and loads of garlic (see Douro & Trás-os-Montes in the Regional Variations chapter). Alheiras are simply superb either fried or grilled.

Then there are blood sausages, which may be sold as **morcelas** or **chouriços de sangue**. Pork blood and meat, bread, red wine and seasonings go into this rich type of sausage, which can be eaten fried and grilled or included in a rich dish such as the sausage and meat packed **cozido à Portuguesa**, where meat, sausages and vegetables are served in their own broth (native to Trás-os-Montes).

Alentejo's famous javali (black pig) presunto, Beja, Alentejo

TAKING THE SNAIL'S PACE

Slow Food is a worldwide grass-roots movement that fosters and protects local, traditional methods of food and wine production in an increasingly technological environment. Not that there's anything wrong with technology, but sometimes flavour and integrity are casualties in the fight to make money. Some people are putting on the brakes – *really* putting on the brakes. From its humble beginnings in Paris in 1989 (although home is in Bra, in Italy's Piedmont region), the movement has grown to encompass over 65,000 members in 45 countries, including Portugal, where agribusiness and aquaculture are having an effect on regionality and the quality of fresh produce.

Across the globe there are about 560 'convivia' – with five in Portugal – that encourage and facilitate the Slow Food philosophy at a local level. They do this by hosting food and wine events that educate people in the enjoyment of quality local products.

To locate areas within Portugal that have a convivium, check out Slow Food's Web site at **www.slowfood.com** (select '*Slow Food Worldwide'*) or call the head office in Italy. Why not support a movement that puts flavour first?

Aves (Poultry)

Chicken is king, queen and foot soldier in the poultry pantry. It comes two ways, **assado** (roasted) or **churrasco** (grilled), and it's eaten at least a couple of times a week. Chickens are so inexpensive, so commonly reared for home cooking – even in Lisbon – and so sumptuous that you would think the Portuguese chicken was the prototype for all others. Many graze on wild herbs and roam free, which makes for wonderful flavour. Actually, we're lying about the number of ways to cook it. There are so many good things done with older chickens (marinating, braising, cooking in a earthenware pot) but it's so hard to go past a good roast or grill. In Madeira you'll find it served with fried banana or dangling on a spit. All over Portugal it is always served with potatoes, and sometimes with rice or eggs as well. Although it probably won't be listed on a menu, look out for **galinha do campo** (free range chicken), which will indicate a fatter, tastier, happier chicken.

Turkey (**peru** in Portuguese) is a fairly recent arrival from, you guessed it, Spanish exploration of South America in the 16th century. Since then it has crept onto the Christmas table in Portugal, and is elaborately stuffed with lots of meats. You can pick one up at the country markets.

Duck is packed with flavour here and often braised with rice (**arroz de pato**), orange or olives as a special occasion meal. From mid-October until Christmas, the Beiras, Algarve and Alentejo become a fresh market for the more delicate quail – delicious (if fiddly) on the grill, but persevere and don't worry about using your fingers to eat them – or their cousins pheasant and partridge. Wild birds have a stronger flavour and firmer flesh than their quick-cooking domestic relatives, and are better suited to slower cooking methods. Look out for wild birds either braised, cooked with cabbage, or as **escabeche** – marinated in vinegar and herbs.

Frango no Churrasco (Char-grilled Chicken)

Ingredients

2	large cloves garlic
1/4 to 1/2 tsp	dried hot chilli flakes
1/2 tsp	sea salt
2 Tbs	olive oil
1	medium free range chicken

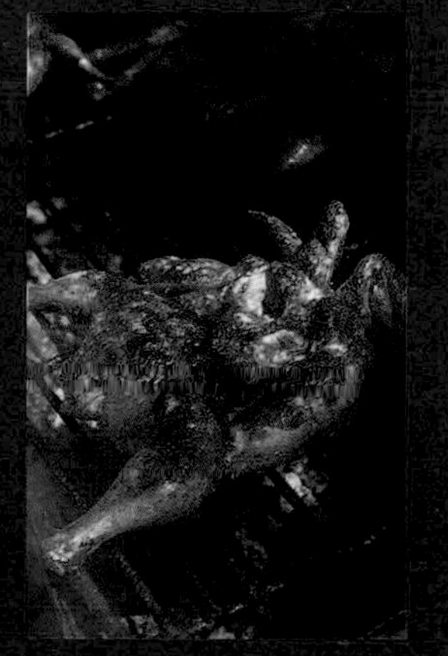

Crush the garlic and mix with the chilli, salt and oil. Set aside.

Remove and discard the chicken's neck and giblets. Wash the chicken in cold water and pat dry with a paper towel. Place the chicken breast-side-up on a chopping board and, using a large sharp knife, cut down the middle right through to the board and all the way up to the neck. Open the chicken out and press it flat. Rub the flavoured oil all over both sides of the chicken. Cover and refrigerate to marinate overnight (or at least for a few hours) to allow the flavours to develop.

Prepare a moderately hot charcoal fire with a grill rack about 15cm above the coals. When the coals are white, lay the chicken on the grill with the skin side up and cook for 12 to 15 minutes, then turn the chicken over and grill the other side for a further 12 minutes or so, or until the chicken is browned. Remove and 'rest' the chicken in a warm spot, uncovered, for 10 minutes – resting ensures the juices stay in the meat when it is cut. Then serve the chicken **piri piri** (red hot chilli pepper sauce), alone as a snack or with potatoes and a salad.

Serves 4

Pão (Bread)

At every meal you will eat bread. If you're very lucky it will have been made by hand by the **padeira** (local baker) – usually a woman – at the back of her home, where she's probably been doing it for decades. Finding a traditional village baker is becoming more difficult but when you do it's magic. It may be that the padeira began baking bread for her family, then friends offered to buy it from her, and eventually the whole community relies upon her. So up she gets at 3am or 4am each day to prepare the woodfired oven and make the dough by hand. Usually there will be two bakings for the day. The bread will be pale and crisp, with a well aerated centre and a thick, chewy crust. She may also have some fresh lettuce or tomatoes from her garden. She'll worry about who will take her place when she's too old – even if she has daughters, it's likely that this is not the kind of profession they'll want to inherit. Sons are even less likely – the work is too hard and the financial rewards too small.

AN UPLIFTING TRADITION

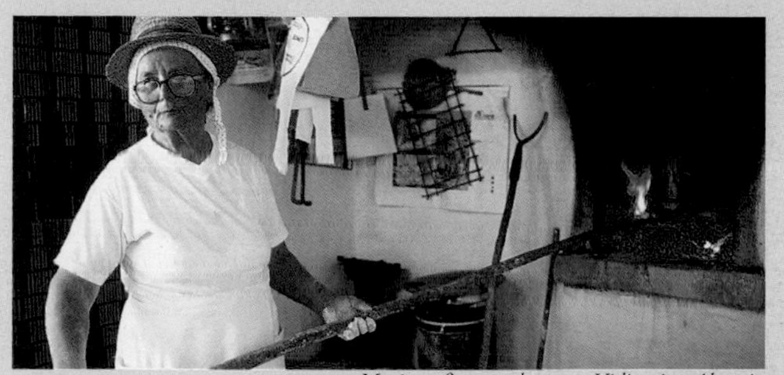

Mariana fires up the oven, Vidigueira, Alentejo

According to the traditional keepers of **pão** (bread) secrets, there's more than a little myth in every batch. The women who make the bread may say prayers during the breadmaking process, make small symbolic gestures, or otherwise imbue their batch with that something special. This does not, however, imply witchcraft. Sometimes it's a sense of humour, or a nod to the sensuality of their craft. Consider this one from the town of Mértola in the Alentejo: the baker would put the bread into the oven, turn her back to it, lift her skirt and say: *"Levanta-te tão alto como a minha saia se levanta acima do meu rabo"* ("Rise bread as high as my skirt is raised above my buttocks"). Bet that inspired her loaves to lift.

Bread dough proving, Vidigueira, Alentejo

These traditional bakers are rare gems, however, and in eateries you'll more likely be given white pap. Being offered **pão caseiro** (bread that's usually been baked on the premises) is increasingly unlikely but should you be so lucky, gobble it up – it's delicious. There are a few special breads to look out for, including varieties of **broa** from Minho (corn bread, which has the same name as small sweet biscuits – see the Doces & Pastéis section later in this chapter), the enriched **bola** dough in the north, and Madeira's terrifically decadent **bolo do caco** (hot, garlic-filled griddle bread – see the Regional Variations chapter). Like the French and their baguettes, the Portuguese like their bread simple and regular, but as with baguettes there's pão and then there's pão. You'll know the difference when you taste it. Plenty of bread turns up in one-pot dishes such as **açordas** ('bread soup' with garlic, coriander and olive oil), **migas** (side dishes with olive oil and garlic) and **ensopados** (stews with toasted or deep-fried bread) and even some of the desserts. Traditionally all meals were served on slabs of bread instead of plates, and the bread soaked with juices was given to beggars or dogs. The tradition of using bread as a plate is a thrifty function that has come to define many regional dishes.

Traditional broa (corn bread), Beiras

Azeitonas & Azeite (Olives & Olive Oil)

Olive trees and olive presses arrived in Iberia with the Romans. But while the Spanish went on to perfect the art of making olive oil, Portugal's output is more rustic. Which is just the way they like it, thank you. The quality of olive harvests is not great, and the olives are often – by design, not accident – allowed to overheat before pressing (creating a strong flavour). Oil from the upper Douro is said to be the best but most is produced for the local market and not for export. The oil makes its way into the food and onto tables across the country, and while it may not be wildly refined, there will certainly be plenty of it. For dishes that you are expected to dress yourself – such as boiled **bacalhau** (dried salt cod) with chickpeas – do not stop pouring until there's enough oil for the fish to swim in. Use buckets. At other times you may be surprised to see a dish arrive in a deep pool of oil. This is not a mistake; you're supposed to mop it up, along with the dish's juices, with a hunk of bread. If you see a dish described as **à lagareiro** (in the manner of the **lagar**, where olives are crushed), it means the dish will contain lots of oil.

Olive grove in the Dão region, Douro

Olives themselves will also be used liberally either as an **acepipe** (hors d'oeuvre), or scattered over a cooked dish. At the markets a single stallholder may offer upwards of 10 varieties but many will be disappointingly tough and unbearably bitter, so try them first. After olive oil, lard is the most popular cooking fat, followed by butter.

REFOGADO

Refogado or **cebolada** is the typical flavour base for lots of traditional soups, stews and braises. It's basically a generous splash of olive oil and a cascade of finely chopped white onion slowly cooked until it is all a molten, golden mass. Then garlic, bay leaves and maybe some tomatoes are added and it's all cooked some more. This intensely flavoured puree then infuses an entire dish of beans, rice, seafood or meat with wonderful depth. It's somewhat confusing having two names for the one item, but technically speaking the process is called **refogado** while the onion mix itself is **cebolada**.

Arroz & Feijões (Rice & Beans)

Apart from bread and potatoes, which appear at every meal, you will also frequently find rice, and maybe even beans or chickpeas. Which is to say that all your meals will be well starched. Rice grows on the plains near the Atlantic coast but its use has spread throughout the country. Long grain is preferred for soups and stews while the ubiquitous rice pudding is best with plump short grains. Rice is white, and don't bother asking for anything else. The rice is often wet and soupy, without the 'every grain must be separate' obsession of other countries. It's there to pick up flavour, and it does so admirably.

Beans and chickpeas are essential to every kitchen, with a long, slow cooking process expanding them with flavour and richness. The chickpeas are enormous and amazingly tender. Don't be surprised to have to dress your own. If a steaming bowl of chickpeas is put down before you with a boiled dish, just add a bucket of olive oil, red vinegar and salt. It will probably have a few onion slices in it, and that's all you'll need. Common dried beans and peas include white, butter, red, black, black-eye and cow pea. And look out for the beloved broad beans.

Feijão com grão (beans with chickpeas), Quinta de São Martino, Mateus, Douro

Sopas & Pratos Completos (Soups & Complete Dishes)

What's the difference between a soup and a stew? In Portugal, sometimes not much. That's because some soups are so thick, so brimming with proud representatives from all the major food groups, that eating anything other than the soup would be sheer piggery. But don't let that stop you. Remember that Portuguese food is food of the people and as a people they have generally not been wealthy. They are masters and mistresses of fuelling themselves on the smell of an oiled broth – which they thicken with bread to make **açorda** (bread soup). All of the soup is soaked into the bread, which becomes squishy and flavoursome, and sometimes it is thickened even more with a beaten egg, or is enriched with sausage or seafood. So it's like a stew without the long, slow cooking. Two of the best known versions include **açorda de marisco**, with prawns, mussels and baby clams, from Estremadura, and **açorda à Alentejana**, a bread soup made with garlic, olive oil, broth, greens, poached eggs and aromatic herbs like coriander or pennyroyal. A variation on this is **migas**, which just means 'soaked bread' and can refer to a bowl of bread soaked in red wine and sprinkled with sugar, or bread crumbled into black coffee, sprinkled with sugar and eaten with a spoon. Migas can also mean a kind of stew, or a well flavoured doughy mix served with a braise. Sometimes it's quite hard to tell the difference between açorda and migas, and looking at the texture won't necessarily tell you.

Ensopados are wet stews in which the excess liquid is soaked up by bread. They can be made from either meat or fish, and are home cooked dishes rather than restaurant dishes, although there's no good reason for that.

The soup category of a menu can include the famous **caldo verde** (Galician kale and potato soup, sometimes served with slices of sausage – see Minho in the Regional Variations chapter), the ubiquitous and delicious **canja** (chicken broth, just in case you need restoration) or **papas** (a gruel, often made from pork), and a bunch of **sopas** (soups) themselves may include fish (**sopa de peixe**), just vegetable (**sopa de legumes**), vegetables and grains, pulses or beans (**sopa de feijão**) or wheat (**sopa de trigo**), or even leftovers (**sopa de cozido**). Or, come to think of it, with stones (**sopa de pedra**) – legend has it a monk tricked food out of peasants by claiming he could make a soup out of stones, but made them supply ingredients to make the 'soup'. **Gaspacho** (cold tomato and onion soup) is popular in the south and is frequently served with grilled sardines. Unlike its northern cousin it is not often pureed, so it's like a wet salad. The soup section also contains **sopa seca** (dry soup), which is neither a soup nor dry. It's more like a hotpot with bread (see Minho in the Regional Variations chapter). The point is that a soupy kind of dish can be light enough to sustain a model without threatening her livelihood, or substantial enough to feed a troop of farmhands.

Canja de Galinha (Chicken Broth)

This broth is common all over Portugal as a restorative, and as a soup is second only to **caldo verde** (Galician kale and potato soup).

Ingredients

1	whole free range chicken
$2\frac{1}{2}$ litres	strong chicken stock
1	medium brown onion, sliced
$\frac{1}{4}$	bunch fresh parsley, including stalks
	zest of 1 lemon
$\frac{1}{2}$ cup	white rice
	salt & pepper to taste
	fresh coriander, chopped
6 to 8	very thin slices of lemon

Wash the chicken and pat dry with a paper towel. Place in a large stockpot and cover with the stock. Add the onion, parsley and lemon zest and bring to the boil. Reduce the heat and simmer for about 45 minutes until the thickest part of the chicken (the thigh joint) is cooked. Remove the chicken and drain, returning the liquid back to the stockpot. Strain the entire stock and return it to the pot. Increase the heat and boil without a lid to reduce it slightly and intensify the flavour. Add the rice and simmer until just tender (about 15 minutes). In the meantime, remove all the flesh from the chicken and tear it into shreds. When the rice is cooked, put the chicken meat into the stock, season with salt and pepper and simmer for 2 to 3 minutes. Divide the soup between heated bowls, ensuring a good mix of rice and chicken to broth. Garnish with a slice of lemon and a sprinkle of coriander and serve.

Serves 6–8

Caldeirada de peixe (fish stew), Viana do Castelo, Minho

So when is a fish soup not a fish soup? When it's a **caldeirada**. This is a soupy stew, or a stewy soup. It is usually, but not always, made with fish, and is another one of the **pratos completos** (complete dishes). There are as many ways to make caldeirada as there are cooks who make it, but what all seafood caldeiradas should have is lots of fresh fish, including shellfish and squid, and layers of potato. They are cooked along the coast, but look out for them in Setúbal and Nazare.

Feijoadas (bean stews) are also a complete meal in which the beans may be stewed with lamb, seafood or rabbit or, in the classic Trás-os-Montes way, with all parts of the pig, as there are lots of them about up there. The stews use dried beans, and the dish will probably also be served with rice on the side. Feijoadas are distinct from broad bean dishes, which are also a complete meal based on dried broad beans cooked with lots of sausage and other pig parts, and served with a lettuce salad.

And just in case this was starting to get clearer, some rice dishes are also complete meals, such as **arroz de lampreia** (lamprey rice) or **arroz de pato** (duck rice) from the Minho region, and **arroz de marisco** (seafood rice) on the coast. Or there's even **arroz de feijão** (rice with red beans). Chickpea-based stews are called **ranchos**, and like the ensopados, **chanfanas** (goat stews) and migas, are a complete meal. So look out. If a dish is described as being 'com arroz', or 'com feijão', it just means that they are served on the side and this alone will not satisfy your appetite. But if you see 'arroz de' or 'feijão de' on the menu, it means a one pot dish is coming your way. Many traditional dishes are truly one-pot wonders with a little bit of everything, so don't go trying to take a mix and match approach because you'll have to face the embarassment of not being able to eat all you've ordered.

"I tell you ... each cheese, one of these round small cheeses, like the Camembert or the Rabaçal, they educate the taste."

– Eça de Queiroz in *A Cidade e as Serras*

Queijo (Cheese)

Cheesemaking was among the many gifts the Romans brought to Portugal as their empire expanded to the north and west. They knew about the use of rennet, the need to reduce moisture by pressing out the whey, and the need for salt as a preservative and drying agent. Sometimes they basted it with wine, smoked it, or dusted it with chives and salt before eating. The Portuguese have kept cheese simple, and many people make fresh cheese from their own milk rather than buy it. This means it can largely be a hit and miss affair, but if you have a few extra sheep and goats out the back, you may as well use them. There's not a lot of pomp and ceremony about cheese in Portugal. It's part of daily life.

As in Greece, Portugal's cheeses are made mainly from ewe's or goat's milk, or a combination of the two. You will eat cheese every day here, either before a meal with a bowl of olives and a glass of wine, in between meals as a snack, or in between bread as a sandwich. You may even eat it for breakfast with honey and spices. It's unlikely, with the exception of the cheddar-like cow's milk **queijo da ilha** (island cheese from the Azores), that you'll find cheese cooked into a dish. While the DOP (see the boxed text Sealing the Quality in the Culture chapter) ewe's milk **queijo da Serra/Estrela** is by far the most expensive and renowned (see Beiras in the Regional Variations chapter), most of the cheeses are less grand. **Requeijão** is the deliciously rich ricotta-like cheese made from ewe's milk whey, and it is eaten fresh as a savoury **acepipe** (hors d'oeuvre); on bread with honey for breakfast; as a dessert with caramelised pumpkin; or even hot and soupy as a nutritious lunch with bread and wine. Common also is an offering of small chunks of **queijo de ovelha** (ewe's milk cheese) either before or after a meal, or in between with a beer or glass of wine. Rabaçal, Azeitão and Saloio are also excellent, as are Évora, Serpa and Nisa from Alentejo, and Monte from Trás-os-Montes.

Many of the cheeses are made with unpasteurised milk, which everyone agrees gives a better quality cheese, but which also presents the health risk of listeria (see Food Poisoning in the Fit & Healthy chapter). If you happen to be passing through a cheesemaking area look out for signs saying 'Queijaria Artesanal'. Here you can buy direct from the producer. Have a look at how the cheese is made and aged, and even try something quite rare: butter made from ewe's milk. This is so loved, and such small quantities are made (ewes don't produce a lot of milk, and what they do produce mostly goes to cheese) that locals will snap it up before it even gets to the market, let alone to a shop. Be wary, however, of fake cheeses that trade off a regulated DOP name, and be aware that finding certain cheeses out of season means that the producer has kept them frozen for the tourist season.

Serra da Estrela cheese, Serra da Estrela, Beiras

Especiarias (Spices)

Vasco da Gama's quick trips made it possible for cinnamon, cloves, nutmeg, pepper and curry powder to creep into common usage (see History in the Culture chapter). His efforts are greatly appreciated every day at mealtimes all over the country.

Açafrão (Saffron)

Too expensive for daily use, and nowhere near as prevalent as in Spanish cooking, saffron is, however, still a staple for the Portuguese.

Canela (Cinnamon)

The favourite spice, it makes its way into almost all sweets, is used to stir coffee, and is added to lots of savoury braised poultry and meat dishes.

Caril (Curry)

Curry powder is a pantry staple but is not used in an obtrusive way. It's more of a subtle seasoning than a dominant flavour.

Colorau (Paprika)

Sweet paprika is **colorau doce**, made from dried and ground sweet red peppers, while hot paprika, **pimentão**, is made from dried and ground hot red peppers. Both are used extensively in flavouring and preserving meats and cheeses. **Massa de pimentão** is a marinating and basting paste in Alentejo, made from roasted red capsicums, crushed with garlic and olive oil.

Cominhos (Cumin)

This is popular in the regional food of Minho and the Azores.

Cravinhos (Cloves)

Although used in the spiced honey cakes of Madeira and in some meat and fish dishes, cloves are nowhere near as popular as cinnamon.

Noz Moscada (Nutmeg)

Around for centuries but only sparingly used, nutmeg is sometimes found in sweets and heavy, spiced cakes.

Pimenta (Pepper)

These are the black and white kind. Surprisingly, food is only very subtly peppered and no pepper will be out on the table.

Pimenta da Jamaica (Allspice)

This spice, from a dried berry tasting of cloves, cinnamon and nutmeg, is important in the cooking of the Azores.

Ervas & Temperos (Herbs & Flavourings)

A pinch here, a handful there and a splash all over – here's what you'll need to put some Portuguese punch in your pot.

Alecrim (Rosemary)

Although it grows abundantly, rosemary is not often used apart from occasionally in some stews.

Alho (Garlic)

If you don't love garlic, you won't love Portugal. This is an absolutely essential element of traditional cooking.

Coentros (Coriander)

Coriander is native to southern Europe, but Portugal is the only country in the region to use the leaves widely in its traditional cooking. Coriander went to Britain in the Bronze Age and was used there up until the 19th century, where the word coriander was also a slang term for money, as in, 'Hand over your corianders or I'll shoot your mother!'. But we digress. For the Portuguese the small and intensely aromatic leaves are as useful as – and arguably tastier than – flat-leaf parsley. You'll find coriander especially in the Algarve and in Alentejo in vegetable dishes, soups and fish stews.

Hortelã (Mint)

Fresh mint leaves are used to season soups and stews in the country's centre and north, where it grows wild.

Louro (Bay Leaves)

An important flavouring in slow cooked dishes all over the country, bay leaves are also used as a flavoursome skewer for grilling meat, with chunks of meat threaded onto the leafy branches.

Orégãos (Oregano)

This herb grows wild in Alentejo, where it is commonly used in meat and fish dishes.

Piri Piri (Red Hot Chilli Peppers & Sauce)

Brought back from Angola, this explosive little chilli, which is made into a sauce (see the recipe), has become a staple to add to everything grilled, especially fish and chicken. In Portugal, piri piri has come to be a generic reference to chilli, even though it's just one type of chilli. In **tascas** (cheap eateries), a large jar of house-made piri piri with a long handled spoon is passed from diner to diner to spread over whatever is before them.

Piri Piri (Red Hot Chilli Pepper Sauce)

You could just go out and buy a bottle of piri piri, but where's the fun in that? Far better to make your own.

Ingredients

1 cup	finely chopped red birdseye chillies
6	medium cloves garlic, chopped
2 tsp	sea salt
½ cup	white wine vinegar
1½ to 2 cups	good olive oil

Put all the ingredients in a large jar, close the lid tightly and give the lot a mighty shake. Leave it in the fridge for a week, give it a stir then start using it. Don't make more than you can eat in about 6 weeks.

Sal (Salt)

The human body has a specialised taste detector for salt, and it has been prized for centuries as a seasoning and a preservative. With all their sun and salty sea the Portuguese are, naturally enough, big producers and users of salt. Most of the salt production occurs along the Algarve coast, but there is also some activity on the mid-north coast at Aveiro. Both of these areas are also traditionally associated with the salting of cod. It's a low maintenance process that begins in May. Saltpans are filled with water and as the water evaporates, the salt concentrates into lumps, which are broken and scraped up to higher levels for more drying. Around mid-September, workers pile the salt into huge mounds and leave it for up to another year to dry, before packaging. This is the natural way, but there are large factories doing it faster with mechanised processing. If a dish is salty it will be called 'salgado' and if you're not brave enough to take well-salted food (which it generally is), ask for a dish to be prepared 'sem sal' (without salt) and bear the brunt of scorn.

Salsa (Flat-Leaf Parsley)

Parsley is found in or on lots of dishes, especially fish and seafood. Only the flat continental variety is used (not the curly).

Sálvia (Sage)

Despite plenty of it growing wild, sage is not popular in Portuguese cooking.

Vinagre (Vinegar)

Plain old white vinegar is used for cooking, and cider vinegar appears in cruets for dressing everything at the table from chickpeas and cod to salad.

Piri piri – don't even think about eating your frango no churrasco (char-grilled chicken) without it

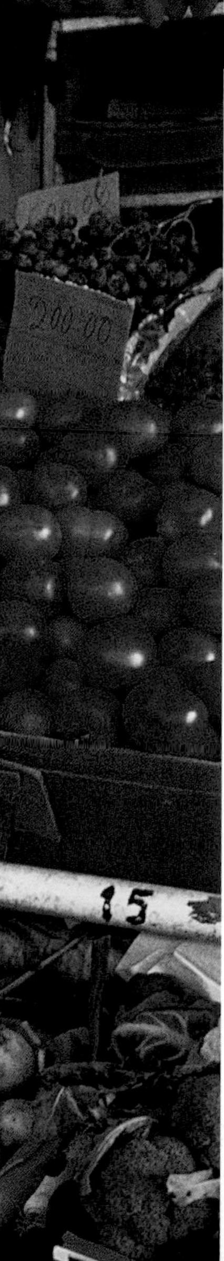

Hortaliças (Vegetables)

Don't make any assumptions about vegetables being savoury and fruit and nuts sweet when it comes to traditional Portuguese food. Moorish invaders left a legacy of mix and match flavours where the most savoury of pumpkins can be rendered into sweet jam (or cake filling), beans can be the crucial ingredient in a pastry, and preserved green tomato a sweet to eat by the spoonful or fill a pie. Potatoes in Portugal are sweeter and better and more moreish than anywhere else, and appear at almost every meal. Steamed, boiled, baked and fried are the favourite ways to prepare them, and just because you have beans and rice and bread doesn't mean you won't get potatoes too. The far north-east of the country, Trás-os-Montes, has DOP (see the boxed text Sealing the Quality in the Culture chapter) spuds, and there's nothing humble about that. Pickles of carrot, cauliflower and capsicum are served over grilled meats with lemon to cut through the fat, but some people also use them to disguise less than fresh meat, so beware.

Abóbora (Pumpkin)

This vegetable is often used in sweets such as **doce de abóbora** (pumpkin jam), and in desserts, or served with **requeijão** (ricotta) for breakfast. **Chila** is a type of pumpkin that is green on the outside, with white spots and black seeds inside. The pumpkin has to be smashed open, not cut, and the inside – which looks like white spaghetti – is cooked with sugar and becomes sweet, crystallized strands that are then used in desserts and sweets (see **doce de chila** in the Doces & Pastéis section later in this chapter).

Batata (Potato)

Why do the potatoes here taste so good? They're universally wonderful, nutty and sweet, and always served in generous quantities. Too many (of which there always are) are never enough. In the Algarve sweet potatoes are baked whole until their skins split, then the flesh is eaten with a spoon, or fried and sprinkled with cinnamon and sugar.

Fresh fruit and veg, Viseu, Beiras

HEY WAITER! WHERE'S MY SALAD?

Notice we don't mention salad very often in this book. That's because in Portugal, it's rarely mentioned either. There is a word for it, **salada**, but you can't have one. Or rather you can, but it will be no more than a few leaves of iceberg lettuce, a few slices of tomato and some slices of onion. It will arrive washed but undressed. You'll have to dress it yourself with the vinegar and oil supplied. No salt, no pepper. If you're really lucky, a few olives, a bit of grated carrot or half an avocado might also appear. But don't get your hopes up. So what happened to all those luscious potential salad ingredients you saw at the markets? They're all to be used in soups, stews and other cooked dishes. So if you like it raw, you'll have to make it yourself. Or stay at home.

Cebola (Onion)
Big and brown, onions are absolutely essential in everything but sweets.

Cenoura (Carrot)
These are often served with meat dishes, simply tossed in butter or cooking juices. They are also so naturally sweet that they are candied or made into jam, and are exquisite pickled with coriander leaves in Alentejo.

Couve Galega (Galician Kale)
This most Portuguese of ingredients is from the Minho region and while kale, savoy and other types of cabbage are used all over the country, this is the crown prince. *The* defining ingredient in **caldo verde** (Galician kale and potato soup), it's also used in lots of other cooked dishes. This is the finely shredded leaves you'll see people buying by the bagful at markets.

Espargo Bravo (Wild Asparagus)
These tiny spears have a short season and are used in **sopa de cação** (dogfish bread soup) or cooked as a vegetable.

Espinafre (Spinach)
Deliciously delicate, spinach is often cooked with garlic in meat juices, and pureed with other fine greens as an accompaniment to meat.

Favas (Broad Beans)
Loved fresh as well as dried, broad beans are cooked with coriander or other fresh herbs, olive oil and spices as side dishes to meat, or as an **acepipe** (hors d'oeuvre).

Feijão Verde (Green Beans)

This is one of the few vegetables to make it relatively unadorned to the table – simply boiled, then drizzled with vinegar and olive oil.

Nabo (Turnip) & Nabiças (Turnip Greens)

Rarely appreciated in other countries, both turnips and their greens are revered in Portugal. Turnip flesh is boiled and mashed with potatoes or tossed in meat juices, while the baby greens are used in soups and accompaniments, and even the tiny flowers are eaten.

Tomate (Tomato)

Along with garlic and onions, tomatoes are one of the most commonly used ingredients and are superbly sweet, too. So sweet that **doce de tomate** (tomato jam – see the recipe) is eaten by the spoonful.

Doce de Tomate (Tomato Jam)

This jam is popular in Portugal, and easy to make.

Ingredients

1kg	very ripe tomatoes
750g	white sugar
1 tsp	ground cinnamon
	juice of ½ lemon

Place the tomatoes in a large bowl and pour boiling water over the top. Leave for one minute, then drain. Peel the tomatoes, cut them in half, scoop out the seeds, and drain off the juice if the tomatoes are watery. Chop the tomatoes roughly and weigh (should be about 750g). Weigh out an equal amount of sugar. In a large saucepan, combine the tomatoes, sugar and cinnamon. Cook slowly over a low heat, tasting and stirring regularly to make sure the sugar is not caramelising. When the jam begins to thicken and takes on the consistency of jelly, add the lemon juice. Cool the mix, then decant into sterilised jars. Use it as you would any sweet jam, on toast or in cake fillings. You could also use cloves or vanilla instead of cinnamon.

Makes about 3 to 4 cups of jam

Fruta, Fruto Seco & Mel (Fruit, Nuts & Honey)

As well as the grapes that grow all over the country, Portugal grows plenty of other fruit. You may never actually see many people eating it, but they do love it and it creeps into all kinds of dishes, usually with plenty of sugar. Between the mid-north-east, central west, south and islands, the supply of fresh fruit is constant. Apricots, citrus fruits and plums are popular while the best figs, strawberries and oranges are transported from the sunny south all around the country. Oranges and lemons are served in wedges with some grilled fish and meat dishes, or cooked in the dish. They're also candied in strips or used to flavour cakes, puddings and homemade liqueurs. Big navels from the Algarve are said to be best for eating fresh while those from Setúbal go into jam, as does almost the entire crop of cherries. After dinner a simple wedge of orange or thin slices of pineapple sprinkled with

Pêra bêbeda (whole pears cooked in red wine), Castelo Branco, Beiras

port can do for dessert. On the banana growing island of Madeira, deep-fried banana is served as a vegetable to accompany fish and chicken rather than as a fruit. In high fruit-producing areas the excess crop is preserved in sugar, dried, or cooked into jam.

A slice of **presunto** (smoked ham), dried Mission figs and a swig of port is one of those perfect combinations that really shouldn't be missed. The famous **ameixas de Elvas** (plums of Elvas) are really greengages (sweet dessert plums) preserved in sugar and served as a kind of sweet snack or as part of a dessert. They will inspire obsession. In the Algarve, dried figs studded with almonds and **doces de amêndoa** (marzipan sweets) flavoured with fruits fill confectionery windows. Quince never goes out of fashion in Portugal and is made into 'cheese' or jelly.

Chestnuts are still used in the remote north as an alternative to potato; cooked in salty water flavoured with aniseed for a snack; or fed to pigs to make their flesh taste sweet. Peanuts are roasted with **piri piri** (red hot chilli peppers). Walnuts can be preserved with fruit and sugar in a jam or baked into spiced cakes.

Fresh honey is harvested across the country, including the islands, and most notably almost all of Alentejo. Where honey is common, dishes will be just as sweet as those in non-honey areas, but are made sweet with honey, not sugar. **Mel da abelhas** is honey from bees while **mel de cana** is honey from the cane, or molasses.

HOW ENGLISH IS MARMALADE?

The word 'marmalade' comes from the Portuguese word **marmelada**, meaning quince jam. The Portuguese presented a marmalade to the English king in 1524, and during the 17th century the Brits went a little nuts and started to use all different kinds of fruit to make what they still called marmalade. The word began to mean a sort of jam but not one to be spread on bread – rather, it referred to a kind of stiff, sweet fruit paste to be sliced and eaten as, or with, dessert. Citrus began to creep into the mix around this time, and by the 19th century it was safe to assume that on English soil, marmalade meant orange marmalade (used as a spread), including the much disputed love/hate element of citrus peel. While the word still refers in French and German to a generic jam or preserve, the Brits were rather attached to their specific version, and an EC edict of 1981 stipulates that marmalade can only legally refer to a preserve that includes oranges, lemons, limes or grapefruit. Everything else has to be called a preserve. But if you want to try the original marmalade, buy some firm quince paste and get into it.

Doces & Pastéis (Sweets & Pastries)

Portuguese life is sweet. Sweeter than just about anywhere else. And rich. Sugar and egg yolks are the two commonest ingredients. And that's thanks to the Moors, who brought sugar cane, almonds and fruit to Portugal, and the nimble fingers of nuns, who made egg yolk sweets as gifts.

But what will you get, and where? At **pastelarias** (pastry shops) you'll find plenty of pastries and liberal doses of sugar with them, while at other eateries the choice varies from the devastatingly calorie- and cholesterol-rich conventual sweets to sweet rice and custards, or cakes. Make sure you try the **toucinho do céu** (a rich, sweet almond and cinnamon cake), the **queijadas** (tarts with a sweet, dense filling) and the famous **pastéis de nata** (technically cream, but really custard, tarts). Apart from sugar, egg yolks, oranges, almonds and lemons, cinnamon is a common ingredient, as is bacon fat or lard, especially in areas where pork products rule.

The **doces conventuais** (conventual sweets) were traditionally made with excess yolks (see the boxed text Is that a Yolk in Your Pocket?) and lots of sugar by the nuns as gifts for noblemen and other important travellers who stayed with them. After the abolition of religious orders in Portugal under the Marquês de Pombal in the 18th century, the recipes were guarded by wealthy families whose daughters had returned from the convents. The recipes are now commercial secrets. They are made by descendants of the daughters, in towns near whichever order created the original sweet. Apart from feeding the locals they also keep the stories behind the sweets alive. As they are rich and labour intensive, they are expensive to buy and are usually given as gifts or eaten at a **casa de chá** (teahouse) or pastelaria that is known for making them. Be reverential when you eat them: everyone else is.

Overlapping the conventual sweets are **doces de ovos** (egg yolk sweets), and chief among them are the strange **fios de ovos** (cooked egg threads), which rely on a skilled cook being able to create perfect strands of beaten egg yolk by pouring them through a sieve and into a boiling sugar syrup. The glossy yellow threads can be eaten as a petit four or baked into a cake or tart to make a dessert. Either way, it's an acquired taste and you'll come across a lot of it. A similarly flavoured base is **ovos moles**, a kind of paste made from egg yolks and sugar syrup stirred and cooked until smooth rather than cooked into threads. It can be spread between pastry or cake layers, smoothed across cake tops as icing, used as a filling for marzipan candies or stirred into other egg desserts. The picture you should be getting here is that egg yolks and sugar dominate everything, and sometimes that's all a sweet will be.

Equally sweet is the dessert preparation of **doce de chila** (candied chila gourd, which is like a spaghetti squash, so named for its spaghetti-like

Don't come to Portugal if you're on a diet – traditional cakes and pastries from Salão de Chá Maltesinhas, Beja, Alentejo

DE ARROZ
DA CASA

A golden breakfast treat – bolo de arroz (cake made with rice and wheat flour), Douro

Pudim Molotov (Soft Egg-white Dessert)

The sweet, wobbly dessert is served all over Portugal, at any time of day. Our recipe was kindly supplied by Fernando Goncalves, of the Portuguese Sagres restaurant in Elwood, Australia.

Sugar water
300g caster sugar
300ml water

Egg mix
600ml cold egg whites
500g caster sugar
2 pinches salt

Pouring sauce
1 egg yolk
30g sugar
1 tsp Baileys Irish Cream, or other creamy liqueur

To make the sugar water, in a heavy-based saucepan dissolve the caster sugar into the water. Simmer for about half an hour, stirring periodically, until the mix is syrupy. Leave the syrup to cool to around room temperature. Preheat the oven to 200°C.

To prepare the egg mix, combine the egg whites, caster sugar and salt in an electric mixer, and whisk until foamy.

Pour the sugar water into the hollow core of a large (30cm) metal ring tin/tube pan, and gently pour the egg mix on top. Place the tin in a wide, deep-sided dish or roasting tin in the oven, and pour warm water into the outside dish, creating a water bath. Bake in the oven for approximately 40 minutes. The egg is cooked when it is golden on top.

While the egg mix is cooking, prepare the pouring sauce in a heavy-based saucepan. Combine the egg yolk, sugar and liqueur in the pan, heating gently and stirring until the sugar has dissolved completely. Allow to cool before serving.

Remove the molotov from the oven and allow to cool. Turn the dessert out, and serve chilled in slices with the pouring sauce.

Serves 10–12

white flesh – see the Abóbora entry under Vegetables, earlier – which retains a thread-like consistency when candied). The prepared chila is used as an ingredient in lots of tarts, puddings and egg sweets and, again, is an acquired taste.

Some desserts are simply a whole egg yolk candied in sugar and wrapped in pastry, or folded in communion wafers. It is impossible to overstate the dominance of these few ingredients on the sweet scene and palate of the country. You'll never get completely away from yolks and sugar, but they can be diluted somewhat.

Desserts in eateries aren't usually of the cake variety. That's why there are pastelarias. For **pudims** (puddings), you should be thinking creamy, eggy, gooey, sweet and definitely not in need of chewing. Pudims usually refer to some type of baked custard (port, tea and lemon are popular) that is either turned out of a mould and covered in dark caramel, or served as a more liquid **leite-crème** (egg custard) in individual, terracotta-coloured plastic dishes (that may look and feel like the base of a pot plant holder, but are supposed to make you think of clay). These are sweet, eggy and delicious and on every restaurant menu. The seasonings will be lemon or orange, cinnamon and maybe vanilla. That is, until you spot something like a **sopa dourada** (golden soup), which is a kind of bread and butter – or cake and butter – pudding traditionally served at Christmas in Minho.

Arroz doce (rice pudding – see the recipe in the Celebrating chapter) is a national favourite, and unlike the English version is cooked on top of the stove much like a risotto. Milk is added slowly to the rice, which slowly plumps up as it absorbs the liquid. It is flavoured with lemon zest and cinnamon, with cinnamon sprinkled across the top in special patterns. You'll see small bowls of this lined up in the refrigerated sweet counter of eateries across the country.

Then there's **pudim molotov** (see the recipe), which rivals arroz doce in popularity. Enormous slabs of snow white, soft meringue are smothered in dark caramel, oozing ovos moles or a creamy liqueur sauce. It's a relative newcomer, first appearing about 50 years ago. Maybe some conscientious cook realised it was un-Portuguese to keep throwing out all those egg whites.

Bolos (cakes) are more likely to be found in a teahouse or cafe, including the classic **pão-de-ló** (sponge cake), which is sold still in the folds of baking paper in which it was cooked. This is not like a French sponge. It's more like an undercooked sponge with a cakeish top and bottom and a centre lush with, you guessed it, sweet yolk. Other bolos are less sponge-like and may be rich with different spices, nuts, fruit or honey. This is for lingering over with coffee or eating as dessert at home rather than eating at restaurants after a meal. Keep an eye out for **broas**, a cross between cake and biscuit (ie, with a cakeish texture but of biscuit size).

IS THAT A YOLK IN YOUR POCKET?

We know the sugar and sweet tooth came with the Moors, but why all the egg yolks? The answer is unclear, but there's surely a story in a single special cake (serving about 10 people) requiring 60 egg yolks. No, that's not a typo. *Sixty.* And all paths lead inexorably back to the convent. Oh, they were wicked. See what happens when you lock up a bunch of reluctant women and make them take vows they didn't want to take? Things get all out of balance and they start making egg yolk cakes.

From the Middle Ages the convents and monasteries became quite wealthy. If a family was rich and wanted to stay that way they had to make sure any daughters were out of the picture. So they sent them to convents, along with 'dowries' that included lots of chickens, and therefore eggs. In addition it seems that tenants on church land paid their dues in produce – more chickens and more eggs.

That explains why the convents had so many eggs on hand, but not why the sweets use such enormous quantities of yolks only. Part of the explanation could be that the yolks might have been viewed as just leftovers (leftovers occupy a special place in the hearts and minds and kitchens of all Portuguese cooks, because they always cook too much and have to think up delicious ways to use the leftovers – some of the best traditional dishes are actually leftovers).

But in a country renowned for thrift, how did the richest part of the egg get become a leftover in the convents? One theory has it that local winemakers 'fined' or clarified their wines with egg whites, which they needed a lot of to remove any particles that might cause cloudiness. More convincing is the theory that when the Cistercians set up shop in Portugal they brought with them the tradition of starched habits. The recipe? Lots of egg whites mixed with flour and water to a paste and spread on the clothes before ironing them. The result? Leftovers of egg yolks. And now, in a land of commercial starch and where the religious orders were destroyed in the 18th century, the egg whites are mostly thrown away.

Formigos (sweetmeats) are a common item on restaurant menus. They are a thick paste of soaked hard bread or biscuit with egg yolks, sugar, honey, milk, cinnamon and wine, cooked slowly over a low heat just until the egg sets. **Gelado** (ice cream) is often the commercial variety and not offered in eateries.

What you will not find much of is chocolate. Although the Spanish have had it since the 16th century, the Portuguese have stuck to their egg yolk and sugar preferences. The exception is chocolate mousse, a dessert section staple.

drinks of portugal

Wine, water, beer and coffee are Portugal's favourite liquids, but don't be fooled by the seemingly limited choice. There are up to 53 wine regions, lots of the same grape varieties with names that change from region to region, a confusing coffee lexicon to navigate, and the temptation of getting up close and personal with that dangerously delicious pickling liquid, **aguardente** (a brandy-like spirit). You'll need help getting around it all.

Vinho (Wine)

If you're used to looking for the characteristics of a particular grape variety, or a blend, you'll be lost for reference points in Portugal: the grapes taste so uniquely of themselves that in truth they can only be compared to other Portuguese wines.

The Portuguese are the most enthusiastic all-round boozers after Luxembourg, France and Italy, and knock back more than double the German quota even though they drink from smaller glasses. There is hardly any wine left to export at the end of each year, which means the rest of us simply don't get to try the good stuff. What we mostly get is Mateus Rosé, which, while it has been most generously described as "a light and cheerful wine with a touch of sparkle", gives no hint of the wine varieties we'll never get to drink unless we get out of the armchair and go.

So just what is so good about Portuguese wine? For a start, some of the country's grape varieties are among the oldest on the planet, and many simply don't exist anywhere else. Secondly, the Portuguese also worked out how to make average wine into superlative fortified wines: the generic Madeira and port, and the branded Moscatel de Setúbal. These are why Portugal is famous, but to ignore the extraordinary range of other wines produced is an easy mistake to commit, because trying to work out each wine's grape variety, region and winemaker is like trying to solve a Rubik's Cube with your eyes closed.

Wine cellar and tasting room, Quinta de Pacheca, Douro

You probably already know that the so-called Old World wines, such as those from France and Italy, tend to be named for the region or even town in which they're produced (think Bordeaux and Barolo), while New World wines from Australia, South Africa and California are identified by grape variety (think Sauvignon Blanc and Semillon).

Even if you've mastered this tricky enough distinction it still won't help because Portugal doesn't reliably label its wine by region or grape. Authorities are attempting to get agreement between producers on what to call the same types of grape. At the moment, the same variety may be called by different names in different regions. But as old habits invariably die a painful and reluctant death, don't hold your breath for speedy change.

It's easy to see how this parochialism came about. Until very recently (like a decade or two back) the road system throughout Portugal was quite primitive, and public transport from region to region less than reliable. So if you had no good reason to go somewhere, why would you? And if there isn't regular communication between towns and villages, there sure isn't going to be any talk between a winemaker in the north and his counterpart in the south. So over thousands of years the same grape varieties became known in different regions by different names.

Dão wines, Viseu, Beiras

In general, the most interesting wines are reds, port and Madeira, then **vinho verde** (light sparkling wine) and muscat. And the most interesting thing to do with them is consume them with food at every meal: that's what they're made for. Despite the complexity of wine types, you'll only be asked to nominate **vinho tinto** (red wine) or **vinho branco** (white wine). Colour is the only distinction made.

The best thing that the local Portuguese wine industry could possibly do is to continue to resist the global trend towards international wine styles. This is done by encouraging awareness of indigenous varieties. There simply isn't the space for vast tracts of Chardonnay or Cabernet Sauvignon anyway, so why not drum up some interest in the flirtatious-sounding Periquita? Or the delightful Alvarinho?

Regional Variations

The following geographic breakdowns relate to a broad categorisation of regionality for wines in Portugal, as referred to in the Vinhos Regionais section of the boxed text Reading the Label.

Minho (including the districts of Viana do Castelo and Braga)

Wine has been produced in the Minho region, in the far north-west, since at least Roman times. Unusually, the vines may grow up to 6m or 7m above ground height, where they like to wend their way through chestnut, poplar or plane tree branches with space enough for vegetable gardens and fruit trees underneath their canopies. Even many of the lower vines are trellised well above head height which can be magical to see when you're driving down the unsealed roads that divide the **quintas** (farms) and their grape-heavy vines. The area produces red, white and rosé wines and is the official DOC region for the famous vinho verde, or 'green wine', which was first referred to in council documents in 1606 (see Vinho Verde later in this chapter).

Trás-os-Montes (including the entire district of Bragança and parts of Guarda, Vila Real and Viseu)

This region is the famous home of **vinho do porto** (port; see Port later in this chapter). The Romans got things going with a system of terracing that still characterises the area. But the big boom occurred in the latter part of the 17th century when a win-win trade deal with England ensured the part of the region called Douro was named as the only official port-producing area in Portugal. The legislation enacted in 1756 delineates an area that remains virtually the same today. But apart from port, the region also has four IPR (see the Reading the Label boxed text) wine producing areas – Chaves, Valpaços and Planalto Mirandês, as well as the rest of the DOC-covered Douro, which is not involved in port production but produces light, aromatic whites and rich, smooth reds with good ageing possibilities. There are also other good wines that are not part of the DOC/IPR system at all. Chaves produces firm, dry young reds, Valpaços produces light, dry fruity wines and Planalto Mirandês produces low alcohol, fresh whites and well balanced light reds that should age well. Touriga Nacional and Fernão Pires are favoured red and white grape varieties respectively. So if you're in the Douro, you're right in the heart of port territory but there's masses more to the wines of the whole region covered by Trás-os-Montes, and Terras Durienses, than that.

Beiras (including the districts of Coimbra and Castelo Branco and parts of Guarda, Viseu and Aveiro)

Again those Romans ... only this time they left grape pressing rooms and documents attesting to their wine making prowess. The Beiras wine region stretches from the Atlantic to Spain across diverse microclimates, and is

READING THE LABEL

Cellars, Casa de Santar, Viseu, Beiras

The division of Portugal into official wine making regions and subregions is confusing, so you'll need to get a grip on some terminology. The tricky element is that the border of a region changes according to certain classifications and does not necessarily correspond to tourism or other regional boundaries. This means any appeal to logic is fruitless. We're telling you straight up: there is no logic. It's more of a stream-of-consciousness type arrangement, so try to relax about it. The bottom line is that the pie gets divided in many different ways depending on who's doing the deed. **Regiões vitivinícolas** (wine regions) are divided in the following ways:

Vinhos Regionais (Regional Wines)

The geographical indications of regional wines cover eight official regions, including Minho, Trás-os-Montes, Beiras, Estremadura, Ribatejano, Terras do Sado, Alentejano and Algarve (see the following Regional Variations section). The wines must be made from at least 85% recommended and authorised varieties of grapes from the particular region. This is the simplest system to follow, and despite the fact that these wines are supposedly more basic than the DOC wines (see the following paragraph) they are actually often a quality choice, and at less cost. So apart from the **selo de garantia** (seal), **certificado de garantia** (certificate) or **garantia de origem** (origin guarantee) you'll also see vinho regional followed by one of the geographical area names listed above. Similarly, the supposedly lower-quality but also delicious **vinhos de mesa** (table wines) are a good choice.

Denominações de Origem Controlada (DOC)
The Denominações de Origem (designation of origin) concept applies to wines that are inextricably connected to a particular area within a geographical zone. They must be a reflection of the specific qualities of the area and are subject to strict controls that cover the entire production process, from vine to glass, as set out in EU legislation. There are 32 official areas, including the island of Madeira and three areas in the Azores. This appellation control or DOC is generally granted to the oldest areas producing the specific wines that meet the criteria. Doubly confusing is that the DOC can refer to a particular wine (such as Bairrada), a town (such as Portimão), an entire region (such as Ribatejo or Alentejo) or a wine style (such as **vinho verde** – light sparkling wine – in the Minho region). So don't even try to work it out. Just fill the glass instead.

Indicação de Proveniência Regulamentada (IPR)
The indication of regulated provenance concept is a lesser version of the DOC, in that it guarantees that a wine currently meets the required characteristics of one of the 32 official DOC areas and that must continue to do so for a period of five years. After that, it may become a DOC wine.

Interestingly, the official wine regions (DOC and IPR) are no barometer of quality, and are often more expensive. You're better off looking for labels displaying 'vinhos regional' and 'vinho de mesa', and looking for a reputable producer. To find the best wines a producer makes, look for bottles labelled **garrafeira** or **reserva**.

So when you read your label, there will at the very least be a seal guarantee. Following this may be the type of wine or the DOC area (such as vinho verde, vinho do porto or Douro DOC) or the words 'vinho regional', followed by the geographical region of, for example, Beiras or Estremadura. You may also see DOC spelled out in full (Denominações de Origem Controlada), followed by an official region such as Bucelas, or even Óbidos VQPRD (Vinho de Qualidade Produzido em Regiao Determinada), which means that the wine is of quality and produced in a specific region, which is another way of guaranteeing quality by conforming to EU conditions. Slight variations in the letters will relate to liquor and sparkling wines. So you'll need to be quite a detective to really work out what's in the bottle. What you will not necessarily find is an indication of grape variety, unless it's printed on the label on the back of the bottle. To further confuse matters you may also find the name of the **adega** (cellar) or wine cooperative that made the wine, or it may be a single estate wine that bears the name of a **quinta** (farm or property) that owns the vineyard.

further sub-divided into Beira Alta, Beira Litoral and Terras de Sicó. It produces the famous DOC wines Dão and Bairrada, both of which exhibit deep colour and good ageing possibilities – but they can also be hard and astringent, which may leave you wondering what all the fuss is about. Despite their similarities, the two are made from different grapes and under different conditions: Dão is made from a number of grape varieties in sandy, granite soil while Bairrada is made with Baga grapes and grown in clay soil. While they are the best known of the region, some say that Dão is overrated. Others to look out for are Távora-Varosa, Lafões and Beira Interior, all of which are DOC wines.

Estremadura (including the district of Lisbon, and parts of Santarém and Leiria)
This is the geographic region most heavily under vine. It was well developed from the Middle Ages onwards by religious congregations established close to Lisbon. Of these the Order of Cister is credited with the greatest contribution, but all of them were actually preparing their own tipple to celebrate communion. They just got good at it. The three most famous brands have been so for centuries: Bucelas (made from Arinto grapes), Carcavelos (often from Arinto or Periquita grapes) and Colares (Malvasia for the whites and Ramisco for the reds). To the north are Alenquer, Arruda, Lourinhã and Torres Vedras, which is gaining in popularity, as well as Óbidos, Alcobaça and Encostas de Aire. Fame can push the prices up, so look for good producers of the lesser known wines and choose a reserva. The red and white wines of Estremadura and its sub-region, Alta Estremadura, show typically complex, close textured and understated qualities that can typify the country's style.

Ribatejano (including parts of the districts of Lisbon and Santarém)
Regional wines from the bullfighting region of Ribatejo are called Ribatejano. Their fame spans centuries and legislative protection against invasion from foreign vines has been in place since the 14th century. The landscape can be distinguished by three major features: the rich, marshy soils along the Tagus river, the limestone and clay soils of the alluvial plains, and the poor soils that stretch down towards Alentejo. Each area produces wines of differing characteristics. DOC sub-regional wines to look out for include Almeirim, Cartaxo, Chamusco, Coruche, Santarém and Tomar, and there are around 60 different grape varieties planted. Red wine varieties include Trincadeira Preta (the most popular), Periquita, Baga and Camarate. For white wines, you can look forward to guzzling Trincadeira das Pratas and Vital (which dominates), as well as Arinto, Fernão Pires and Tália.

WINE TOURISM

Portugal has only recently seen the potential for wine route tourism since, to the Portuguese, making wine is about as routine and normal as breathing. So if you're looking for a common thread through different regions, follow the signposted Rota dos Vinhos (wine routes) of Alentejo, Bairrada, Beira Interior, Bucelas, Carcavelos e Colares, Dão, Port Wine, Ribatejo, Templars, Vinhos Verdes, Oeste, Vinhas de Cister or Costa Azul. Look out in the future for the planned routes of the Algarve, Azores and Madeira. All the participating properties (each is called a quinta) should have symbols at the roadside which indicate what facilities it has to entertain cruising wine tasters. Here's what the corresponding phrases mean:

turismo em espaço rural	'tourism in the country', or accommodation on a working farm or vineyard
vinhas	vineyard
visita de cave/ adega	cellar or wine cooperative tours
marcação prévia	visits by appointment only
prova de vinho	wine tasting
venda de vinho	retail wine sales
museu ou coleção temática	wine museum
possibilidade de participação em actividades vitivinícolas	the possibility of participating in agricultural activities

Terras do Sado (including the district of Setúbal)

The geographical region of the Setúbal Peninsula is referred to as the regional wine Terras do Sado. (These confusing distinctions, while they may make sense to locals, can be a nightmare to wrap your brain around.) This is another ancient wine growing area: the Phoenicians and Greeks both thought this was a fine spot for vines, and planted accordingly. Later the Romans followed suit, then the Moors and Francs. There's an extraordinary range of grape varieties here. Setúbal and Palmela are the two DOC-covered sub-regions within Terras do Sado. Setúbal is renowned for its branded fortified white wine, Moscatel de Setúbal, which is uniquely delicious. Deep golden in colour, with floral aromas and a hint of date, orange or honey on the nose, this is one of Portugal's famous exports, and deservedly so. Made since 1834, the muscatel contains 70% muscat grapes and 30% non-muscat local grapes of four different varieties, which give the blend its freshness and vitality. It is aged for a minimum of five years and is best served chilled or over ice as an aperitif. The area's less well known red version, Moscatel Roxo, is slightly drier, more complex and tends to develop well with age. Palmela produces red, white, rosé and sparkling wines, and liqueurs.

Alentejano

From ruins near the town of Vidigueira it is apparent that Romans settled on the baking plains of Alentejo and were busy making wine. The first written documents on wine making in the region date from the 12th century. Alentejo produces some of the best wines in the country, known as Alentejano, and some say the reds from here are preferable to the better known Dão and Bairrada. It's also known as the cork growing capital of the world (see the boxed text Cork Wrecked Your Wine? Blame Portugal!). The premium soils are reserved for cereals and grazing stock, especially the delicious black pig. So vines and olives get the tough soil. Alentejo and its eight sub-regions are all DOC covered and include Redondo, Portalegre, Borba, Reguengos, Vidigueira, Évora, Granja/Amareleja and Moura. Perhaps the most renowned wines are reds from the Alt Alentejo to the north: in Portalegre you'll need plenty of soft, plummy reds to match all the inescapable pork products. The Aragonez caste – known elsewhere in the world as Tempranillo, the variety from which Spain's famous Rioja is made – is common in the reds of the region. Generally you'd expect deep garnet colour, and intense, ripe fruit bouquet and a soft, slightly astringent (too astringent in poor examples) quality. They should be well rounded and improve with age. The whites should show a fresh, aromatic bouquet and a well balanced complexity from the blending of different varieties.

Algarve

Heading down to the Algarve means majestic, rocky coastline and lazy days on the beach with occasional breaks for freshly grilled fish. And, of course, wine. The region is important in the history of wine making because during the Moorish occupation wine was produced for export as well as to keep the locals quiet. When the Christians overthrew the Moors, they thought the infrastructure set up by those vanquished was a good one – so they continued with it. The region is protected from chilly northern winds by mountains, and faces onto the hot, dry and almost always sunny Mediterranean coast. There are four specific DOC wine areas – Lagos, Portimão, Lagoa and Tavira – within the whole region, whose **vinho regional** (regional wine) is also DOC. You'll find straw-coloured, delicate whites and soft, smooth reds reflecting the laid-back nature and low acidity of a warm climate.

Azores

The Azores were colonised in the mid-15th century. Vines are thought to have been introduced here by the Franciscan friars who were in need of a tipple to celebrate Mass. Noticing similarities between conditions on the islands and on Sicily, varieties that did well there were introduced. Verdelho from Pico became especially famous. Of the nine islands, three boast IPR wine growing areas: Graciosa on the island of the same name, Pico on the island of the same name, and the region of Biscoitos on the island of Terceira. All produce white wines, including fortified whites from Pico and Biscoitos. Grape varieties include Arinto, Boal, Fernão Pires, Terrantez and Verdelho dos Azores, and even if you never get around to visiting the islands you can still taste the wines.

Vinho Verde ('Green Wine')

These wines are tart, slightly sparkling, lowish in alcohol (from 8.5% but creeping up these days to around 10% to 11%) and may be either red, white or rosé. The wine is 'green' because it is made from immature grapes, and the result is meant to be drunk within a year of bottling. All vinhos verdes, including the reds, benefit from a slight chilling before drinking. There are six sub-regions officially allowed to produce vinho verde, including Monção, which is renowned for using Alvarinho grapes and is by far one of the best white examples of this wine. If a bottled vinho verde (many are not bottled) says Alvarinho anywhere on the label, it will be a good one to try. Alternatively, look for one made from the Loureiro grapes of Ponte de Lima town – sometimes the two are blended. Alvarinho aguardente and vinho verde vinegar are also worth a try.

Fortified Wines

Any wine that has been fortified with alcohol to stabilise and strengthen it is called a fortified wine. Portuguese examples include the branded Moscatel de Setúbal (see Terras do Sado earlier in this chapter, under Regional Variations) and the generic Madeira wine and port wine.

Vinho da Madeira (Madeira)

The Madeira archipelago, about 750km off the coast of Morocco, was discovered in the early 15th century by lost Portuguese sailors searching for the west coast of Africa. When they saw its biggest island, all they saw was wood, so they called the island Madeira, meaning 'wood'. Having named it for its main feature, they set about clearing the lot to make way for crops, including vines, in fires that allegedly burned for seven years. The wine itself was mediocre until an accidental discovery: adding brandy to

WINE REGIONS

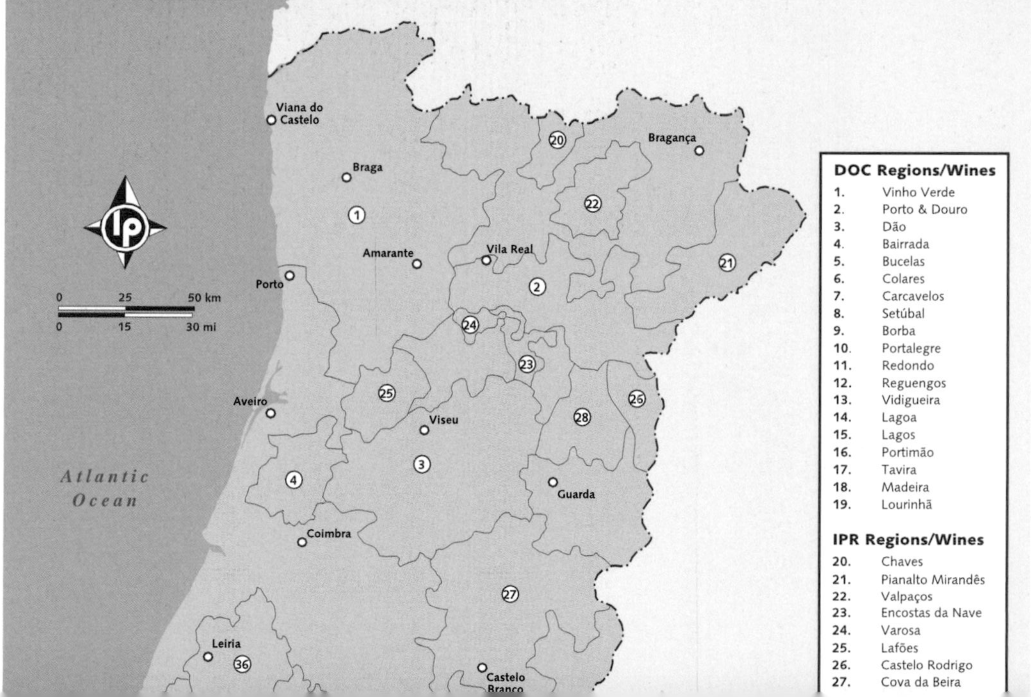

Viana do Castelo
Braga
Amarante
Vila Real
Bragança
Porto
Aveiro
Viseu
Guarda
Coimbra
Leiria
Castelo Branco
Atlantic Ocean
0 25 50 km
0 15 30 mi
DOC Regions/Wines
1. Vinho Verde
2. Porto & Douro
3. Dão
4. Bairrada
5. Bucelas
6. Colares
7. Carcavelos
8. Setúbal
9. Borba
10. Portalegre
11. Redondo
12. Reguengos
13. Vidigueira
14. Lagoa
15. Lagos
16. Portimão
17. Tavira
18. Madeira
19. Lourinhã
IPR Regions/Wines
20. Chaves
21. Pianalto Mirandês
22. Valpaços
23. Encostas da Nave
24. Varosa
25. Lafões
26. Castelo Rodrigo
27. Cova da Beira

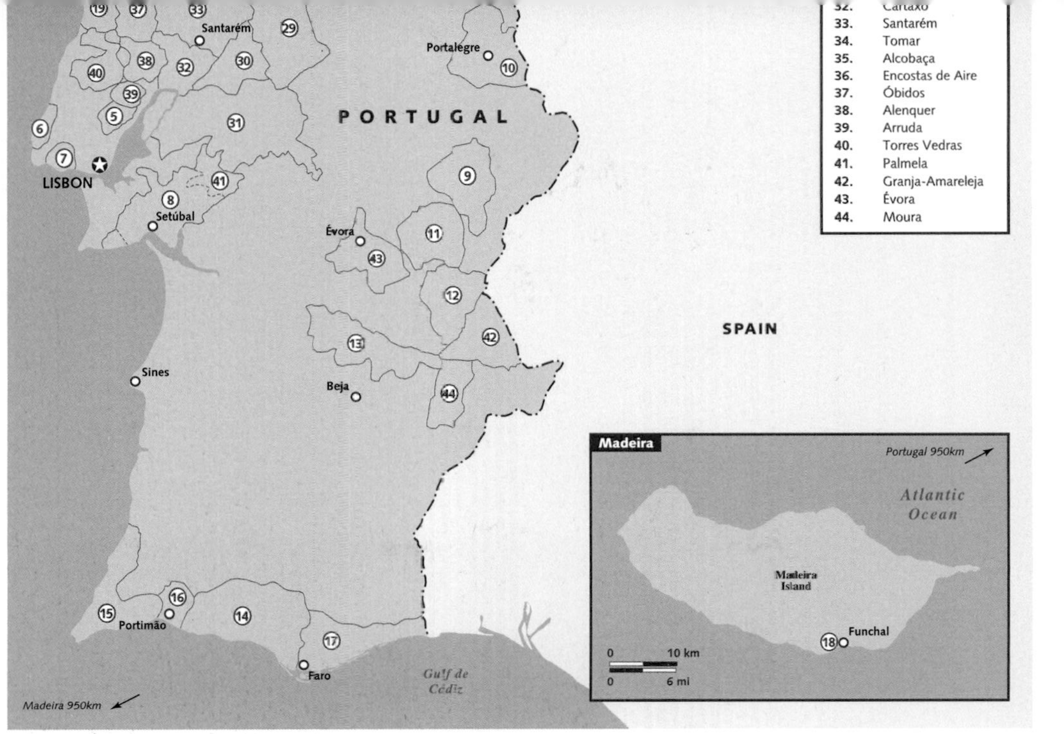
32. Cartaxo
33. Santarém
34. Tomar
35. Alcobaça
36. Encostas de Aire
37. Óbidos
38. Alenquer
39. Arruda
40. Torres Vedras
41. Palmela
42. Granja-Amareleja
43. Évora
44. Moura
PORTUGAL
SPAIN
Santarém
Portalegre
LISBON
Setúbal
Évora
Sines
Beja
Portimão
Faro
Gulf de Cádiz
Madeira 950km
Madeira
Portugal 950km
Atlantic Ocean
Madeira Island
Funchal
0 10 km
0 6 mi

CORK WRECKED YOUR WINE? BLAME PORTUGAL!

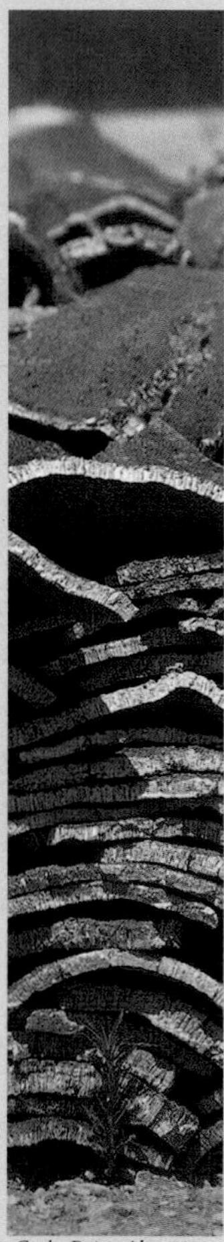
Cork, Beja, Alentejo

Something like one in a dozen bottles of wine is, in winespeak, 'corked'. This doesn't mean it has cork in it, but that the cork itself is tainted by a chemical called trichloroanisole, otherwise known as TCA, and it in turn wrecks the wine. Since over half of the world's cork comes from Portugal's Alentejo region, and TCA contaminates the cork during the cleaning process, there's a fair chance that because someone in Portugal took their eye off the cleaning ball you've now got a dud bottle of wine on your hands.

Nevertheless the process is not as lax as the TCA problem might suggest. The cork oak trees must be at least 25 years old before they're ready for harvesting. A thick layer of bark is stripped from the outside of the lucky tree for drying and processing and this can only be done every eight to 10 years. A good tree can go through this between eight and 10 times before it dies.

So how do you know that strange smell is not what the winemaker intended? For a start, any wine that smells like a damp dog is probably not what the winemaker intended. Other descriptions include wet cardboard or mustiness, neither of which any self-respecting winemaker would want you to smell on opening one of their bottles of plonk. And for the budget wine buyers out there, you should be able to smell these faults regardless of how cheaply you've purchased. Always take a corked wine back to the vendor, or send it back if you're in a restaurant. They'll pass the message on.

In the meantime, there's the Stelvin (screw) cap or closure. It looks just like the seal on a bottle of spirits, and has the double benefit of sparing those tired cork trees whose offspring are becoming ever more expensive for winemakers to buy, and of reducing wine wastage through tainted corks. There's really nothing wrong with a screw cap bottle, except that most people count that inimitable sound of a bottle yielding its cork – the last physical barrier between us and what's in the bottle – as being among the numerous pleasures of wine drinking.

fortify and preserve it during its sea travels aged it into the refined drink we know today. Because of this Madeira became known as '**vinho da roda**' or 'wine of the round voyage'.

Madeira is made from any of four so-called 'noble' grape varieties, including Sercial (dry and light), Verdelho (medium and golden), Boal or Bual (medium sweet and dark gold) and Malvasia (sweet and chestnut brown), which is called Malmsey when sold. Terrantez is a rarer style that falls somewhere between Verdelho and Boal.

Madeira may also be classified by age as well as by grape variety. Vintage is dated and made exclusively from one of the noble grape varieties. It has a minimum ageing period of 20 years in wood and two years in the bottle. Extra Reserve is made from 85% noble grape wines and is aged for a minimum of 15 years. Special or Old Reserve must be over 10 years old and Reserve at least five.

The grape juice is fermented (with natural sugars converting to alcohol), and at various stages of fermentation the wine is fortified with sugar cane spirit or neutral grape brandy. It is then heated. The heating process that so transformed Madeira's poor quality wines during 17th century travel was actually a by-product of crossing the equator and back on a long

BREAKING THE RULES

Matching food and wine in some parts of the globe has become impossibly complicated. But Portugal is a practical place, and drinking wine with food has evolved so organically over centuries that anything produced for the plate and the glass in the same region has a good chance of tasting good together. If you are in a modest establishment chances are you won't have a lot of wine choice anyway. Choose either white or red depending on the richness of your dish: some lighter pork dishes are good with white, while a rich cod dish will happily stand up to a sassy regional red. If you like to torture yourself with something more complex, you've missed the point completely. The flavours are simple, and that's their strength.

Ever wondered what works well with port and Madeira? White port is a favourite aperitif with roasted almonds, olives, cherry tomatoes or small cubes of **presunto** (smoked ham). If you're drinking Madeira, the dry **Sercial** and **Verdelho** styles are excellent as aperitifs either chilled or at cellar temperature (cool). Sweeter styles are best served alone instead of dessert, or can be drunk with dessert. **Bual** can be served as an alternative to port with cheese, and **Malmsey** is a fine digestive.

W. & J.
GRAHAM'S
ESTABLISHED 1820
PORT

sea voyage. Today the **estufagem** (heating or 'cooking' process) occurs in the cellar with the heat of the sun and well-placed hot water pipes. After this process, taking about six months, the wine is aged and – depending on the style – blended, eventually reaching an alcohol level of about 17%.

During the Spanish occupation of the island from 1580 to 1665, the sherry-producing 'solera' system was introduced to the making of Madeira. This is a tiered barrel system that allows younger wines to be gradually added to a cask of old wine, thereby taking on the older wine's characteristics. The advantage of the system is that the wine remains consistent over different vintages. The end result differs little from its original inspiration, which may be over a century old. This is something like the mother mix of a sourdough, or the Chinese practice of keeping back a little of each red sauce batch to start off the next: continuity, consistency and connection. The practice is very expensive and requires quite a bit of cellar space, which is something Madeira lacks. The solera system is now used only on a small scale and only with Madeira's exceptional vintages.

Incidentally, if you're wondering how Madeira differs from sherry, it's in the grape variety and the source of the grapes – Madeira can only be made in Madeira from specified grapes, while sherry – the English word for Jerez – can only be made in the Jerez region of Spain from specific local grapes. The processing is also different. While sherry is made using the solera system and is fortified with neutral grape brandy, it does not undergo the heating process that determines the unique character of Madeira. Some have said that no drink, no foodstuff of any kind, shares the apparent immortality of old vintage Madeira, so if your kind host offers you an aperitif with four score on it, revel in the knowledge that you're drinking from the cup of history.

Vinho do Porto (Port)

The history of port goes way back to the naming of the country as Portucale. As was the case with Madeira (see the preceding entry), the creation of port was a happy accident. This time it was British merchants who realised that adding brandy to the fresh wines of the Douro not only preserved them during transit, it also made them taste better. The more strength and sweetness the wine had, the better. They probably had to do a lot of tasting to work this out, so spare a thought for their suffering ...

Although this high alcohol wine (around 20% alcohol content) is named after the town of Porto, the action begins about 100km upstream in the vineyards of the middle and upper Douro. The vineyards stretch a further 100km or so east to the Spanish border. The wine is made at the source from up to 40 different grape varieties, including Arinto (Padernã), Boal and Sercial (white port) and Bastardo, Cornifesto, Donzelinho,

White port wine

OFFICIAL PORT STYLES

Here's what to look for and what you'll taste:

Vintage
This is port from a single high quality harvest which can only be officially approved after two years ageing, at which stage it should be full bodied, dark and high in tannin (which means it will continue to age well). There are only about three years per decade declared as vintage years, so these ports are expensive. Vintage years are determined by the famous port houses, who every year choose the best grapes from several vineyards in a region, then blend and age them and decide whether the port quality constitutes a vintage year. Ready to drink vintages include 1960, 1963, 1966, 1970 and 1975 with the 1970 the best of those so far. Still languishing in the cellars of the fortunate are the 1977, 1980, 1983, 1985, 1991 and 1994. While they're still just babes, the 1977 and 1983 vintages are currently leading the race. The best of the 20th century are 1900, 1908, 1912, 1937, 1945, 1963 and two young maybes: 1970 and 1994. So if you find any of these lurking about in an obscure location, keep them laid flat to preserve the crust, then decant the contents and drink the lot – once it's open, you've only got 24 hours to enjoy it at its premium.

Port with an indication of age
A tawny port (see later in this boxed text) blended from wines of various ages and matured in wooden casks should have its age indicated on the label as 10, 20, 30 or over 40 years old. Over time the wine loses its youthful characteristics and develops a more complex bouquet that may set you thinking about wood and spices as well as a few nuts like walnuts, hazelnuts or almonds.

Malvasia and Marufo (ruby port). It is then fortified with brandy or, more accurately, neutral grape spirit, which arrests fermentation and leaves the wine naturally sweet but still with plenty of alcohol. Traditionally, barrels were then floated down the Douro to Porto on ancient, high-tillered wooden boats that remain now only as a curiosity, having since been supplanted by the less picturesque but probably more efficient road tankers.

But to be quite correct, the barrels actually head to Vila Nova de Gaia, which was established in the 13th century on the riverbank opposite Porto, in defiance of shipping tolls. Over 50 port companies reside here, because this is where port is blended and aged before being shipped to the four corners of the globe. And since you can walk across one of Porto's many

Port with a date of harvest
This is port from a single high quality harvest that has aged in wood for at least seven years before bottling. As with the aged tawny port blend (see the previous entry), the single harvest version loses its youthfulness and develops woody, nutty, spicy characteristics. Ideally over time it will become soft, well rounded, harmonious and complex. The colour may become tawny, or display a green tinge in the older wines.

Late bottled vintage (LBV)
Port from a single good year is blended from wines specially selected for colour and depth of flavour, and that have already been aged for five to six years before bottling. This port has good fruit flavours, and is supple and full bodied.

White port
Dry and medium dry white port should show complex floral aromas and be quite pale in colour. A sweet port will be more golden, and show more mature characteristics.

Tawny port
This port is a blend of different wines of varying ages that have been matured in small casks. It combines the youthful fruity qualities of a young wine with the smooth, toasty maturity of older wines.

Ruby port
Wines from many different years are blended to produce a young, full and fruity wine with a deep colour. Ruby port is aged for a maximum of three years (usually less) in large wooden vats, which helps maintain the colour, bouquet and flavour of the wine.

bridges to get here, it may as well be part of the city. All the big names hang out here, including Taylor's, Sandeman, Warre's, Graham's and Dow's. Vintage port is bottled at two years and ages in the bottle. The rest ages or matures in oak casks and, once bottled, is ready for immediate drinking.

As port has always been made for export (especially for the insatiable Brits), the Portuguese actually don't drink as much port as you might think for a product that was conceived on their turf. After all that clever invention and trade, they're still more likely to be drinking vinho verde and aguardente. This means that if you want to look like a local, don't go around the country ordering a glass of port after every meal. You'll stick out like a grapevine in the must.

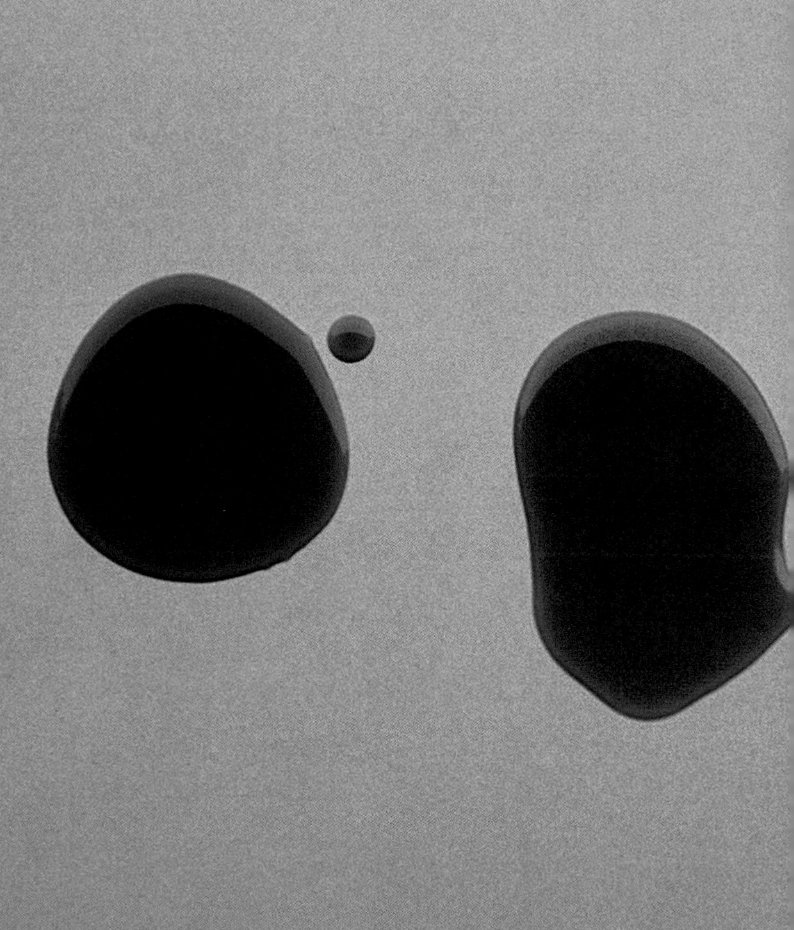

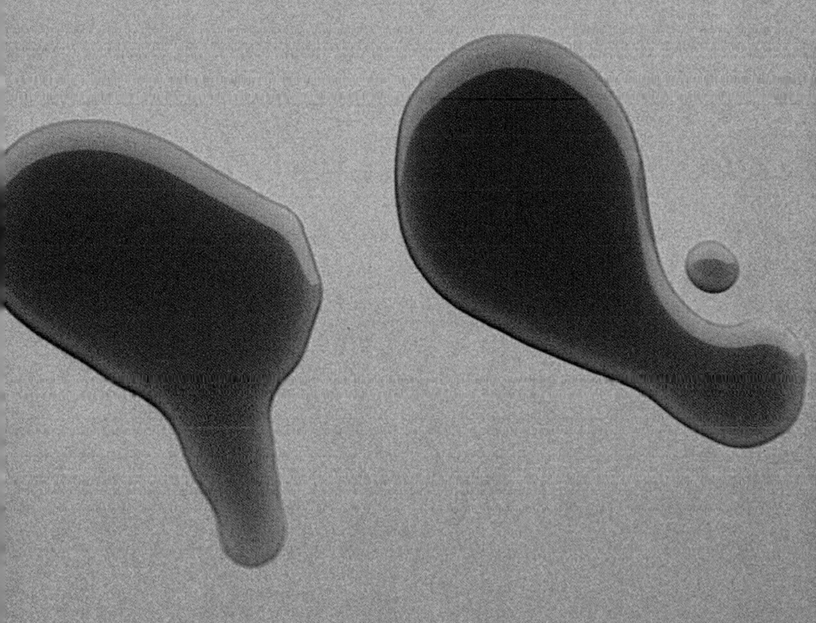

Port becomes lighter during the ageing process – from left, port aged five, 10, 20 and 40 years, Douro valley

Cerveja (Beer)

Portuguese beer is both strong (over 5% alcohol) and inexpensive. It's also wonderfully refreshing. It's best in draught rather than bottled form and is ordered as **um imperial** (200ml), **um principe** (330ml), **uma caneca** (500ml) or **um girafe** (1L). Sagres is the runaway winner for flavour, and the favourite in central and southern Portugal. It is mostly a pale yellow blonde beer, but there are also the rarer brown versions. Cristal is also scattered about, and is dominant on the island of Madeira. You'll know which beer the locals favour because it will be the only one available on tap. The rest will be bottled, if they're stocked at all. Super Bock is the northerners' preference and it's a heavier lager at almost 6% alcohol, with a robust, malty flavour.

The best place to get a beer is a **cervejaria**, or beer house, where you'll find snacks as well (see Cervejaria in the Where to Eat & Drink chapter). There's plenty of beer in **tascas** (cheap eateries) and restaurants too, but look out if you decide to either begin or end your meal with a beer – looks of fascination and horror will accompany your choice because, of course, you should be drinking wine with your food. Beer is for drinking at all other times of the day, preferably with a nice and salty deep-fried pig's ear. Beer for breakfast must also be tried at least once: the branded Martini com Cerveja, a draught beer with a shot of red vermouth, is a heart starter to rival caffeine. Less well known are tango, a draught beer with a shot of Manelho (alcoholic raspberry syrup), and the oddly named Pinochet, a Sagres and lemonade shandy.

"This one's mine", Alentejo

Cold Sagres beer – a favourite in Alentejo

Aguardente (Brandy-like Spirit)

This firewater will threaten your health in the most seductive way. It's a type of brandy, except it can be made from just about anything, and sometimes is. The unidentifiable homemade type is best avoided – it will almost certainly make you sick. Brandy is a spirit distilled from fruit and, in the case of cognac, from wine. This makes it more expensive than grain based spirits. (The term brandy can also refer to fruit flavoured grain spirits.)

Enjoying aguardente, Baixa, Lisbon

Poor people used to distill their spirits from the leftover grape skins and seeds, which resulted in the drinks that remain today as marc in France, grappa in Italy, aguardiente in Spain and aguardente in Portugal. A true Portuguese brandy is **medronho**, which is made by fermenting the berries from the strawberry tree for a few months then distilling it – it's available all over, but some say springtime in Monchique, a small village in the Algarve with access to loads of the raw materials, is the best time and place to taste it.

While the best aguardente is said to rival cognac, try not to drink too much of the stuff. It's potent (see the boxed text Look Out! Here Comes the Hangover! in the Fit & Healthy chapter, for hangover cures). Virgin visitors may be shocked to see grandmothers knocking back a shot of 50% proof aguardente before breakfast, but rest assured its purpose is strictly medicinal and the bottle will remain untouched until tomorrow. Other brandies to try include **bagaçeira** (grape skin spirit), **aguardente de figo** (fig spirit) or **ginjinha** (cherry spirit). Good luck.

Non-Alcoholic Drinks

Chá (Tea)

Tea is usually served in a relatively weak form, and often in a glass. More women than men seem to drink it standing at the **pastelaria** (pastry shop) counter with an enormous pastry in the other hand. If you like tea with milk, ask for **chá com leite**, but it probably won't make you happy because the water will most likely be out of an urn instead of freshly boiled. Now for some confusion. **Chá com limão** is, predictably enough, black tea with a twist of lemon. But **um chá de limão** is lemon tea, which means a glass or cup of boiling water with a generous twist of lemon rind. It smells delicious, and is probably the healthiest way to start the day. This is why so many people, especially women, order it at breakfast time or as an afternoon palate cleanser when it's too late for coffee. Younger women here love iced tea, and this market seems to have been cornered by Lipton's, whose canned product is popular all over. Some even like iced tea with their morning pastries.

Café (Coffee)

The history of coffee is one of global economic importance that spans six centuries, and Portugal was in on the drama. It remains a product mostly made by poor countries and drunk by wealthy ones, and is now one of the most important traded agricultural products in the world. Portugal, along with Italy, Greece and the UK, has the oldest European trade ties with the coffee industry but is only a moderate consumer. That said, Portuguese coffee is excellent, inexpensive, and arguably among the finest in the world. Regardless of where you order **uma bica/um café** (short black or espresso) across the country, it is of a consistently high standard. This is also the best form of coffee to order; the rest is a confusing mess that will have you begging, in a caffeine deprived muddle, to be allowed to make your own. See this chapter's Bean There boxed text for a way of making sense of it all.

Água Mineral (Mineral Waters)

The benefits of Portuguese mineral waters were enjoyed as far back as Roman times, both as a way to quench thirst and as a therapeutic release from the stresses of the day. Today, if there's a medicinal benefit to the water you're drinking it will be noted on the bottle's label as **água mineromedicinal**. The great strength of Portugal's waters is that they are almost all sourced from remote rural areas that are happily free from pollution. And they're cheap. Some of the big names in the bottled water that flows freely around the country are Luso, Alardo, Pizões/Castello, Carvalhelhos and Pedras Salgadas. If you're ordering mineral water in a restaurant, still water is **sem gás** and carbonated is **com gás**. **Água natural** refers to room temperature water, while **água fresca** is chilled water.

Luso

Sourced from the town of the same name, half way between Lisbon and Porto, Luso dominates (at about 37%) the country's mineral water market. Visitors have lounged about in Luso's therapeutic waters since the mid-19th century, and still do. But there's plenty left over for bottling. If you like a still table water that crosses all social classes, this one's for you.

Alardo

This water bubbles up to the surface on the remote south-eastern slopes of the Serra da Gardunha in central Portugal, near the border with Spain. A still, soft-tasting water, it has the unseen benefit of having picked up loads of apparently rare and healthy trace elements on its way through ancient rock strata.

Pizões & Castello

These are the still and carbonated versions of water from Pizões-Moura in south-eastern Portugal. Pizões is still and sold in PVC, while Castello – which is highly carbonated during bottling – gets the glass.

Carvalhelhos

This is easier to drink than to ask for, and sees the surface at a village called Boticas in the Serra de Alturas in northern Portugal. It's lightly mineralised, bicarbonated and contains fluoride.

Pedras Salgadas

Famous throughout the country as a digestive aid, Pedras is therefore good to drink during a meal. It is an alkaline, strongly bicarbonated water comparable to France's Badoit. It's the gastronome's choice, so if that's how you fancy yourself don't be caught sipping the others during meals. They're for consumption in between meals.

Other Non-Alcoholic Drinks

Portugal is refreshingly free from the all pervasive advertising of many developed countries, which may in part explain why drinks remain simple and relatively (with the exception of Lipton's canned iced tea) unbranded. While there are plenty of soft drinks, they don't appear to have displaced the basics. It's not even embarrassing to sit yourself down in a swish cafe and ask with confidence for **um copo de leite** – a glass of cold milk. Now you've got to love a country for that. Most cafes make fresh orange juice, **sumo de laranja**, and chocolate flavoured cold milk is also a breakfast favourite. Hot chocolate is **um chocolate quente**. Any fruit juice is **sumo**, while soft drinks are **refrigerante** and cordials **sumo sem gás**.

A village's public drinking water, Alentejo

BEAN THERE

Ordering a coffee in Portugal can be a complicated process – here's a guide for when you desperately need a coffee made just the way you like it.

Uma bica (in Lisbon and the south)
Um café (in the north)
Short black/espresso. It may arrive at the table with a cinnamon stick on the side – this is not a joke, but is to stir the coffee and add a little spice.

Um carioca
A weak short black/espresso

Uma bica cheia (in Lisbon and the south)
Um café cheio (in the north)
A short black/espresso topped with hot water

Um café duplo
A double espresso

Um café pingado
A short black/espresso with a dash of cold milk. Don't even think about trying to communicate how very easy and delicious it would be to use a stain of hot milk froth, or just a quarter dash of cold milk, to make a macchiato. Too hard.

Uma bica com uma pinga
A short black/espresso topped with **aguardente** (brandy-like spirit). Alternatively, do as the locals do: order a coffee and a separate shot of aguardente, then add as much liqueur as you like to your coffee, slugging the rest of the spirit.

Um garoto or **um café com leite**
A popular drink of ready-made filter coffee of dubious quality topped with warm or hot milk

Um galão
A large glass of hot milk with a dash of filter coffee, common at breakfast but probably not nearly enough caffeine to help you get started for the day

Um galão bem escuro
A stronger version of **galão**, but again, it's hard to taste the coffee

Um galão claro
An even milkier version of the already milky **galão**

Short and black – a classic Portuguese break

Uma meia de leite (in the south)
Um café com leite (in the north)
A medium sized cup of half milk and half filter coffee

Uma meia de leite de máquina (in the south)
Uma meia de leite directa (in the north)
A medium sized cup of half milk and half espresso coffee. This should not be confused with your splendid vision of a perfect caffe latte, but it is the closest you'll get.

home cooking & traditions

Eating and cooking (and sharing both) is what Portuguese people excel at. So it's no surprise to find that home kitchens are busy places where family secrets are passed on, and everyone is known for doing at least one dish well. Maybe.

Taking in the streets of Lisbon

We've mentioned previously that Portugal spent most of the 20th century in the dark (see History in the Culture chapter). This has kept the food fairly traditional – the Portuguese were mainly an agrarian nation, and are still accustomed to home grown food.

It's also a Catholic country, and there are plenty of adult kids still living at home in anticipation of moving out when they marry. Their parents are most likely to be continuing the traditions of their forebears by remaining connected to nature and seasonal produce, and are very likely to be conservative in their tastes. This means consuming traditional dishes at traditional times of the year. But it seems that younger people still living at home find traditional cooking way too fatty, too oily and without enough salad and fresh vegetables to be eating it every day. And naturally enough they're also looking for new flavours. Kids often complain about the richness of the food and how boring it is compared, say, to South-East Asian or Italian food.

When papá eats at home it may well be that the food is what he wants: regional, local and predictable. He may or may not help cook, but usually would only on special occasions, or if the dish is one of his specialities. Otherwise it's down to mamã, who may prefer traditional but lighter food since she's possibly watching her weight, or worried about cholesterol, or both (too many conventual sweets). If it's down to the kids to cook, you may well end up with an Asian favourite. But watch what happens when the adult children finally leave home. They'll be back on a regular basis for fresh produce from the garden, homemade cheese or bread, or whatever special (read: traditional) dish either parent made that they so loved while growing up. If they're unwell they almost invariably come by for healing **canja** (chicken broth) or **caldo verde** (Galician kale and potato soup), or creamy **arroz doce** (rice pudding). They may also drop by for a freshly killed chicken, and will inevitably eat all the traditional foods at festive times of the year.

Recipes will be passed on to family members by demonstration and woven through stories. Family dynamics around food in Portugal are, as they often say about many things, 'muito complicado' (very complicated). Kitchens can be tiny, and many of the important family celebrations are held at restaurants so no-one gets lumped with all the washing up and chaos, or maybe just because it's a family tradition to all go to a restaurant together at a particular time of the week or for a particular dish. But when push comes to shove, nowhere is food as good as it is at home.

This love for traditional, home cooked food is based upon a consistent supply of chemical free, home grown, fresh produce. In the not so distant past many Portuguese people raised their own stock – or at least chickens – and had animals for fresh milk, from which fresh cheese would be regularly made. They also tended an extensive vegetable garden that would supply most daily needs. It's likely the whole lot was, by default, organic. But industrialised food processing and better transport later meant that it was cheaper for Portugal to import fresh produce from – dare we say it – Spain. All things being circular, many people are reverting back to home grown, or organically grown, produce. When arable land is at a premium, it makes sense for primary producers to grow a smaller amount of higher quality foods for which the market will pay more. Organics are one way to do this,

Colourful homes in the village of Sardoal, Ribatejo

and as organic production in Portugal has multiplied more than tenfold in less than a decade, it can be assumed this will continue. If you're buying produce in Portugal, an organic product should have the words 'biologica' or 'bio' somewhere on the label and be certified by an organisation recognised by IFFRO (the international registry body for organisations deemed to be qualified to certify and monitor organic practices). For more on the state of organics in Portugal email agrobio@teleweb.pt. They will also be able to provide contact details of any organically run agro turismo properties. In the meantime, try very hard to get yourself invited back home for a meal with a traditional family. Chances are the home grown cabbages and cows haven't ever come within spraying distance of a chemical – you'll taste the difference.

FOOD-RELATED FAMILY NAMES

How important is food to Portuguese people? Very – so much so that there are lots of food-based family names. Read on ...

Mr Fig and Mrs Fig Tree were filled with consternation. That morning, they had visited Mrs Sardine who had told them the bad news. Mr Male Fox had eaten Mr Rabbit in front of Mrs Little Chicken, and she'd fallen down in shock. So Mr Fig and Mrs Fig Tree hurried over to see Ms Milk River and Ms Olive Tree to ask them to come and help. On the way they saw Mr Pigeon flying along at speed – had he heard? They all rushed to help Mrs Little Chicken, who was lying passed out in front of Mr Pear Tree's house. Her sister, Ms Little Parsley, had burst into tears. What could they do? They ran to get Dr Suckling Pig, who pronounced her dead and recommended grilling her. They would have a feast.

Sound like a kid's story? Maybe, but these names are all popular Portuguese family names and you'll find them all in the phone book. Meet the cast:

Mr Fig	**Sr Figo**
Mrs Fig Tree	**Sra Figueira**
Mrs Sardine	**Sra Sardinha**
Mr Male Fox	**Sr Raposo**
Mr Rabbit	**Sr Coelho**
Mrs Little Chicken	**Sra Pinto**
Ms Milk River	**Sra Leite Rio**
Ms Olive Tree	**Sra Oliveira**
Mr Pigeon	**Sr Pombo**
Mr Pear Tree	**Sr Pereira**
Ms Little Parsley	**Sra Salsinha**
Dr Suckling Pig	**Dr Leitão**

Frying sardines, Viseu, Beiras

Utensils

Portuguese kitchens are generally very small and stocked with rudimentary equipment. Until recently domestic ovens were not common, which is why so many dishes are either grilled or boiled up on a hotplate. Dishes called **no forno** (from the oven) are most likely found at restaurants, perhaps even cooked in a woodfired oven. Dishes described as **a padaria** refer to pre-domestic oven dishes (usually assembled in an earthenware pot) that were taken to the village baker for slow cooking in the woodfired oven after the bread was baked. No kitchen would be without **pratos de barro cozido** (earthenware cooking dishes) of various sizes, some of which have quite a specific purpose. **Tigela** means bowl, but more specifically an earthenware bowl in which individual **tigeladas** – spongy egg custard flavoured with vanilla, lemon or cinnamon – are cooked and served. A **tacho de barro** is an earthenware casserole dish that comes in numerous shapes and sizes and of which every kitchen will have plenty, partly because they are so practical and partly because they cost next to nothing. The dishes may be sealed or unsealed, plain or brightly painted. They have the advantage of going from oven to table, and food cooked in them tastes different from when it's cooked in other materials.

Near Vila Real in the upper Douro the pottery is grey from the wood smoke that circulates during slow firing, and the pots are used for cooking and for storing olives, oils and water. Earthenware spirit burners are also made for individual **chouriço** (a garlicky pork sausage flavoured with red pepper paste) grilling sessions at the home table, and are also typically seen in fado restaurants. **Púcaras** (earthenware jugs) are especially made for cooking poultry and game, usually in their own blood. Since you can't buy fresh chicken blood unless you know who's killing the chook, chances are the chicken is one of your own. A **frigideira** is a frying pan or skillet, and an **assadeira** is a large, shallow roasting pan for big birds or joints of meat. And then there's the **cataplana**, an ingenious invention that typifies cooking in the Algarve, consisting of a clam-shaped metal container with a heavy lid. It looks like a couple of saute pans with curved sides that are hinged together and fastened once food is inside, which means it can be shaken all around or even turned upside down when it is quite full. Whatever is cooked in it has intense flavour and may include fish, shellfish, lamb or kid. A cataplana comes in many different sizes and should only ever be opened in the presence of the intended diners (as proof it was cooked in the real thing, and so you get to smell the aroma as it's opened).

celebrating with food

Do they love a festival in this country or what? Breakfast, lunch and dinner, there's always something special around the corner to celebrate and much of it is linked to – or inspired by – the harvest, the Christian calendar, or a great date in a proud history.

To the roughly 15,000 Muslims and the rest of the non-Christian 2% in Portugal, we apologise. But 97% of the country claims to be Roman Catholic, with an extra 1% sprinkling of Protestant, which means that when you're talking about religious festivals, you mean those that spring from strong Christian beliefs, albeit with a hearty connection to a pagan past. Non-specific festive events are either **festas** (festivals) or **feiras** (fairs), while those with a religious dimension are referred to as **romarias** (saints' days or pilgrimages, depending on who you talk to). While there are occasions when the whole country celebrates at once, just about every city, town and village will have their own particular saints' days at which eating and drinking are central to the celebrations.

A contemplative pause before the festive crowds descend, Campo Maior, Alto Alentejo

A Calendar of Celebrations

Here's a month-by-month rundown of traditional Portuguese celebrations, as well as other annual gastronomy events. There's a festival for all occasions, with both predictable dates and exquisite local surprises. Slot these into your party habits:

January

Dia de Ano Novo (New Year's Day)

1 January – New Year's Eve means spectacular firework displays that are held all over the country.

Festa dos Rapazes (Festival of Boys)

25 December–6 January – At this festival, held near Bragança (Alentejo), boys dress up and rampage in a pagan rite of passage.

Dia de Reis (Day of Kings)

6 January – The end of the Christmas season is celebrated all over the country with the eating of shared bolo rei ('king's cake'). Displayed in bakery windows since November, the cakes are spiced fruit breads in a ring shape, which symbolises the crowns of the Magi, and inside is a fava bean or lucky charm. If you happen to get the bean or charm in your piece of cake, it basically means you're honour-bound to buy the bolo rei the following year and share it with the same people. Think of it as a kind of social glue. The cakes also turn up again in some areas at Easter. On Madeira you might be eating **bolo de mel** (a honey cake that isn't made with honey – see Madeira in the Regional Variations chapter for more information) and children will plant barley or corn in pots and place them around decorative cribs to symbolise bounty and renewal. All up, New Year is the time of year you're most likely to walk away from with a bit of extra baggage around the waist.

Festa de São Gonçalinho (Festival of St Gonçalinho)

Second week of the month – Sometimes it's hard to tell the difference between religious and pagan customs, especially with the romarias, which may also coincide with the solstices. All the celebrations and worshipping are not for nothing. Saints, like pagan gods, have to work for it: they're asked to perform special miracles. Take the Festa de São Gonçalinho at Aveiro (Beiras). Loaves of bread (light ones, we hope) are tossed to the crowd from the top of the chapel, either in gratitude for the safe return of a fisherman, or for finding a husband. Are we right in thinking the participants might mostly be women? Can we see any religion in here? But no matter. The St Gonçalinho festival provides a good excuse to eat and drink and revel.

February

Feira da Queijo da Serra (Celebration of the Serra da Estrela cheese)

Second week of February – Serra da Estrela's cheese contest and fair is held in different towns (including Fornos de Algodres, Seia, Celorico da Beira and Manteigas). Oliveira do Hospital hosts the fair at the beginning of March.

Domingos Gastronómicos (Gastronomic Sundays)

Every Sunday from February to May – Some parts of Portugal are so proud of their culinary heritage they don't even need a reason to celebrate it. In the Minho area Domingos Gastronómicos have run from February to May each year for over 20 years. Every Sunday during that time a local restaurant will prepare traditional dishes and any stories or meanings behind them will be published. It may be that **caldeirada à pescador** (fisherman's stew) will be cooked by a restaurant in Caminha one day, while **lampreia** (lamprey, an eel-like fish) is due to be cooked in Monção the following week. The program was initiated by Alto Minho Tourism to encourage restaurants to cook regional dishes and Portuguese people to seek them out. This has been so successful that now the children of the region have joined in. They are encouraged to ask their families for traditional recipes, which they also look up in the school library. They then choose some favourites and, with the help of staff, cook them up and eat them. Schools may even have a vegetable garden so that children develop an awareness of where food comes from and how it is part of their heritage. To encourage the preservation of traditions, some regional restaurants charge lower prices for regional dishes.

Carnaval (Carnival)

Dates depend on when Easter falls – Carnaval always begins 40 days before Easter. It is celebrated all over the country, but most ferociously in Ovar (Beiras), Funchal (Madeira) and Loulé (Algarve). Many of the Christmas dishes crop up (see December later in this section), as does the almost mandatory – despite it being an everyday dish – **cozida á Portuguesa**, where meat, sausages and vegetables are served in their own broth. Since the pig-killing season will also have just finished, there are plenty of special pork dishes to be had.

If held in February, Carnaval coincides with the **Almond Gatherers' Fair** in Loulé.

March

Ovibeja (Sheep Fair)

Mid-month – Starting around 20 years ago as a cattle fair, this is now the Alentejo's biggest agricultural and regional food fair. Many restaurants and **tasquinhas** (small taverns) in Beja feature the region's **sopa de cação** (dogfish bread soup) and local sausages, cheese and wine.

April

Comemorações da Semana Santa (Holy Week Festivities)

Starts 15 days before Easter – If Christmas is the most important family celebration then Páscoa (Easter) is the most important religious one. Semana Santa culminates with Easter Sunday after a solemn week of religious activities, particularly in Braga (Minho), Portugal's religious capital. The end of Good Friday may be marked with an omelette garnished with bacon and on Easter Sunday families would roast a lamb, piglet or kid, or bake a pie of mixed meats and whole eggs. Either way, the symbolic egg has been around since about the 15th century.

Festas do Espirito Santo (Festivals of the Holy Spirit)

Every Sunday from Easter to Whit Sunday – While there are lots of special cakes and breads made around Easter (especially decorated with boiled eggs on top), one of the most important treats is **amêndoas da Páscoa** (sugared almonds), which godfathers give to their godchildren. On the Azores, elaborate festas do Espirito Santo are among the most fervent. Locals ask the Holy Spirit to protect them against natural disasters through a series of rituals, including the distribution of bread to the poor and making Holy Spirit soup (with calf meat, water and mint). The festivals take place every Sunday between Easter and Whit Sunday (seven weeks later), when the great feast is held.

FIAPE (International Fair of Agricultural, Cattle and Handicrafts of Estremoz)

Last week of the month – Make your way to Estremoz (Alentejo) for its international agricultural and cattle fair, where local restaurants participate in a gastronomy contest. Enjoy foods such as **ensopado de borrego** (lamb stew served on toasted or deep-fried bread) and doces conventuais (egg- and sugar-based conventual sweets).

Dia de 25 Abril (Liberty Day)

25 April – Liberty Day celebrates Portugal's 1974 revolution.

May

Festa das Cruzes (Festival of the Crosses)

Early in the month – Held in Barcelos and Guimarães (Minho), the very serious celebrations of the Passion of Christ are followed by a huge country fair, at which you can eat and dine like a royal.

Peregrinação a Fátima (Pilgrimage to Fátima)

12–13 May & 12–13 October – Head here not for the food, but to experience the mood of tens of thousands of penitents, each with candles alight.

June

Festa de São Gonçalo (Feast of St Gonçalo)

First weekend of the month – This is something you don't want to miss. In Amarante (Douro), young, unmarried men and women swap cakes in the shape of phalluses.

Feira Nacional da Agricultura (National Agricultural Fair)

Early in the month – Held in Santarém (Ribatejo), this is an agfest of the highest order.

Festa de Santo António (Festival of St Anthony)

Mid- to end of the month – Poor old Santo António (St Anthony) of Lisbon is surely one of the most overworked saints. In a season of saintly celebrations from the middle to the end of June, he and his other popular colleagues, St John and St Peter, are celebrated in Lisbon at a time that also coincides with pagan solstice celebrations. St Anthony has the tricky job of finding lost things, and of finding husbands for single women. Altars are erected in the old parts of the city and all-night festivities are punctuated by the aromas of sardines grilling over terracotta braziers. These celebrations are held outdoors, and it is the time of year you are most likely to get a free feed, as happy Lisboetas will give away their fish to anyone who wants it. Single men give pots of fragrant basil as presents to their girlfriends, and unattached young people jump over bonfires and enact pagan love divinations by singeing thistles to see if they will flower the next day. Beware if your thistles don't bloom: it means your mate is certainly not around the corner.

Festa do Vinho Verde (Vinho Verde Feast)

Late in the month – Held in the town of Ponte de Lima (Minho), this festival features various wines and sausages.

PIMEL (Honey, Pine Nut, Fruit and Sweet Desserts Fair)

Last week of the month – This regional products fair is held in the town of Alcácer do Sal (Alentejo).

Festa de São João (Festival of St John)

End of the month – Porto goes wild in late June with its Festa de São João, which is characterised by all-night eating and drinking, and the playful practice of whacking each other over the head with bunches of leeks or lemon balm and eating tender roast kid (see the recipe). In Braga, the country's religious capital, the Festa de São João is one of the best festivals on the calendar and involves the classic combination of grilling sardines and all night outdoor revelry.

Cabrito à Padeiro (Baker-Style Roast Kid)

Steel yourself. This recipe calls for a kid – a baby goat – of just a month old. If you can't find one, aim for half a small lamb (about 3kg). It's only recently that Portuguese homes were kitted out with domestic ovens, so villagers previously took their prepared dish off to the local baker to be cooked in his or her oven after the bread baking.

Ingredients

1	whole kid (about 3kg)	2	bay leaves
100g/80g/50g	softened lard (pork fat)	2 tsp	sweet paprika
4	cloves garlic, crushed	100ml	white wine
2 tsp	ground black pepper	100g	smoked bacon, diced
1	medium brown onion, peeled and sliced	1kg	roasting potatoes
			salt & pepper

Remove the offal from the kid. Wash the offal, chop it finely and set it aside. Wash the kid inside and out, and pat it dry with a paper towel. Mix 100g of lard with the garlic, bay leaves, paprika, pepper and wine, and smear this paste all over the inside and outside of the kid. Mix any remaining paste with the finely chopped offal and stuff it inside the kid. Seal it in with skewers. Refrigerate the kid for a few hours. Preheat the oven to 190°C. Smear another 80g of lard over the skin and roast the kid for one hour, basting a few times during cooking.

Meanwhile, peel and halve the potatoes, put in a pot with a pinch of salt and cover with water. Bring to the boil and remove immediately. Drain the potatoes well and toss with the remaining 50g of lard, then season with salt and pepper and add the onion and bacon. Spread flat on a roasting tray and place in the oven.

After the kid's first hour of cooking, turn it over. Cook for a further 1½ to 2 hours, turning once more and basting regularly. A skewer inserted into the thickest part of the kid should release clear juices. If the juices are pink, continue cooking. When the kid is cooked, remove it from the oven and keep warm for 15 minutes before slicing, to rest the meat. Remove the roasted potatoes when cooked and serve with slices of kid. Alternatively, roast kid may be served with rice cooked with the kid's offal, smoked ham, onion and saffron.

Serves 8–10

July

Festa do Colete Encarnado (Festival of Red Waistcoats)

First weekend of the month – Named for the costumes of the Ribatejo horsemen, and celebrating bullfights and the running of the bulls, this festival is held in Vila Franca de Xira (Ribatejo).

Festa dos Tabuleiros (Festival of the Trays)

Mid-month, but held only every three to four years – This harvest feast in Tomar (Ribatejo) is one of the most extraordinary festivals. The word **tabuleiros** (trays) refers both to tall crowns made from loaves of bread decorated with paper flowers and wheat, and the beauties who wear them. Since the crowns take up to four months to make, the festival is held only every three or four years in July. About 400 young girls are chosen from the two parishes of Tomar, and its neighbouring 15 parishes. On festival day, the maidens, bedecked with the heavy crowns (which are measured to be as tall as the girl who wears it), form part of a procession. They are accompanied by a male relative or fiancé who gives them wine to keep them going. After the procession the 17 most gorgeous tabuleiros are chosen, oxen are slaughtered and everyone gathers for the formal blessing of the year's meat, bread and wine. The next day, families line up to receive their blessed portions of each – including bread from the tabuleiros (but the tabuleiros themselves are not actually eaten) – and the party begins. At various times the rite has given thanks to Ceres (the wheat goddess) for a good harvest, and the Christian Holy Spirit for favours rendered or under consideration.

Festa dos Tabuleiros, Tomar, Ribatejo

August

Festival Internacional da Cerveja, (International Beer Festival)

Early in the month – Held in Silves (Algarve), this festival is as you'd expect, with beer, food, dancing and mayhem.

Rally do Vinho da Madeira (Madeira Wine Rally)

Early in the month – Although it's a car rally (and the most important sporting event in the region), there's plenty to eat and drink too.

EXPOTUR (Gastronomy and Ethnographic Fair)

Second week of the month – Various regions come together in Caldas da Rainha (Estremadura) to present foods typical of their regions, including fried and stewed river fish and cockles. Regional wines are also represented.

Festival do Marisco (Seafood Festival)

Mid-month – What do you think you'll be eating here in Olhão (Algarve)?

September

Festa das Vindimas (Wine Harvest Festival)

Month-long – Held in the demarcated region of the Douro valley, celebrations of harvesting and crushing take place at different vineyards.

Mercado de Santana (Gastronomy Festival)

First week of the month – Held in Leiria (Estremadura), this festival features dinners held in restaurants by the riverside, with a panoramic view of the castle. Dine on sausages, cod, shellfish, cheese, wine and **cozido à Portuguesa**, where meat, sausages and vegetables are served in their own broth.

Festa do Vinho da Madeira (Madeira Wine Festival)

Second week of the month – This festival, held in Funchal and Estreito de Câmara dos Lobos (Madeira), celebrates wine, with grape picking and the pressing of the grapes, and with a typical Madeira feast.

Feiras Novas (New Fairs)

Third Sunday of the month – Vast markets are held on the banks of the Lima Ponte de Lima (Minho), for a festival dating back to the 12th century. Enjoy **arroz sarrabulho**, a regional stew made with rice, cuts of pork, beef and chicken, and sauce made of onion and pig's blood.

Festa de São Mateus (St Matthew's Fair)

Last week of the month – The popular festival is held in Elvas (Alentejo), and features **sericaia**, a very soft cake with an almost creamy texture served with a stewed plum in syrup, and **açorda à Alentejana**, a bread soup made with garlic, olive oil, broth, greens, poached eggs and coriander.

10 WAYS TO SEDUCE A LOVER, PORTUGUESE STYLE

So we all know that the desire for food and sex are kind of related, but as grown-ups we keep the drives separate. Sort of. But that doesn't mean there isn't food that gets us in the mood. And if you're in Portugal, or planning a celebration, you may want to bear some of this stuff in mind. It's about texture, aroma, flavour and that oh-so-indefinable sensation that you can't describe but know when you've got it – 'mouth feel'. Even sounds naughty, doesn't it? But it's actually a technical term that even professionals use in polite company. The Chinese and Japanese know all about it, which is why some of their incredibly bland dishes are among the most revered. These dishes feel wicked on the tongue, and when rolled around the mouth, eyes close involuntarily. It's mouth feel. So here's a list of mouth-feel inspiring foods to seek out in Portugal, should you want the mood to grab you.

1 **Polvo assado** (fried octopus tentacles) in the Algarve. They are finger-thick, flexible, tender, sweet. Lascivious.

2 **Tripas à moda do Porta** (tripe in the Porto style). Slippery, rich, sensuous and seductive. Just don't think about where it comes from and you'll be fine.

3 Any of the rice dishes that are meant to be wet and slippery, especially the fishy ones like **arroz de lampreia** (lamprey and rice stew). The rice is so rich, flavoursome and moist, even the Portuguese call it 'arroz maroto' ('naughty rice').

Deep-fried octopus, Tavira, Algarve

4 Sweets from Trás-os-Montes, many of which appear to have been created to facilitate friendly relations between men and women. **Pito de Santa Luzia** is a sweet made from a rich yeast dough filled with sugar, cinnamon and pumpkin. On 13 December every year, wives and girlfriends offer the sweets to husbands and lovers in anticipation of, as they say, either a good time, or fertile results.

5 Inhaling the steamy, wet juices of clams cooked in a **cataplana**. As the lid is flipped open at the table, rush in and immerse yourself in aromas of fresh herbs and the iodine ocean smells of the clams. Then wolf them down.

6 **Pastéis de nata** (custard tarts) straight from the oven. Lick out the warm, oozing centre with your tongue and pop the shell in whole. These are guaranteed to melt you on the inside.

7 The burn of a single hot rush of short black coffee, spiked with fiery **aguardente** (brandy-like spirit) and spiced with a cinnamon quill.

8 Sharing your spicy, just-grilled at the table **chouriço** (a garlicky pork sausage flavoured with red pepper paste) with a new friend at a restaurant where poignant fado singing is performed. Everybody's longing for love in the land of fado.

9 Fat, spoonfuls of delectable young Serra cheese, scooped straight from the centre of the round. Ripe, sensuous, buttery, rich and sticky.

10 **Bacalhau** (dried salt cod) – if you don't experience a luscious salt cod dish that makes you grateful for your each of your senses, then you don't deserve Portugal.

Spicy chouriço & a good red

October

Peregrinação a Fátima (Pilgrimage to Fátima)

12–13 October – (see earlier under May)

Festival Nacional de Gastronomia (Gastronomy Festival)

Month-long – Featuring absolutely the best of national food and cooking, as well as wine, folklore and handicrafts from all over the country, this festival is held at Casa do Campino in Santarém (Ribatejo).

Feira de São Simão (St Simon's Fair)

Last week of the month – Celebrated in Alcobaça (Estremadura), this handicrafts and gastronomy fair lets you sample dried fruits and nuts and **ginjinha** (liqueur made from cherries).

November

ExpoAlentejo

Second week of the month – This national gastronomy festival is held in Beja (Alentejo), and features honey, dried fruits and nuts, olive oil from Moura, sausages from Estremoz and Beja, and **Queijo da Serpa** (sheep's milk cheese) from Serpa.

December

Festa do Natal (Christmas)

24 December–6 January – Christmas is arguably the most important family celebration of the year. On Christmas Eve **bacalhau** (dried salt cod) is king as families all over the country gather around for **bacalhau com todos** (salt cod with the lot). This means the best quality slices of boiled salt cod are served with separate bowls of potatoes (boiled in their skins and scraped while hot), boiled **couve gallego** (Galician kale) or baby turnip tops, and hard-boiled eggs. These are all served with olive oil and cider vinegar that appear in cruets on the table, freshly chopped garlic, salt and pepper, and a hot garlic dressing. But this is just one of the courses. Other dishes served at the same time might be **arroz de polvo** (octopus with rice), **pastéis de bacalhau** (fried salt cod cakes), and in the north perhaps **folar** (brioche dough baked with chicken, spicy sausages and **presunto** – smoked ham), and all served with lashings of **vinho verde** (light sparkling wine). Sweets could be **arroz doce** (sweet rice – see the recipe), the northern speciality sopa dourada ('golden soup' - slices of sponge covered with egg and almond sauce) and various fried cakes such as **sonhos** ('dreams' – sweet fried dough, sprinkled with sugar and cinnamon), **fatias douradas** (similar to French toast, smothered in a sweet syrup and sprinkled with cinnamon) or **bolos podres de natal** ('rotten cakes' of Christmas – lightly spiced honey cakes), depending on the region.

Arroz Doce (Sweet Rice)

Ingredients

1.2L	water
½ tsp	salt
2 cups	short-grain white rice
	zest of 1 lemon
2 cups	fresh milk
2 to 2½ cups	white sugar
2 to 4 tsp	ground cinnamon

In a large non-stick saucepan, bring the water and salt to the boil (using a heat mat may help prevent rice sticking). Add the rice and lemon zest and gently simmer until all the water has evaporated, without stirring. Add the milk and sugar and stir well. Simmer very gently, stirring constantly, until all the milk has evaporated and the texture is rich and creamy. This will take 15 to 20 minutes. Pour the mix into individual serving dishes while hot. Sprinkle with cinnamon, using a paper cut-out to make shapes such as stars or hearts (as the Portuguese do according to the occasion). Leave at room temperature to set.

Serves 6–8

TASTY MORSELS

Some Portuguese words are so sensuous that you might be tempted to slice them up and fry them for breakfast. Read this list out loud with a lover while you decide what to eat.

apaladado	tasty
apimentado	spicy
aromático	aromatic
aveludado	velvety
avinhado	winy
claro	clear
condimentado	seasoned
espesso	thick
fofo	fluffy
fresco	fresh
herbáceo	herbaceous
intoxicação	intoxicating
maduro	ripe
sedento	thirsty
tenro	tender

Apart from wine you'll probably also drink either **vinho quente** (mulled wine) or **porto quente** (mulled port), just to put a cap on the celebrations. You can even dip your bread in it. Note you could eat almost all of these dishes during the year, and you probably have many times. But at Christmas they become special, and are enjoyed all together and with family after midnight Mass. Christmas Day lunch might start with **canja de galinha** (chicken broth – see the recipe in the Staples chapter) followed by stuffed roast turkey or a reheated dish of bacalhau leftovers, and more of the same sweets. There will always be too much to eat.

regional variations

Bread, cheese, wine, pork and fish. This is what awaits you in a country in love with its ocean and the fresh produce of a dramatic landscape. It's food of – and like – the people themselves: proud, generous and well seasoned.

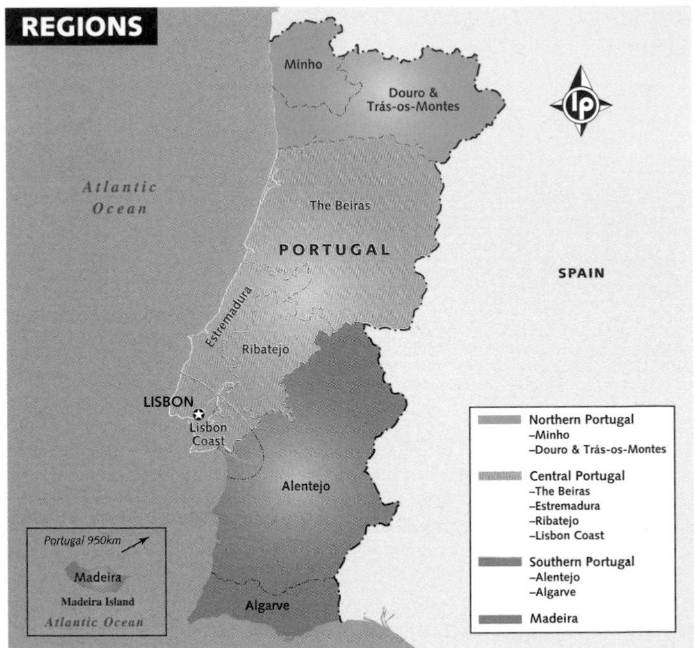

Is regionality important in Portugal? You bet it is. So much so that various government, tourism and private bodies are getting together to work out exactly what food and drink belong to different regions, sub-regions, cities, towns, villages and even streets. Unlike France and Italy, such a task has not yet been undertaken in Portugal and many are waiting with bated breath to find out just what belongs where. Although the country is not inundated with multinational feeders (at least not yet) there is still concern among the various regions that traditions and techniques need to be preserved. While different groups within regions have attempted to look at their own regional dishes, this is the first time a coordinated, official approach has ever been taken. The results will, hopefully, yield a definitive regional guide to a country that has so far been reluctant to give up its culinary secrets to strangers. But for now, this chapter will arm you with all you need to know.

Northern Portugal
Minho

The Minho region is bordered by the rivers Douro to the south and Minho to the north and its lush, dramatic landscape has always been productive. The Romans had introduced wine making in the region by the 2nd century AD and it is the famous home of **vinho verde**, or 'green wine', which can be either red, white or rosé (see Vinho Verde in the Drinks chapter).

Caldo verde (Galician kale and potato soup) can be had all over the country but here is where it's best, because this is where the correct cabbage comes from; other regions may make it with shredded kale or other types of cabbage instead of the dark and slatternly **couve galega** (see Hortaliças in the Staples chapter). It's suitable for breakfast, lunch and dinner and scarcely a menu is without it. **Broa de Milho**, the golden corn loaf of the region, is mandatory at every meal. The massive loaves, sold by weight, are especially impressive at the Thursday market at Barcelos.

Sopa seca ('dry soup') is especially popular in Minho, and is a dish based on thrift. Shredded cooked poultry or meat, such as pork, veal, ham or sausage, is layered in a earthenware dish with slices of cooked carrot and potato, doorstop slices of bread and plenty of finely chopped mint. Boiling stock is poured over the top and the dish is baked in a hot oven for up to half an hour. During this process, it 'dries'. This is a dish your mother would be proud of you for eating: wholesome, nourishing and sensible. It can also be sweet, as in the spicy bread pudding also called sopa seca, served as dessert but also containing a stock made from boiling up sheep's head and pork.

While there's plenty of coastal fish this is also the zone for lamprey, trout and salmon dishes. The eel-like lamprey spawn in Minho's rivers, peaking in spring, and an excellent way to try them is in **arroz de lampreia** (lamprey rice). Rather like good oyster months in France, local fishermen say crabs are best in months that have an 'r' in them, while oranges are the exact opposite: best in months with no 'r'. Trout are often served stuffed with bacon fat, grilled and served with **presunto** (smoked ham) on top. In fact, many fish dishes are cooked with meats, or their fats. Unlike the olive oil-dominated southern regions, northerners cook with far more butter and meat dripping. Vegetarians be warned: even breakfast can be a hazardous offering of **agua d'unto**, soup made with boiling water, dripping and crumbled broa.

Rejoada no Minho (the annual killing of the pig) is an event for those of stout constitution. There's none of this sterilised pre-packaged meat for the traditional Portuguese. Young pigs are generally bought for fattening around a year before the annual slaughter in November. The slaughter is a time of celebration. The day starts early, with the butcher arriving first thing to end the pig's life with a single stab to the heart. The blood, later to be

VINHOS VERDES TRAIL
Monçao Adega Co-op
Match the Alvarinho grapes with shellfish or the sought after lamprey in spring.
Ponte de Lima Adega Co-op
Pick a red and don't be shy about trying rojões, a dish of cumin-spiced pork cooked in wine.
Quinta dos Abrigueiros
A red to match the hearty cozida à Portuguesa: meats, sausages and vegetables served in their own broth.
Paco d'Anha
Try a sweet vinho verde ('green wine') with the local sopa dourada, a sponge cake and almond dessert.
Quinta do Paço
Pick a big white to match sardines grilled on Braga's streets during the Festival of St John's, held on 24 June each year.
Casa de Sezim
As the nation's birthplace, Guimarães is a fitting place to try a national dish, caldo verde (Galician kale and potato soup).
Quinta da Franquiera
Barcelos is home to the famous cock and to the rich broa (corn bread).
Quinta do Assento
Amarante is a good spot to try just-caught trout.
Quinta da Aveleda
Match this fresh wine with the renowned presunto (smoked ham) from nearby Lamego.
SPAIN
PORTUGAL
Minho
Douro
Atlantic Ocean
Minho River
Lima River
Homem River
Cávado River
Ave River
Douro River
Tâmega River
SERRA DA PENEDA
SERRA DE ARGA
Parque Nacional da Peneda-Gerês
Area de Paisagem Protegida do Litoral de Esposende
Monção
Valença do Minho
Castro Laboreiro
La Guardia
Paredes de Coura
Caminha
Vila Praia de Âncora
Arcos de Valdevez
Lindoso
Ponte da Barca
Afife
Bravães
Ponte de Lima
Campo do Gerês
Viana do Castelo
Feitosa
Terras de Bouro
Vila do Gerês
Cabril
Caldelas
Vila Verde
Guilheta
A3-IP1
Esposende
Ofir
Fão
Apúlia
Barcelos
Braga
Bom Jesus do Monte
Póvoa de Lanhoso
Nine
Guimarães
Fafe
Póvoa de Varzim
Vila do Conde
Vila Nova de Famalicão
A7-IC5
Caldas de Vizela
Aves
Felgueiras
Trofa
E1
Santo Tirso
Paços de Ferreira
Amarante
Maia
A4-IP4
Penafiel
Livração
Marco de Canaveses
Porto
0 5 10 km
0 3 6 mi

made into blood sausages, is caught in a bowl containing a little wine, and needs to be stirred to prevent it from coagulating. Small bunches of straw are lit and passed over the body to singe the hairs, then the body is washed and scraped down with a stone. The butcher slits the belly, removes the contents and cleans the inside. Everything is kept, as the lunch on the slaughter day is always a special one that includes plenty of blood and offal.

DON'T MISS – Minho

- **Caldeirada de peixe** – fish stew made with conger eel, skate, monkfish and red mullet layered with potatoes, tomatoes and sometimes rice. With broa on the side, scrumptious.
- **Pudim do Abade de Priscos** – from around Braga in Alto Minho this dessert is rich with caramel, spiked with port and spices and flavoured with bacon. A bacon flavoured crème caramel, if you like.
- **Domingos Gastronómicos** (Gastronomic Sundays) – special traditional regional dishes offered at certain restaurants on Sunday from February to May each year, lest the locals forget their culinary heritage. A must (see the February section of the Celebrating chapter).
- **Caldo verde** (Galician kale and potato soup) with **broa de Milho** (corn bread) and **vinho verde** ('green wine') – kill three birds with the one stone: these basics are found all over, but most especially associated with Minho.
- **Arroz de pato** (duck rice) – a truly delicious celebratory dish made, if you're lucky, with flavoursome free range ducks.
- **Cominhos** (cumin) – that spicy note you probably can't put your finger on, but can taste in everything.

Caldo Verde (Galician Kale & Potato Soup)

Caldo verde is like **bacalhau** (dried salt cod). It's found all over the country in one form or another. It should only be made from **couve galega**, (Galician cabbage), which is native to the Minho region. It needs to be shredded so finely, and so much of it is made and eaten, that most people buy it freshly shredded from their local market. But to make it at home, it's fine to use ordinary cabbage, or kale.

Ingredients

250g	cabbage or kale
150g	**chouriço** (a garlicky pork sausage flavoured with red pepper paste)
500g	potatoes
1 to 1½ litres	water
1 to 2 tsp	salt
⅓ cup	olive oil
good pinch	freshly ground black pepper
	fresh coriander

Wash the cabbage or kale and shake dry. Bunch up the leaves and slice them into unimaginably thin shreds (less than 1mm thick). Set the shreds aside. Prick the sausages and either simmer them in water (if you don't like too much fat) for about 15 minutes, or pan fry them (if you want more fat) until cooked through. Cool and slice into 1cm-round slices. Peel the potatoes and slice them into 1cm-thick rounds. Place the potatoes in a saucepan and cover them with the water, adding the salt and bringing to a boil. Simmer until tender, about 15 minutes, then drain the potatoes but *do not throw the cooking liquid out.* Mash the potatoes lightly with a fork, then return them to the pot with their cooking water, adding the olive oil and pepper. Bring to a boil, then drop in the shredded cabbage or kale. Simmer for a few minutes. Add the sausages so that they reheat, then check the seasoning. Spoon the soup into bowls, garnish with sprigs of coriander, and serve with plenty of **broa** (corn bread).

Serves 4–6

The pig is then hung in the cellar, washed with wine and stuffed with bay leaves until jointing the next day. At this stage some of the flesh is salted down and some made into sausages before smoking. But back to lunch: **sarrabulho** (a variety of meats, cooked in pig's blood) will definitely be on the menu, either as a soupy rice dish including the lungs, heart and liver, or the cumin-flavoured porridge **papas de sarrabulho. Rojões**, cubes of belly pork cooked in lard and suet with cloves and cumin until crisp, and **bicas**, small spicy blood sausages made with cumin and maize flour, are served with boiled potatoes, and perhaps even more fresh pork, including the ears, in **cozido à Portuguesa** (boiled meats, Portuguese style). The blood can also be made into **bolachos** (a type of dumpling), and served with the fatty cooking juices of the rojões. Even the stomach, stuffed with eggs, bread, sugar and cinnamon, can be eaten as dessert called **bucho doce**. All up, a pork fest.

The blood of lamb and chicken also features in the recipes of the region, which presumes that many people still raise and slaughter their own animals. Sweets include some pastries from the convents, and many using spaghetti squash strands or other pumpkin and squashes in cakes, and lots of fritters and **fatias douradas** (soaked stale bread with spicy syrup). But don't think there aren't any eggs: **pudim de ovos e laranja** (egg and orange pudding) contains 22 eggs. **Sopa dourada** ('golden soup') is, confusingly, a famous dessert from the town of Viana do Castelo of sponge fingers covered with **ovos moles** (thickened, sweetened egg yolks). Best not ordered before mains.

REGIONAL VARIATIONS

PUDIM DO ABADE DE PRISCOS

This delicious northern pudding, named after the abbot who invented it, is a vegetarian no-no. It's a bit like a crème caramel except that it's cooked with scraps of **presunto** (smoked ham). Why? In this part of the country, there's part of the pig in everything. Sugar, presunto and port are all cooked together with water, then cinnamon and lemon zest are added. This is strained, then cooked until a caramel forms. The caramel is whisked together with lots of fresh egg yolks then poured into a mould with a fluted edge to set. The presunto acts something like gelatine and causes the pudding to set. The pudding wobbles like custard when sliced to serve and, unless someone told you, you'd be hard pressed to identify the presunto. It gives a depth of flavour that you can easily fool yourself into thinking is just a rich form of caramel. If you're not vegetarian, enjoy. If you are, bad luck. The abbot knew how to make a pud.

Douro & Trás-os-Montes

Phoenician traders were busy in the Douro region as far back as the 9th century BC and it remains a thriving commercial centre, expanding out from Porto, the regional capital and the country's second largest city. When the Roman settlements of Portus and Cale, on opposite sides of the river, became united, Portugal was born. Porto itself is on the opposite bank to the wine houses that age, blend and bottle port wine. The wine itself is made upriver in the dramatic Douro valley, where steep roads wend through the terraced vineyards (see Vinho do Porto in the Drinks chapter).

Further to the north-east is the remote and less visited Trás-os-Montes ('behind the mountains'), where the rugged landscape makes for a harsh life. The food is rich with meat, and especially good are presunto and sausages. About 500 years ago Jews fleeing the Inquisition and claiming to

DON'T MISS – Douro & Trás-os-Montes

- Port wine – you may be surprised to find that there's not a great tradition of port drinking in Portugal, but don't let that slow you down.
- **Cozida à Portuguesa** – a beloved, now national dish from the region, in which various meats, green vegetables, offal and sausages are served together in their own broth with rice and potatoes.
- **Toucinho do-céu** ('bacon from heaven') – rich and luscious almond, pumpkin, egg and cinnamon (and maybe bacon) cake said to originate in the town of Murça, where pigs are traditionally revered.
- **Chouriço** – the small spicy sausages are especially good in this region.
- **Batatas, batatas** and more **batatas** – the very best potatoes in a country full of delicious ones.
- **Presunto** (smoked ham) – sweetest and sassiest from the towns of Chaves and Lamego. Eat it for breakfast. Eat it for lunch. Eat it for dinner. Even try it for dessert.

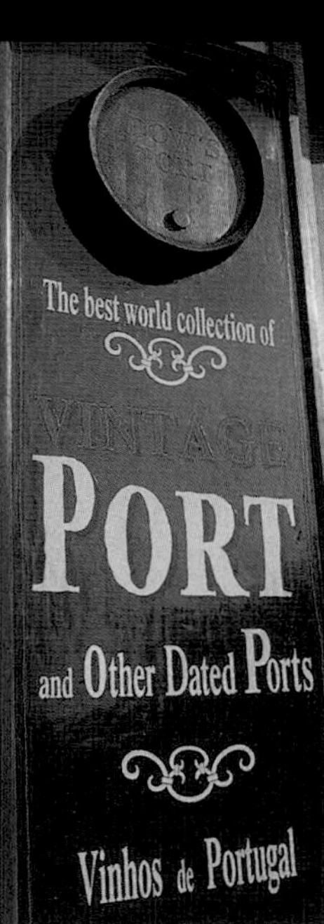

Bife de Presunto Panada com Arroz de Feijão (Smoked Ham with Beans & Rice)

From Vila Real in Trás-os-Montes, this is a kind of posh schnitzel for most people, as it requires generous slabs of **presunto** (smoked ham), which is just as expensive as its Italian cousin, prosciutto. That is, unless you run a **fumeiro** (smokehouse), where smoked legs of ham hang from the rafters in abundance.

Ingredients

4	slices presunto, each about 1.5cm to 2cm thick
1 cup	dried white beans, soaked
1	small brown onion, chopped
2 cups	tomato sauce
1 cup	cooked white rice
2	eggs, beaten
1 to 1½ cups	fine fresh breadcrumbs
	vegetable oil for frying

Place the presunto slices in a large bowl of cold water and soak for an hour to reduce their saltiness. Meanwhile, in a large saucepan, simmer the beans until tender, then drain and toss with the onion, tomato sauce and cooked rice. Keep the mixture warm. Pat the slices of presunto dry with a paper towel. Dip the ham in the beaten eggs, then in the breadcrumbs. In a frying pan, heat the vegetable oil (to a depth of 1cm) and fry the ham until golden and crisp on both sides. Drain the ham and serve immediately with the warm beans and rice.

Serves 4

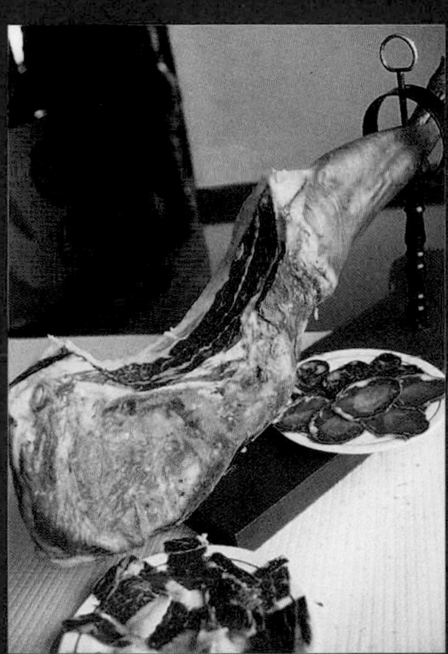

Freshly sliced presunto, Alentejo

be New Christians set up camp in Trás-os-Montes. Because not eating sausages was a clear sign of practising Judaism (as sausages were traditionally made from pork products), they invented **alheira** sausages to reduce suspicion. These were made in sausage-like shapes from white meats such as chicken, rabbit, partridge or pheasant with bread, flour and spices and lots of garlic. While alheiras remain the lightest of the lot today, pork has certainly crept into the mix. A cold, harsh landscape inspires rich food, and this region has plenty of it: smoked meats, veal, partridge and wild boar are popular and meat dishes generally dominate.

An Iron Age granite pig in the town of Murça was probably used in Celtic fertility rites thousands of years ago and is evidence of just how long the region has relied on pork products. Pigs are often hand fed, and dine well on cooked potatoes, corn, chestnuts and wheat. **Feijoadas**, rich kidney or butter bean and cured meat stews, are popular throughout the region and dishes enriched with chestnuts such as **sopa de castanhas piladas** (chestnut, bean and rice soup) are a meal in themselves.

Being called a 'tripeiro' (tripe eater) is not some cruel slur. It means you, or your family, are probably from Porto. There are a few theories about why they are known as such. One has it that when Henry the Navigator was preparing to sail to Morocco in the early 15th century the loyal supporters from Porto donated all their good meat to feed his sailors while those who remained kept the scraps – offal – for themselves. Another theory has it that during a siege, the people of Porto outwitted their enemy by giving them all the good cuts of meat and keeping the offal for themselves, thus defeating them by giving the impression that they had such a lot of good food they could afford to give it away. There's also a rumour that during invasions Porto sent all its good meat down to Lisbon to strengthen the front lines and kept the scraps for itself. We think the tripeiros are simply hooked on the luscious, mucilaginous texture of cooked cow's stomach. So look out for **tripas à moda do Porto** (in Porto, of course), which will be a slow cooked dish of dried beans, trotters, tripe, chicken, sausages, vegetables and cumin. It's rich and gelatinous, as those brave enough to try it will duly discover.

It's not all meat, though. The warm, Mediterranean climate of the Douro valley encourages rich crops of figs, cherries, almonds and oranges, and Trás-os-Montes cheese, **Monte**, is one of the few cheeses made from the milk of cows and ewes. This is also home to much of Portugal's mineral waters, both for soaking in and drinking. Naturally you'll also be in need of something stronger, in which case **bagaçeira** (**aguardente** – a brandy-like spirit – mixed with distilled wine lees) will warm the cockles. Desserts are sweet, rich and spiked with cinnamon. And possibly with pig too.

Central Portugal
Beiras

What to eat? There's salt, salt cod and **ovos moles** (thickened, sweetened egg yolks) in Aveiro; egg cakes, and **chanfana** (goat or lamb stews) made with lots of red wine in Viseu; cream and Rabaçal cheese from Coimbra; hams, sausages and firmer cheese throughout the forests towards Spain; and seafood and fish down the Atlantic coast.

The Beiras has a little of everything but what it's renowned for is the Serra da Estrela, where goats and sheep graze the slopes, providing both milk and meat from kid, goat, lamb and mutton. And although there's lots of cheese throughout the country, one is especially famous: Serra cheese (Queijo da Serra/Estrela). It's made from the winter milk of ewes that graze in the Serra da Estrela.

Dão wine tasting, Casa de Santar, Viseu, Beiras

DON'T MISS – Beiras

- **Leitão** or **Cabrito assado no forno** (roast suckling pig or baby goat) – they're young and innocent, but maybe you could bring yourself to try them just once (see above).
- **Manjar branco** – a very traditional pudding recipe for roast chicken coated in egg and fried, served atop bread dipped in egg and fried, with cinnamon and sugar syrup poured over the top. A reminder that in the Middle Ages sweet and savoury flavours were mixed together, and the practice continues in Portugal.
- **Serra cheese** and **requeijão** (ricotta-type cheese) – the former is eaten scooped straight from the cheese round with a spoon or later when it is hard and piquant, and the latter sprinkled with cinnamon and sugar, drizzled with honey, served with pumpkin or tomato jam or baked into cakes.
- **Torresmos** (pork crackling) – what can we say? Lush with lard, seasoned with salt, hot or cold, the crisp salted strips are available everywhere as a quick snack with beer or as a lead-in to more substantial dishes.
- **Pão de-ló** – the famous 'collapsed' sponge cake particularly associated with the town of Ovar, rich with egg yolk and sugar and sometimes left barely cooked in the centre and spooned out like a pudding. It's eaten at Easter and Christmas, but is also eaten all over the country and for any special occasion.
- **Pastel de molho da Covilhã** – an exceptional dish of thrift from the city of Covilhã. Flaky layers of crisp lard pastry are covered in a saffron broth soured with vinegar. A unique experience (see left).

Pastel de molho, Covilhã

Local fisherman, Espinho, Beiras

Then there's the sucking or suckling pig in the towns around Coimbra. In the town of Mealhada it seems this is the only dish on restaurant menus, and people travel for miles to get it. The whole suckling pigs are rubbed with garlic, lard and salt, staked with a thick metal rod and roasted in a woodfired oven. Served simply with bread and wine, the skin is papery, golden and crisp and the flesh underneath meltingly good. It is eaten hot or cold, on site or as a takeaway. There's no way to get away from meat really, but alternatives include heavenly breads such as **pão centeio do Sabugueiro** (a rye bread particular to the town of Sabugueiro) and **broa serrana** (highland bread), honeys, chestnuts, apples, peaches and cherries. The Beiras are also home to some of Portugal's best wines, including Dão and Bairrada (see Regional Variations in the Drinks chapter), so there's no excuse for not eating and drinking up.

SERRA CHEESE MAKING

Unlike many cheeses that rely on rennet (an enzyme from the lining of a cow's stomach) or genetically engineered or microbial coagulators, Serra is made with the ancient and far less predictable 'thistle' method.

The cream is separated from the bulk of the milk. An artisanal producer may do this by filtering it through layers of sheep's wool. The milk is then heated and cardo, a thistle that grows wild in the fields, is blended with water and allowed to ferment. It is then added to the warm milk to cause it to coagulate. No-one seems to know why thistle causes coagulation, but it does.

Cardo, the thistle used to curdle milk in cheese making, Serra de Estrela, Beiras

The curd is drained and hand pressed into moulds to drain further. The whey is heated with the cream, then drained to make the exquisite requeijão (see Queijo in the Staples chapter), a kind of fat-enriched ricotta.

The fresh Serra rounds are kept in a temperature-controlled room on slotted trays for further draining for 15 days. Any mould is washed from the rounds, which are then transferred to a ripening room for a further 10 days. Each cheese is hand wrapped in cloth to maintain its shape. The cheese then goes to a third ripening room with higher humidity and temperature. After the ripening, women scrub the outside of the cheese with wire scourers, and the cheese is then packaged for ageing.

Young Serra is pale and almost runny. When served, an entire round may have its top cut off, a spoon inserted and the whole cheese (about 1.5kg to 2kg) will be brought to the table to be scooped at will. This is hugely indulgent, and, in the interests of self-education and being thorough about the whole travel experience, should be undertaken at all cost. As the cheese matures (should you be able to keep your hands off it) it becomes entirely different in that it is harder, more intensely flavoured, and more expensive.

Estremadura

Fish, fish and more fish. That's the mantra of the region and it includes such delicious dishes as **escabeche** (also popular in Ribatejo, and associated with Lisbon). The word comes from the Arabic 'sikbaj', meaning 'vinegar stew' and it started out as marinated meat, but is now more often fish. Especially good are small oily fish such as sardines and small mackerel, fresh tuna or firm white fish fillets. First they're cooked, then left to marinate in vinegar, oil and flavourings for up to three weeks – a delicious snack.

Estremadura is bordered by the Atlantic to the west, which means lots of **sopas de mariscos** (shellfish soups) and **caldeiradas de peixe** (fish stews), and Ribatejo to the east, meaning meat. Try **morcelas de arroz** (blood and rice sausages) or **tortulhos** (sheep's tripe stuffed with more sheep's tripe) or, confusingly, meat caldeiradas made from kid or lamb. This is also where you absolutely must try **batatas à murro**, small, salted potatoes baked in their skins then 'smashed' open with the palm of the hand and seasoned with olive oil and garlic. Sweet teeth will love the **bolinhos de pinhão** (pine nut cakes) and those worried about cholesterol can have the guilt-free olive oil cakes and biscuits from the Convento das Clarissas of Louriçal. But it wasn't just the nuns who made sweets (see the boxed text Is that a Yolk in Your Pocket? in the Staples chapter) and the monks who made wine. The wealthy monks from Alcobaça made a mean seasonal fruit jam rich with walnuts, which is still made today: Delícia do Frei João.

Grilled fish with kale

DON'T MISS – Estremadura

- **Açorda de marisco** – seafood bread soup from the coast. It's pricey, though.
- Mosteiro de Santa Maria de Alcobaça – Portugal's largest church, and when we say large we mean absolutely massive. Home to the wealthy Cistercian order from the early 13th century, this place was also a hub of culinary invention. Check out the kitchen, whose dimensions are such that there was room to roast whole oxen on a spit in its fireplace.
- Alcobaça – the National Wine Museum, where you'll find every stage of traditional wine production is meticulously recorded.
- **Magusto** – a beloved dish of charcoal grilled **bacalhau** (dried salt cod) served with crumbled **broa** (corn bread), cabbage, dried beans and seasoned with lots of fruity olive oil.
- Nazaré – the coastal town where racks and racks of shark and horse mackerel lie drying in the sun (see below).

SAGRES

Bacalhau à Bras

(Shredded Dried Salt Cod, Fried Potatoes & Scrambled Eggs)

This is one of the easiest and most delicious salt cod recipes. This dish is native to Estremadura but is found across all regions of Portugal and in innumerable households. It can also be called **bacalhau dourada** ('golden bacalhau').

Ingredients

750g	bacalhau (weighed after trimming)
750g	potatoes
	vegetable oil for deep frying
3 Tbs	olive oil
150g	butter
375g	onions, peeled and sliced
2	cloves garlic, chopped
	salt & pepper
9	eggs
½	bunch parsley, washed and finely chopped
1 cup	small black olives

Trim the cod's tail fins and remove its large bones.

Weigh the remainder of the cod, then cut into chunks about 10cm square. Cover the chunks completely with water, then soak for 24 hours, draining and covering with fresh water at least three times at roughly 8-hour intervals.

Drain the cod thoroughly, flake the flesh and cut the rest into fine strips. Set aside.

Peel the potatoes and cut them into fine matchsticks. Pat them dry with a paper towel, then deep-fry the sticks in hot oil until they begin to colour. Remove and drain on a paper towel.

Heat the oil and half the butter in a large frying pan and gently cook the onions for about 10 minutes until soft and beginning to colour. Increase the heat, add the garlic and then stir the cod through the mix. Continue to cook for 5 to 6 minutes, until the mix becomes golden. Add salt and pepper to taste, then transfer the mix to a bowl and toss through the potatoes.

Heat the remaining butter in the frying pan and add the potato and fish mix.

Beat the eggs and stir them gently through the mix so they just bind the fish and potatoes but don't scramble.

Remove from the pan and serve on a warm plate, with parsley and olives sprinkled over the top.

Serves 6–8

Bacalhau à Bras (shredded dried salt cod, fried potatoes & scrambled eggs)

Ribatejo

Hmm. We promised ourselves we wouldn't mention bullfighting but this region is its capital, and you're likely to come across it so here goes. It's stressful, the bull gets hurt, the bull dies. And even though the much cited claim that the Portuguese – unlike their Spanish neighbours – do not kill the bull is true, what they *really* mean to say is they don't kill it in front of the audience. It happens out of sight, but believe us, it still happens. We simply can't think of any good gastronomic reason for it, so we're not supporting it.

Now onto the food. Mix tomatoes, rice and melons, olives and oil, market garden produce, livestock and figs. What do you get? Something good to eat – plenty, in fact. Ribatejo is home to the best horses in Portugal, has a proudly traditional past, and you can eat really well here. So what are you waiting for? Eat! Head to a **taberna** (tavern) with the locals, and start with bitter but still flavoursome olives and a hunk of bread. Here you can eat the daily special dish – very likely to be pork, goat, lamb or chicken – with rice, chips, more bread and wine straight from the barrel. Share a table – this is how it's done here. You'll get to know your dining companions – friendly, open people with tanned faces and ready smiles.

You'll be eating the produce of the fields and rivers, along with the mandatory bacalhau imports. And herring, served with moist and flavoursome rice. Since Ribatejo borders Alentejo, you'll also find plenty of bread dishes here, all the richer for being made with corn rather than wheat bread. Try **migas** (side dishes made with bread) with corn bread and cabbage, or

Bulk vinho tinto and vinho branco at Taberna do Quinzena, Santarém, Ribatejo

DON'T MISS – Ribatejo

- **Enchidos** (sausages) and **carnes** (meats) – and in particular **bucho recheado, chouriço, farinheira, morcelas de arroz, morcelas de sangue, negro** and **presunto** (see right).
- **Arroz de tomate** – 'tomato rice', which sounds simple and plain but is actually a divinely rich dish, often served with fried fish.
- **Delícia de batata** – leftover mashed potato turned into luscious little cakes, with plenty of almonds and cinnamon.
- **Migas carvoeiras** – dumplings made with corn bread and seasoned with dripping, and served with thick, juicy roasted ribs. Definitely one to eat with the fingers.
- **Enguias** (eels) – we *know* you haven't tried them yet. Go on. They slip down a treat.
- **Melões** (melons) – the green-skinned variety from Almeirim are justly famous for sweetness and juice.

delicate turnip tops with fried sardines or a slab of grilled bacalhau; cobs of wheat bread grilled with garlic butter and served with grilled bacalhau; **sopa de pedro** (vegetable soup with red beans and sausages); sweets made with mashed potato and cinnamon; migas made from crumbled maize bread with olive oil, garlic and hot water to serve with sausages or fried fish; eel stews and lamprey; apples, beef, honey and pears. Regional grapes have high concentrations of sugar, which means higher alcohol content in the wines, but that's OK because the bread gets heavier (and so does the rest of the food) to match it. Pagan rituals are also alive and well in Ribatejo. The first official day of spring each year sees people off from work to look for signs of fertility in the land. That means they're picking poppies, olive branches and ears of wheat in the hope of a good year.

ENCERRAMENTO DA FEIRA DO MILAGRE
2.ª GRANDE
CORRIDA DOS AGRICULTOR
NAZARÉ
SÁBADO
PEDRITO DE PORTUGAL
GUSTAVO ZENKL
VILA FRANCA
6 TOIROS

Lunchtime rush at Taberna do Quinzena, Santarém, Ribatejo

Lisbon Coast

The Lisbon coast area includes, naturally enough, the city of Lisbon itself. There's plenty to be had here that comes from all over the country, and while the traditional 'regional' dishes of the Lisboetas are known, they are not necessarily what everyone eats.

Lisbon became the capital in the mid-13th century, but despite this there are still community level activities around eating and drinking that perpetuate tradition. Local fishing and farming, wine making at Colares and Palmela, and rice growing and salt panning all continue on the cusp of the city while the Tagus river remains, as ever, a working waterway. This is spiny lobster territory and a good spot to try them. They're caught off the coast but do check the price because it will always be expensive. The very best are said to come from Peniche, about 100km further up the coast in Estremadura, but you'll do fine to order them here too.

And don't forget to try the utterly scrumptious **Queijo de Azeitão**, a cheese made from raw sheep's milk and weighing in at a delicate 100g to 200g. It is cured and has a buttery, semi-soft texture with a good dash of piquancy, depending on the age. One of Portugal's best cheeses, this one is so good that unscrupulous producers try to get away with fakes. So check the label for DOP certification (see the boxed text Sealing the Quality in the Culture chapter) and know that you're most likely to be finding the real thing in the councils of Setúbal, Sesimbra and Palmela. Avoid social death by remembering that Azeitão is eaten with a spoon, not cut, and try it with **marmelada**: not the Seville orange jam we know, but a very stiff quince paste (see the boxed text How English is Marmalade? in the Staples chapter).

One is never enough, Pastéis de nata (custard tarts with a flaky pastry shell)

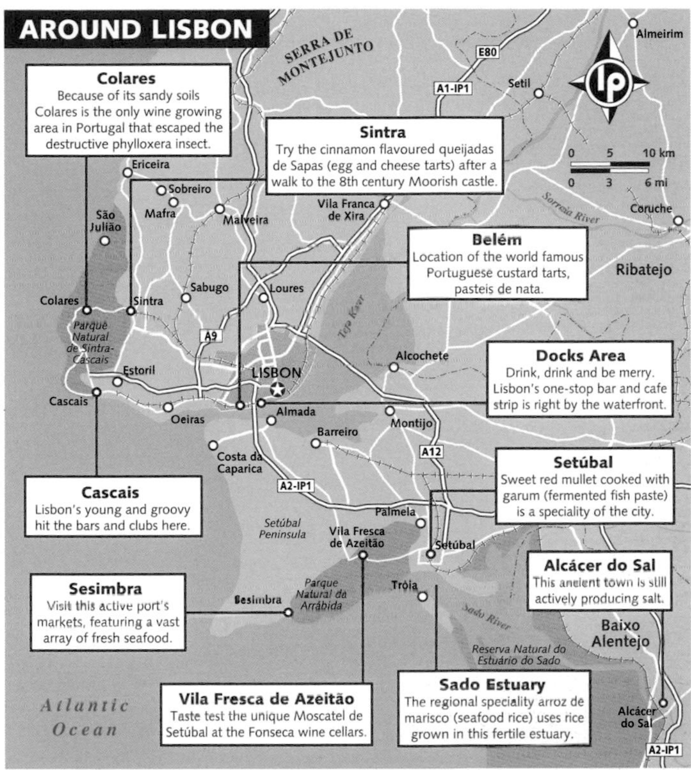

A visit to Lisbon's Belém district would be sadly lacking if you didn't try the ubiquitous but legendary **pastéis de nata** (custard tarts with a flaky pastry shell) from the Antiga Confeitaria de Belém. It's said the tarts were invented by monks from the nearby Mosteiro dos Jerónimos. The monks sold the recipe to a local family in the early 19th century, and the family's descendents run the perpetually frantic cafe and pastry shop, churning them out at a healthy rate of 10,000 a day. They're served warm from the oven and dusted with icing sugar and cinnamon – if you've never had a Portuguese custard tart, here's where you start.

DON'T MISS – Lisbon Coast

- **Queijadas da Sapa** – the most famous bite-sized cheese, egg and cinnamon tarts are from the Pastelaria Sapa in the town of Sintra, where they have been made since the late 18th century. Pretenders will be sold at the town's roadside, but only accept the real thing (see below).
- Belém's **pastéis de nata** – custard tarts with a flaky pastry shell; try these at the tart's spiritual home, Antiga Confeitaria de Belém.
- **Ginjinha** – sweet cherry liqueur; look for this in Lisbon, and elsewhere if you can get it. It's served at tiny streetside bars.
- **Batatas fritas** (potato chips), **vinho do casa** (house wine) and grilled, salt-crusted baby chickens – a cheap way to get to heaven over lunch, at Bonjardim in Lisbon (Travessa de Santo Antao 11–12).
- Cascais – hanging out in this sheltered bay town at the mouth of the Tagus is what the fashionable people have always done. Be one of them.
- **Caldeirada rica** – rich fish stew. Rich with variety (up to eight different types of fish) and flavour. Check the price, though.
- **Salmonetes** – red mullet, a speciality of Setúbal, south of Lisbon. You may be surprised to find these fish cooked with salty, intensely fishy and fermented **garum** paste, thought to have been used in this area by the Romans as a seasoning.

Southern Portugal
Alentejo

What can we say? Even Portuguese people *not* from this region wish they were. The baking plains, the olives and oil, the wild boar, the bread-based one-pot dishes, the sassy reds. Wines, that is. Welcome to the land of megaliths, ancient stories and whitewashed villages. Everyone loves the Alentejo, and they especially love to sup on its bounty. The heat, often reaching a sweltering 40°C from May to October, slows the pace, and life in this sparsely populated rural region is sweet. Cork trees and orange groves stretch across the gentle slopes, interspersed with vineyards and wheat fields. The rivers are rich with fish; the hills are home to the famous wild boar that snack on its fallen fruits and roots (which sweeten its flesh); and the plains are home to many grazing animals, cereal crops, orchards and olive groves.

There's probably only one important thing to remember here, and that is that pork will confront you at every repast. Oh, and bread. Bread figures heavily, not just on the table, but also in cooked dishes. In summer you'll be eating **gaspacho**, a chilled tomato and garlic soup ladled over thick slices of bread, and sometimes served with a slice of ham or sausage and a few ice

Recommended Restaurants

1. **O Aqueduto** – Rua do Cano 13-A
2. **Adega do Isaías** – Rua do Almeida 21
3. **Ouro Branco** – Campo da Restauração
4. **A Maria** – Rua de Deus 12
5. **O Barro** – Rua D. Arnilda e Eliezer Kamenesky 44
6. **A Grelha** – Rua de Corvalinho 1
7. **O Bacalhau** – Ave Sacadura Cabral 25
8. **O Escondidinho** – Rua Estevão de Almeida 6-A
9. **Refugio da Vila** – Largo Dr. Miguel Bombarda 8
10. **Afonso** – Rua de Pavia 1
11. **Bar Alentejano** – Ave Sacadura Cabral 25
12. **Adega Velha** – Rua Dr. José J.V. Gusmão 1
13. **Luar de Janeiro** – Travessa do Janeiro 13
14. **A Moagem** – Rua do Fábrica 2

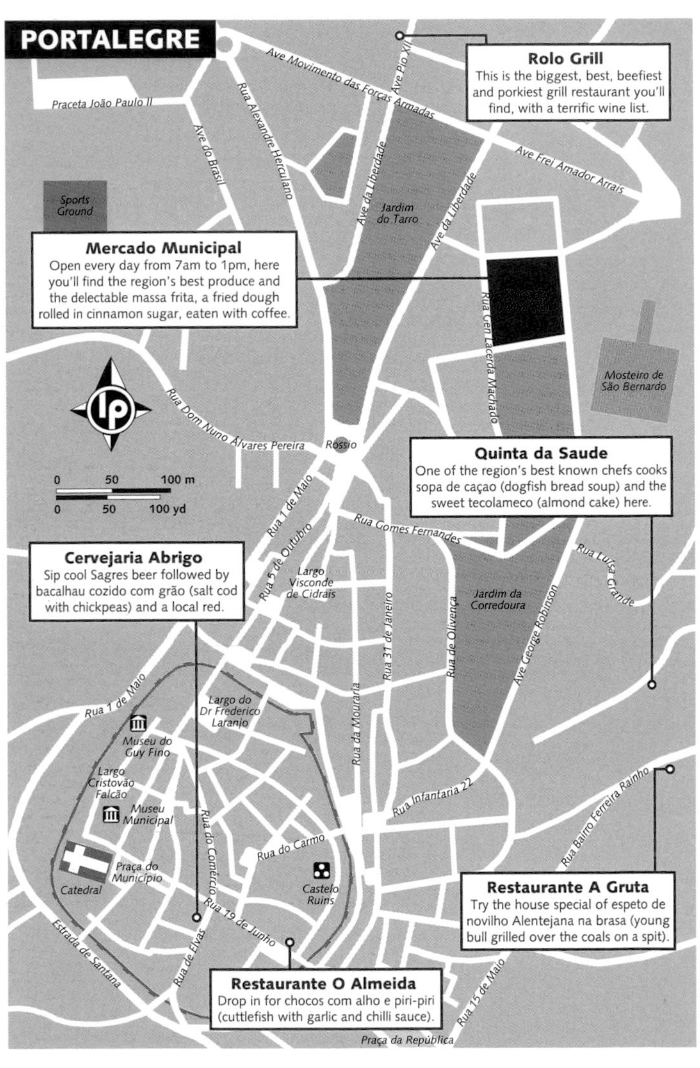
PORTALEGRE
Rolo Grill
This is the biggest, best, beefiest and porkiest grill restaurant you'll find, with a terrific wine list.
Mercado Municipal
Open every day from 7am to 1pm, here you'll find the region's best produce and the delectable massa frita, a fried dough rolled in cinnamon sugar, eaten with coffee.
Quinta da Saude
One of the region's best known chefs cooks sopa de caçao (dogfish bread soup) and the sweet tecolameco (almond cake) here.
Cervejaria Abrigo
Sip cool Sagres beer followed by bacalhau cozido com grão (salt cod with chickpeas) and a local red.
Restaurante A Gruta
Try the house special of espeto de novilho Alentejana na brasa (young bull grilled over the coals on a spit).
Restaurante O Almeida
Drop in for chocos com alho e piri-piri (cuttlefish with garlic and chilli sauce).
Praceta João Paulo II
Ave Movimento das Forças Armadas
Ave Pio XII
Rua Alexandre Herculano
Ave do Brasil
Ave da Liberdade
Ave Frei Amador Arrais
Sports Ground
Jardim do Tarro
Rua Gen Lacerda Machado
Mosteiro de São Bernardo
Rua Dom Nuno Álvares Pereira
Rossio
0 50 100 m
0 50 100 yd
Rua 1 de Maio
Rua 5 de Outubro
Rua Gomes Fernandes
Rua Luísa Grande
Largo Visconde de Cidrais
Jardim da Corredoura
Rua de Olivença
Ave George Robinson
Rua 31 de Janeiro
Rua da Mouraria
Largo do Dr Frederico Laranjo
Museu do Guy Fino
Largo Cristovão Falcão
Museu Municipal
Rua Infantaria 22
Rua Bairro Ferreira Rainho
Rua do Comércio
Rua do Carmo
Praça do Município
Catedral
Castelo Ruins
Rua 19 de Junho
Estrada de Santana
Rua de Elvas
Rua 15 de Maio
Praça da República

DONA ANA PINTO'S CHICKEN

Dona Ana Pinto has cooked the traditional dishes of her region at Restaurante Os Infantes in Beja, Alentejo, for over 30 years. Her very good reputation builds on her mother's, in a culture where inheriting your parents' profession is still common. Her family name, Pinto, means baby chicken. There is no tradition of official technical training in Portugal; rather, the secrets of the kitchen – and they are very much secrets – are passed on orally, preferably to another member of the family.

Dona Ana is teaching her young cousin to take over the reins, and he has so far spent four years by her side at the stove. She says he has 'sensação' (feeling) for the food, but that he won't be ready to take over for another five or six years yet. While she says lots of people can make the same dish, and she could even try to teach them, no-one else will be able to make it taste like she can. She never tastes the food, and she doesn't measure ingredients: she simply knows when it's perfect and knows that the same ingredients can vary from day to day, so any 'measuring' must be intuitive.

Knowing what the local produce tastes like and how it varies is crucial. When Dona's restaurant is invited to cook at international food fairs, they take absolutely every ingredient with them, including the water. Fresh produce for the restaurant comes from the local farmer's market at the castle nearby where local growers sell their wares. For this dish a supermarket chicken simply won't do: the dish relies on fresh chickens from the country that roam wild, eating insects and herbs that give their flesh the flavour, and taking the exercise that darkens the colour and gives texture. Dona also needs lots of their blood, so they must be freshly killed for the restaurant to prepare this dish. On weekends the queue to eat her food stretches out to the street, and among the dishes they queue for is **arroz de cabidela**, chicken cooked with rice in its own blood. It is served in a clay pot, also traditional of the region, which is thrown and fired at a village near the restaurant.

Dona Ana's instructions for Arroz de Cabidela

Although recipes are rarely written down, Dona Ana has revealed to us the secrets of her arroz de cabidela (so consider yourself an honorary member of the family). Here's how she told it to us:

"Put some olive oil and butter, diced onion and garlic, parsley and bay leaf, salt and white pepper in a cold pot and put over a low heat. When onion is translucent, add a whole jointed chicken, cover with white wine and cover the pot and cook. When wine has evaporated add a little water. When the chicken is cooked (about 45 minutes), remove from the heat, rest and cool. Add blood, then bring the liquid to a simmer. Serve with rice cooked in water and salt. Put rice in a clay pot, cover with juices from the chicken and put chicken on top. Serve with any white wine of the region."

cubes if the day is really hot. As in the Algarve with grilled sardines (see the Algarve section later in this chapter), in the Alentejo this soup is also served with fried fish on the side instead of sausage. In the pit of winter, **migas** (seasoned fried bread) provide sustenance, and you are likely to face them for breakfast and possibly also at lunch. Pork is a typical version, where garlic is fried in lard (pork fat), with bread and water added. The mix all pulls together to form a solid, flavoursome 'dough' that is sliced and served hot with different cuts of pork such as spare ribs, lean meat and smoked sausage. See why a glass of wine is necessary at breakfast too?

All year round you will eat **açorda** (bread soup), which is, at base, just bread and water. There are variations, but you will usually taste crushed garlic, salt and aromatic herbs (coriander or pennyroyal). Add olive oil, hot water and sliced bread, and whammo – the makings of a feast. You can then poach eggs in the liquid, and add various types of fish, and potatoes.

You will eat fried wild asparagus with scrambled eggs; oozingly rich Serpa cheese; carrots preserved with coriander; rabbit fried with thyme; eel stew fragrant with mint; hare stewed with butter beans; mullet **caldeirada** (stew); roasted partridge; dogfish açorda; white beans cooked with fresh spring truffles and the famous pork and clams. You will drink the reds of Borba, Reguengos de Monsaraz, Granja, Redondo and Portalegre, and finish with the impossibly rich conventual sweets. You will not be allowed to move on until your appetites have been exquisitely trampled upon by some of the best regional foods of the country. Don't worry if you eat too much food – if you've covered the Alentejo, then you've actually covered a third of Portugal.

BREAKFAST IN BEJA

Corte Ligeira is just out of the picturesque town of Beja, in the Alentejo region. It is both a family-run wild pig farm and an **agro turismo** (agricultural tourism) property. Just one feature of many that will put you in touch with the workings of the region is breakfast. Apart from coffee, you'll try **requeijão** (the fresh cheese made from whey), which is similar to ricotta, or fresh **queijo de cabra** (goat's cheese). Smearing them on freshly baked bread is completed with a drizzle of locally made honey flavoured with the wild flower **rosmaninho**, or a scoop of sweet tomato jam (see the Doce de Tomate recipe in the Staples chapter).

Naturally in a family-run business everyone has responsibilities, and in the de Matos family, it falls to grandmother to make the **javali salame** (wild pig salami) and **chouriço de sangue** (pork blood sausage). And they too are served cold for breakfast, along with fine slices of **presunto de javali** (smoked wild pig ham). Followed by **bolo podre** (olive oil, honey and spice cake), such a feast will set you up for a hard day's volunteer work.

DON'T MISS – Alentejo

- **Requeijão** – fresh ricotta cheese with **bolo podre** (local spiced honey cake), sausage and cheese (such as Évora) for breakfast (see below).
- **Açorda à Alentejana** – the delicious bread soup made with garlic, aromatic herbs like coriander or pennyroyal, olive oil, broth, greens and eggs. Look out especially for one with fresh purslane.
- **Empadas de galinha** – small chicken pies from the spectacular World Heritage-listed town of Évora. They are the perfect picnic or snack food, any time of day or night, and are so rich and sweet and delicious you just *know* they can't be good for you.
- **Carne de porco à Alentejana** – a famous dish of pork and clams, cooked in a traditional **cataplana** (enclosed copper dish) with lots of coriander.
- Red wines from the north of the region around Portalegre – said to be among the best in the country.
- **Ervilhas com ovos** (peas with eggs) – on offer in restaurants and at home in the spring months. Peas and slices of **chouriço** (a garlicky pork sausage flavoured with red pepper paste) are cooked with lots of lard, olive oil, onions and parsley and served with poached eggs.
- **Pastéis de toucinho** – flaky, sweet, luscious bacon tartlets from the town of Arraiolos.

Carne de Porco à Alentejana
(Alentejo-style Pork & Clams)

Ingredients

1kg	pork neck, chopped into 2cm cubes
6	cloves garlic, chopped finely
1	bottle young, dry white wine
2	bay leaves
	salt & pepper
1 tsp	paprika
3 Tbs	olive oil
1	onion, chopped
1kg	fresh baby clams, thoroughly washed and scrubbed (all sand must be completely removed)
	fresh coriander
	wedges of lemon

In a glass or china bowl, combine the pork, garlic, half the wine, bay leaves, salt & pepper and paprika. Cover and leave to marinate for at least 8 hours. Stir occasionally.

Heat a deep saucepan (or cataplana) over a high flame, adding the olive oil. Let the oil come to near-smoking point. Remove the pork from the marinade and add it to the saucepan in batches, gently frying the meat until it is browned. Return all the meat to the pan, lower the heat to medium and add the chopped onion, stirring until the onion is just cooked. Add the marinade mixture to the pan, along with the rest of the wine, and cover and cook for about half an hour, or until the pork is tender. Remove the lid and simmer until most liquid has evaporated.

Add the clams to the pan and simmer for about 5 minutes, when the shells should begin to open. Garnish with sprigs of coriander and wedges of lemon, and serve with fried potato.

Serves 4

Algarve

This is possibly what you came to Portugal for: beaches and fish. But it seems everyone else comes here for this too, so don't be surprised to find yourself in the company of non-native speakers. And, more importantly, non-native eaters and drinkers. Nowhere in the country is evidence of the bland internationalisation of local food so apparent (done to please wealthy visitors). It's tragic. So to discover regionally specific dishes that have avoided tourist influence, you'll need to get off the beaten track, heading to the north of the region where other tourists – and their requests for toasted sandwiches and Caesar salad – rarely venture.

The Algarve is the ex-Arab dominated southern strip of the country. Over the 600 years or so of their time in the sun, the Arabs did lots of good things for the table. Sugar, spices, figs, almonds and corn mash are all of Arab origin, and all consumed daily. The region can be divided into three types of geography: the coast, the hills, and the bit in between. On the coast fish dominates, in the hills it's pork and game such as hare and partridge, while in the middle there's agriculture and the raising of livestock.

The coast itself is lined with greenhouses full of tomatoes for the rest of the country, but that does not mean they dominate in the local cuisine. The coast is the place to eat snails, but you'll also eat lots and lots of grilled sardines, because although they are served all over the country, this is home. You'd be mad not to try the octopus, squid and cuttlefish. The octopuses can be large, with thick tentacles, and are exquisite freshly caught (that's what the fishermen's terracotta pots are for) and fried, served with lemon and **vinho branco** (white wine). They're so good they should be illegal: sweet, tender, sinful tentacles to suck and chew with your nearest and dearest (see the boxed text 10 Ways to Seduce a Lover, Portuguese Style in the Celebrating chapter). The Algarve coast used to be a tuna fishing hub so there are plenty of local dishes of tuna – curiously, what many non-Portuguese would call dry and overcooked is the preferred way – but the tuna stocks are depleted and the industry has deteriorated over recent years.

This is definitely a bivalve zone, so here's where to try clams, oysters, mussels, cockles and whelks, the fisherman's favourite cooked with kidney beans in **búzio com feijão**. Horse mackerel (bonito) or cuttlefish with tomato sauce; seafood açorda and rich fish, eel and shellfish soups; squid stuffed with ham and sausage; unctuous rice with red wines and octopus; and **xerém** – a cornmeal porridge made here with cockles, pork and corn mash – are dishes to try. Soupy seafood rice or corn dishes are really what this part of the coast is about, and indulgence is the key. Just mop everything up with bread, and even a splash of wine in the dish if you feel it needs some. One of the very best dishes is freshly gathered cockles steamed

DON'T MISS – Algarve

- Local fishing boats coming into port at Tavira, particularly with freshly caught octopus. Superb fried and served with lemon.
- Almond and dried fruit sweetmeats from the many **confeitarias** (patisseries) along the coast, and especially those made with almonds and figs, such as the luscious **morgados**.
- **Medronho – aguardente** (a brandy-like spirit) made from the fruit of the strawberry tree, which is prolific around Monchique, home also to superb **presunto** (smoked ham).
- **Berbigão** – steamed baby clams, freshly gathered and succulently tender.
- A summer feast of **gaspacho** (chilled tomato and garlic soup) with a side serve of freshly grilled, salt encrusted plump sardines.
- While we don't wish to be sour, the Algarve also has a stern 'do miss'. We implore you to avoid the tourism-destroyed coastline (see below) in favour of out of the way, local eateries and drinkeries, if you can still find them.

with a little white wine and seasoning and scattered with chopped coriander. If this crops up on a menu on the coast, try it.

Seafood and shellfish dishes will often be enriched with meats or sausage, as will chicken or vegetable dishes. Partridge, hare, pork, lamb and poultry are popular in the hills, but you're never so far away that fresh fish can't get there too. This is **cataplana** country – seafood and sausage or other meats cooked in a special enclosed copper dish (see Utensils in the

The ultimate seaside lunch – polvo com batatas (octopus with steamed potatoes), Tavira, Algarve

Home Cooking chapter) – but it's a dish that visitors have latched onto. Chances are that you'll be spotted as a visitor and will pay through the nose for the privilege of eating this dish. It's best to get invited back to someone's house for the real thing. The **presunto** (smoked ham) from Monchique is among the finest in the country, and look out especially for pork dishes with rice and beans, or chick peas. Add **piri piri** (red hot chilli pepper sauce) to just about anything you like and get used to eating salt: this is a centre of the industry and the food is always generously salted. Coriander sauces will also make regular appearances.

On the sweet front, it's almonds and dried fruits, for which the Algarve is renowned. **Doces de amêndoa** are crafted marzipan sweets, while the delicious **figos cheios** (dried figs studded with almonds) make an excellent choice for the not so sweetly inclined. Honey, superb through the region, also crops up in many cakes, while the abstemious can indulge in oranges, the best in the country. This is home to **medronheira** (**aguardente** – a brandy-like spirit – made from the fruit of the strawberry tree and sweetened with honey) and **amarguinha**, an almond liqueur. Or just try **melosa** – a mixed drink of brandy and honey. So drink up, eat up, and get a good tan.

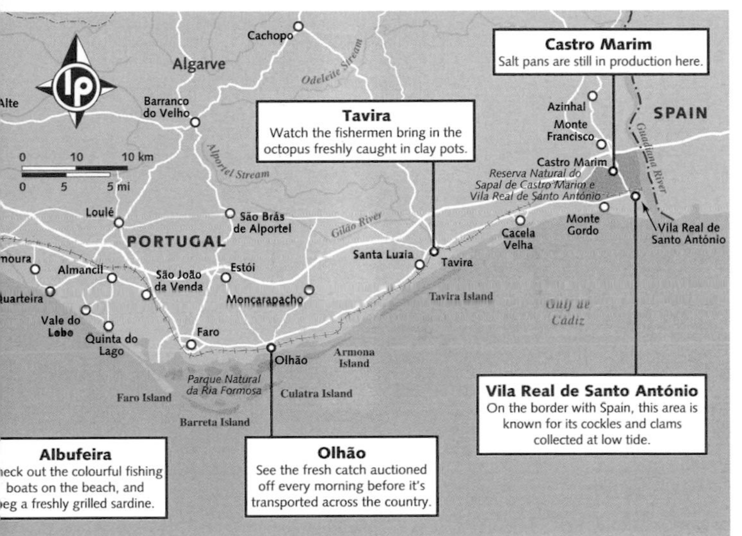

IT'S SNOWING IN THE ALGARVE!

The sunny Algarve is the lush lap of the country and stamped with the influence of the Moors. Everything that grows here does so with abandon, including the almond trees whose yearly profusion of sweet white flowers is linked to legend.

The story goes that a Moorish prince married a Scandinavian princess and took her to the Algarve to live. Instead of living it up in the sunshine, she did a bit of pining during her first warm winter. She was missing the snow, and there certainly wasn't likely to be any falling in the Algarve. Her health deteriorated rapidly (obviously she had none of the Portuguese fortitude) and in a desperate bid to save her, the Moorish prince gave the Algarve dense plantings of almond trees. They were in full bloom in January, the middle of a warm winter, and the thick, white almond blooms blanketed the earth and shimmered like snow in the evening light. Her health recovered, and the Algarve now has lots of yummy almond dishes. Sigh.

Madeira

If more people knew what was on the menu on Madeira, it might receive more visitors. It is not like mainland Portugal. How could it be? The island is closer to Morocco than Lisbon, and has all the laid-back charm that a tropical island should have. And it has fantastic food. The Portuguese claimed it in the mid-15th century and set about establishing a colony where the 'white gold' of sugar cane made the locals rich. The island is just 19km by 56km, but thousands of kilometres of irrigation channels mean that every square inch of land gets water, so its impossibly rugged landscape is completely under cultivation. Vines, exotic flowers, bananas and market gardens dot the terraced hillscapes in tight patches. The serious business of eating and drinking provides a great reason to explore the island.

The capital, Funchal, was named for the fragrance of the wild fennel that once grew abundantly. Like the wood that Madeira was named for (Madeira means 'wood'), the fennel was cleared to make way, it seems, for bananas. So naturally enough lots of dishes are served with grilled or fried bananas on the side. And while that may sound rather rank to some, it actually works a treat.

Madeira is where you should learn to enjoy crisp, cold beer: the climate is hot year round, so you'll need it. And with it will come **tremoços**, the salted, preserved yellow beans that you deftly pop from their skins and chew until they release their nuttiness. Quite delicious. You should also try the extraordinarily marine-flavoured limpets, served grilled on the half shell with garlic butter, bread and more beer. Madeira has loads of fresh fish, and foremost in volume and quality are **bifes de atum** (tuna steaks). But there's one problem – as with other meats, tuna will not be deemed cooked here until every last trace of pinkness is banished, which means it can be very dry. If you're Portuguese this won't bother you, but if you prefer tuna pink and tender, you'll need to suffer the ignominy of ordering it 'mal passado' (rare), which no-one will really understand, but go ahead and try anyway. They do love **bacalhau** (dried salt cod) here, just as much as everywhere else in Portugal, and so much so that they catch a similar local fish, then gut it, splay it, salt it and dry it in the sun, and call it false bacalhau. You may catch a glimpse of these much loved fellows baking in the coastal sunshine, and although considered not as 'good' as the really good (and really expensive) imported real thing, it's still highly enjoyed.

Madeira is also home to cows and wonderfully happy chickens. Chunks of chicken – and we mean huge chunks – are spiked with an **espetada** (skewer or kebab) and cooked over the coals or in a woodfired oven. Back in the even better old days, men and women harvesting crops in the mountainous terrain would skewer chunks of fresh meat with green sticks of the

Madeira's rugged west coast

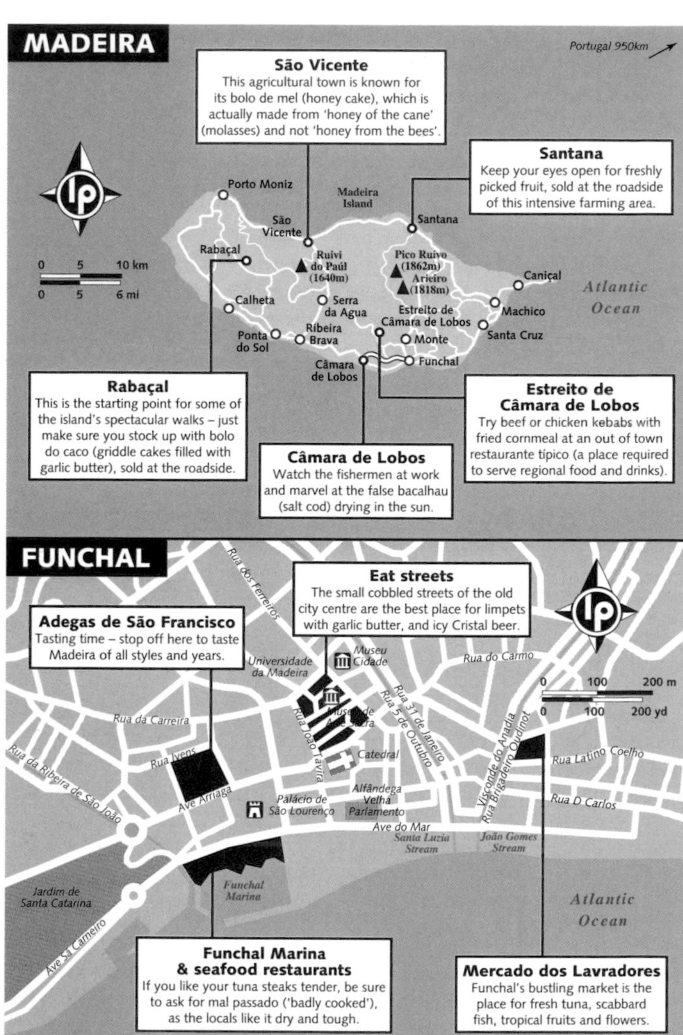
MADEIRA
Portugal 950km
São Vicente
This agricultural town is known for its bolo de mel (honey cake), which is actually made from 'honey of the cane' (molasses) and not 'honey from the bees'.
Santana
Keep your eyes open for freshly picked fruit, sold at the roadside of this intensive farming area.
Porto Moniz
Madeira Island
São Vicente
Santana
Rabaçal
Ruivi do Paúl (1640m)
Pico Ruivo (1862m)
Arieiro (1818m)
Caniçal
Atlantic Ocean
Calheta
Serra da Agua
Estreito de Câmara de Lobos
Machico
Santa Cruz
Ponta do Sol
Ribeira Brava
Monte
Câmara de Lobos
Funchal
0 5 10 km
0 5 6 mi
Rabaçal
This is the starting point for some of the island's spectacular walks – just make sure you stock up with bolo do caco (griddle cakes filled with garlic butter), sold at the roadside.
Estreito de Câmara de Lobos
Try beef or chicken kebabs with fried cornmeal at an out of town restaurante típico (a place required to serve regional food and drinks).
Câmara de Lobos
Watch the fishermen at work and marvel at the false bacalhau (salt cod) drying in the sun.
FUNCHAL
Rua dos Ferreiros
Eat streets
The small cobbled streets of the old city centre are the best place for limpets with garlic butter, and icy Cristal beer.
Adegas de São Francisco
Tasting time – stop off here to taste Madeira of all styles and years.
Universidade da Madeira
Museu Cidade
Rua do Carmo
0 100 200 m
0 100 200 yd
Rua da Carreira
Rua João Tavira
Rua 31 de Janeiro
Rua 5 de Outubro
Catedral
Rua da Ribeira de São João
Rua Ivens
Ave Arriaga
Palácio de São Lourenço
Alfândega Velha Parlamento
Visconde do Anadia
Rua Brigadeiro Oudinot
Rua Latino Coelho
Rua D Carlos
Ave do Mar
Santa Luzia Stream
João Gomes Stream
Funchal Marina
Jardim de Santa Catarina
Ave Sá Carneiro
Atlantic Ocean
Funchal Marina & seafood restaurants
If you like your tuna steaks tender, be sure to ask for mal passado ('badly cooked'), as the locals like it dry and tough.
Mercado dos Lavradores
Funchal's bustling market is the place for fresh tuna, scabbard fish, tropical fruits and flowers.

DON'T MISS – Madeira

- **Espetada** – substantial skewers spiked with excellent quality meats and poultry, served sizzling (see right).
- Mercado dos Lavradores, Funchal – an absolute joy: massive fresh tuna lined up for butchering, and slippery scabbard fish waiting to be stripped of their skins; brilliant tropical flowers and fruits; and a mood of indulgence and warmth. This is a definite 'do not miss' under any circumstances (see At the Mercado in the Shopping & Markets chapter).
- **Bolo do caco** – hot, garlic-filled griddle bread, sometimes cooked with spicy **chouriço** (a garlicky pork sausage flavoured with red pepper paste) inside and bought freshly made at the roadsides on the weekends. Let it all ooze down your arms while you eat and chat to the streetside seller. And definitely partake of any freshly char-grilled chicken at the same time. Guaranteed to be the best quality chicken you can get – smokingly fresh and full of flavour.
- Walking trips through the spectacular countryside filled with man-made waterways, which visitors from mainland Portugal come for especially.
- Stocking up on rare vintages of Madeira, and tasting lots of others.
- Lapas (limpets) with garlic butter and Cristal beer – intensely marine-flavoured and particular to the island.
- Eating the sumptuous local **peixe espada** (scabbard fish) with fried bananas and ignoring incorrect translations that would have you confuse it with **espardarte** (swordfish). They are two different fish, and the former is hard to get elsewhere.

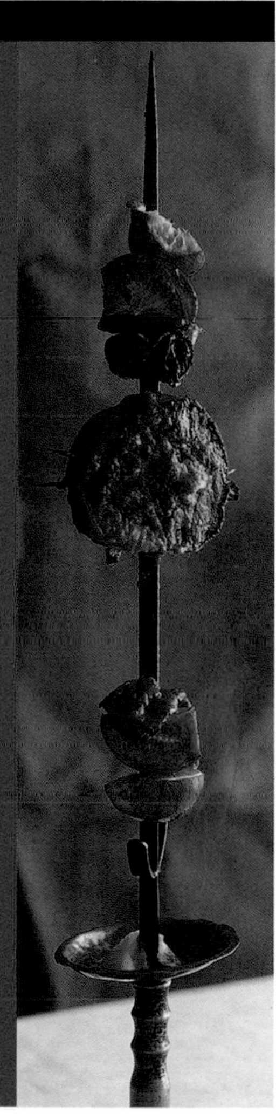

laurel tree (the parent of bay leaves) and grill them over hot coals. The **restaurantes típicos** (see the Where to Eat chapter) near Funchal now grill them on long metal skewers that are hung from hooks above the table, and from which the hungry eat the chunks of flesh, mopping the juices caught by a plate at the base with **bolo do caco** – hot, garlic-filled griddle bread. Try a local wine if you like, but even the locals will probably suggest one from the mainland because while the island's (relatively) inferior grapes can be, and mostly are, turned into the liquid gold Madeira (see Madeira in the Drinks chapter), they make only average table wine. But don't let that stop you trying it. Oh, and don't forget to order a side dish of **milho frito** (fried cornmeal), which, apart from being made with the white cornmeal, will make you think you've landed on a polenta farm in Italy. Crisp outside, soft inside. Apart from Madeira wine, you should also try **aguardente de cana** (sugar cane brandy) and, since it's a tropical island, **pudim de maracuja** (passionfruit pudding) or **licor de maracuja** (passionfruit liquor). They are all happy companions to Madeira's famous **bolo de mel**, a heady, spiced 'honey' and walnut cake made with lots of delicious ingredients, none of which is honey – molasses is used instead.

shopping
& markets

Shopping for food in Portugal is one of life's great pleasures. It is not only a necessity, but a celebration of fresh produce and the people whose livelihoods are still linked to nature's rhythms. Markets are for catching up on gossip, buying and selling and passing an entertaining day outdoors. What's not to like?

Speciality Shops

There are plenty of specific shops in which to browse, as well as the one-stop shopping centres. Hours are roughly from 9am to 7pm most days, and smaller shops may close for lunch between 1pm and 3pm. They may also close on Sundays. Large shopping centres usually operate from 10am until 11pm every day. In addition to speciality shops, it's well worth looking out for artisanal producers, especially in regional areas, where farm fresh produce can be delicious. This is particularly good for cheese and for bread made by the village baker. Other shops to look out for, especially near dock areas of cities, are those with no special name that sell **bacalhau** (dried salt cod) and other dried fish, spirits and maybe wine, and bulk dried pulses and legumes. Remnants of the days of stocking up ships for a long voyage, they stink of fetid fish, but are well worth a visit.

Charcutaria (Delicatessen)

The equivalent of a delicatessen, this is somewhere to stock up on smallgoods, olives, some cheeses and other traditional deli fare. And alcohol too, if you want it.

Confeitaria (Confectionary/Pastry Shop)

Pop in here for special cakes or pastries, perhaps of a limited type, either to take away or eat with a quick coffee.

Doçaria (Specialist Sweet/Dessert Shop)

This is a shop specialising in regional sweets that may be either a type of cake, dessert, pastry or biscuit. Often they're family-run businesses, making and selling the same specialities for generations.

Ervenaria (Medicinal Tea Shop)

You can purchase herbal concoctions here, mixed to remedy specific ailments such as a sluggish liver (now why on earth would you be suffering from that?), poor digestion or the appearance of cellulite. No solutions are offered for world peace, but just about everything else is covered.

Padaria (Bakery)

With the decline of the village baker tradition comes the rise of the bakery shop. While the quality varies, these are worth a look both for fresh bread and an often small range of pastries, or for a quick sandwich and a coffee.

Pastelaria (Pastry Shop)

Pastry or cake shops are all over the country but most common in the cities where lots of people want a daily sweet fix. There are dozens of pastry varieties, hopefully 'fabrico próprio' (made on the premises).

Pastéis de Tentúgal (flaky pastries with a creamy egg yolk and sugar paste filling) made to a 16th century recipe by master pastry chef Snr Cacilda Correia, Beiras

Peixaria (Fishmonger)

The fishmonger may be part of a **mercado municipal** (see At the Mercado later in this chapter), or have its own shopfront. What you don't want to buy is any fish that has the word 'congelado' near its name. This means it's frozen, and really, you're better off eating chicken if you can't find fresh fish in Portugal.

Local fish markets, Viseu, Beiras

Tabacaria (Tobacconist)

This is the place to buy cigarettes and chewing gum for nerve-wracking road trips.

Talho (Butcher)

While plenty of people still get the butcher to come over and slaughter their own hand-raised beast – or do it themselves – the village butcher is the place to go if you're just after a few chops for dinner. Helpfully, many butcher shop signs have cartoon pictures of the type of fresh meat they sell. Especially guilt provoking is the fact that the animals are often drawn with smiles on their faces.

At the Mercado (Market)

Markets are central to Portuguese life. These may be daily municipal markets, weekly town markets, monthly regional markets or any of the mini, super, or hyper markets.

Most towns have a **mercado municipal** (municipal market) that will usually be open for business every day but the Sabbath. If you want to plunge face first into regional produce, let the markets be your guide. And, if following your snout is the basis of your entire travel itinerary, this is a great way to get to know the people in town: if you know what they eat, you should be able to work out who they are.

Some days are better than others to visit the market. Saturday is likely to be a better day for variety, volume and people watching. Inland markets may get fresh fish from the coast on, say, Wednesday and Saturday, so be on the lookout for that. Weekly mercados or **feiras** (fairs) are usually held in a central town square, and monthly country markets will be on the edge of town where there's plenty of space. The monthly markets are huge, and notices will be up to indicate which day they're held. As with markets all over the world, early birds will be best fed and only the more touristy markets remain open into the afternoon.

While some markets are definitely of the 'don't miss' variety, there's no point desperately trying to be in the right place at the right time for whatever specialist market your guidebook tells you about. Let yourself off the hook. You're bound to come across a fantastic market somewhere and it will be all the more fun because you don't expect to find it (see the boxed text Market Monthly).

It's quite acceptable to look at and even touch the fresh produce at market stalls, but only if it would then normally be washed before eating. Don't go handling cheese or sausage or you'll annoy stallholders. If you plan to pick something up, try to catch their eye first and say "Bom-dia senhor/a" (Good morning sir/madam) and motion to what interests you. In the country areas this will be especially appreciated, and in the city it won't harm to be polite either. The stallholder will probably offer a taste, and you can then work out what to do next. Nibble your way around the lot if you like – why not. No-one will expect you to buy something you haven't had the opportunity to taste.

Mercado da Ribeira (or de 24 Julho), Lisbon

No visit to Lisbon would be complete without checking out the Mercado da Ribeira, as it's known locally (guidebooks refer to its correct name of Mercado de 24 Julho, but you may get blank looks if you do the same). From very early in the morning, fresh produce streams in by van, truck,

LISBOA
ÓBIDOS
Hospital
Museus
Parque D. Carlos I
Vida

cart or ferries docking at the nearby terminal. A huge flower section, as well as meat, poultry, fish, dairy, bakery goods, fruit and vegetables, fills the domed building daily. Look for the machines grinding their way through freshly shredded kale for **caldo verde** (Galician kale and potato soup); a wide variety of potatoes; fresh and dried chillies, corn and herbs; and the specialist snail sellers. The cafe at the markets is open 24 hours, which means it can attract a fun, late-night crowd or danger from the Docks area. It's open from 3am to noon Monday to Saturday.

Mercado de Bolhão, Porto

In the impossibly constricted centre of Porto, the semi-enclosed Bolhão market is worth visiting for its Art Nouveau facade alone. But inside is an excellent indication of the region's produce. Look out especially for the hefty loaves of **broa** (corn bread) including the **branca** (white), **escura** (dark) and **trigo** (wheat). All are sold by weight. Marvel too at the sausage skins for sale – what could possibly be going in them all? The market is closed on Sunday, and is quiet on Monday.

Mercado dos Lavradores, Funchal

This market is a joy, and is possibly one of the finest fresh markets to be found. Madeira's fisherpeople, farmers, flower growers and basket weavers congregate in the centre of town to flog their wares in the tropical warmth. The market is partly undercover – housing the entire fish section and three levels of fresh produce – while a central courtyard is shaded with brightly coloured umbrellas. Watch massive fresh tuna lose their heads, and silvery scabbard fish slipped from their skins, and taste the fruit warmed by the sun. On Friday the market spreads beyond its building to the backstreets of the old fishermen's quarter. It is closed Sunday and public holidays.

Feira de Barcelos, Barcelos

Held in the Campo da República every Thursday, this is the town's big drawcard. It's enormous, and you can find almost anything in the edible department, including livestock, should you care to take some away with you. Massive loaves of broa are sold still scented from the oven, and straight from the back of a truck. This is also home to the ubiquitous Barcelos cock, replicas of which are found all over the country. Legend has it that a pilgrim, falsely accused of stealing and therefore sentenced to a hanging, pleaded with the judge that if he was innocent the roast cockerel dinner the judge was about to tuck into would get up and crow. It did, and with a bit of drama the whole sordid mistake was sorted. The result? Brightly painted carved cocks all over Portugal. The moral? Haven't a clue.

Market day in Caldas da Rainha, Estremadura

MARKET MONTHLY

Getting lost sometimes heralds the start of an excellent adventure, and trying to follow directions in Portugal is bound to get you lost on more than one occasion. It was our luck to get lost recently, and the idea to go 'where all those other cars are going' landed us at a monthly country market in Vila Fresca de Azeitão, south-west of Lisbon.

Struggling to get to the market centre through traffic and parked transport lorries was well worth the effort. Here was just about any kind of farm equipment, plants, clothing, kitchen equipment and fresh regional produce imaginable. In the midst of crowded rows of stallholders, whole chickens turned on the grill with flames licking at their juicy thighs, thin slices of fresh beef were fried for hot sandwiches, one-pot stews bubbled at the edges, a local band played music and lots of happy market-goers relaxed with beer and wine. An oasis for rest and restitution.

Out in the rows of stalls the buzz was palpable, and blended with sounds of live animals for sale. Tiny newborn pups snuggled at their owners and smooched in cardboard boxes, hopefully destined for a life on the land with a kind family. An infinite variety of fresh poultry paced about nervously: they seemed to know what they were destined for and that it wouldn't involve much fun – from tiny chicks and ducklings up (and out) to their plump cousins, the geese, and nimble quail scampering about, perhaps hoping to escape the plate.

Trade was a little calmer over at a **bacalhau** (dried salt cod) stall, where the proud owner balanced a whole splayed salt cod in the palm of his hand, then showed a client that the fat flesh was still flexible. This is how they show that their wares are of quality; bacalhau should be dry enough to stand straight up from the palm, but soft enough to yield when touched. **Presunto** (smoked ham), thickly packed in bright red paprika powder, swayed in the open air, and fat strings of sausages all but obscured the vendor. A nod from the left and a sample was slashed down, wrapped and traded for cash. A leg will do a family for a month.

This was the time to stock up the larder with other bulk purchase items such as **garrafãos** of local wine (wicker-covered 5L flagons), gallons of olive oil, clay pots full of olives preserved in brine, bags of grain, and sacks of dried beans, nuts and dried fruit. There were five different kinds of fig, more of olives. Cheeses, properly handled, can continue to age and feed the family until the next monthly market.

We headed off late amid families cramming hay bales, caged young poultry and tired kids into the backs of cars. We endured the usual traffic chaos, but we actually didn't care – we were set. We'd stocked up with the kind of fresh food – bread, olives, cheese, wine, cured meats and fruit – that needed no planning or equipment. We were headed for the hills nearby for an evening picnic at the foot of castle ruins and views across the countryside. And this time, we didn't get lost.

At the Supermercado (Supermarket)

Apart from the fresh food ones there are **minimercados**, **supermercados** and **hipermercados**. A minimercado is like a convenience store with a little of everything, and may be open when the others are closed. You'll pay more for the convenience, of course. A supermercado (like Pingo Doce) has more of everything, and is for the weekly shop. They have plenty of fresh food too – not everyone is into the fresh marketing scene – and are open from 9am to 8pm, seven days. If you're after a spare toilet seat or new microwave, try a hipermercado (like Continente or Jumbo), which has lots of household stuff other than food. Hipermercados are slightly cheaper than supermercados, and are open from around 9am to 11pm Monday to Saturday, and from 9am to 1pm Sunday.

Things to Take Home

Portugal's pretty relaxed about what you take out of the country in the way of comestibles. But unless you're driving out you'd better make sure you can get them home safely, otherwise you'll be lugging all that weight around just to toss it in the bin at customs. Take whatever you want to the rest of the EU (domestic quantities only please, nothing that would arouse suspicions of professional looting), but take care elsewhere. North America and Australasia have strict quarantine laws to protect native wildlife and agricultural industries, so everything must be declared. This includes any visits to farms or rural properties, so pack your boots on top. Not everything you declare will be confiscated, but it simply isn't worth the risk. Declare the lot. Fresh fruit and vegetables are definitely out and basically all you'll get through with is some, but not all, dried packaged foods and your quota of booze. There isn't that much in the way of rare and precious items that you won't find at home, so stick with the bottles. And since **aguardente** (brandy-like spirit) has a higher alcohol content than **vinho verde** (light sparkling wine), it's better to try taking that, or something preserved in it, like fruit. The same goes for port and Madeira, but only if it's something you won't find at home.

If you are driving out, however, whack a **presunto** (smoked ham) in the boot and feast on preserved ham in the months to come. Sweets won't last long, and neither will much else that's edible. It's far better to stock up on utensils. Get yourself a **cataplana** (enclosed copper dish) or three – they come in different sizes, serving two to 10 – and some of the terracotta cookware that makes one-pot dishes, such as chicken with bloody rice, taste so good. The terracotta olive containers are cute too. Logically, they have a spot for the olives, and one for the stones. The really daring could also toss in a **presunteiro** (ham slicing machine).

A Portuguese Picnic

Well, the Portuguese don't picnic much, but there's absolutely nothing to stop you from searching out some castle ruins or heading into the grounds of an awesome monastery with your stash of treats. One of the best possible picnic foods has to be **bola de carne** from the north. Rich bread dough is layered with different kinds of cured meats and sometimes cheese into a rich and satisfying sandwich that can simply be cut off in appropriately thick wedges. Alternatively, just gather local fresh bread, olives, slices of presunto, a hunk of cheese, some fruit and local pastries and a bottle of wine, and scout out a scenic view for your feast. Don't forget the bottle opener.

where to eat & drink

To live is to eat, to eat is to drink, and to drink is to raise a glass to friends, family and life itself. Portuguese people love to eat and drink. They love sharing eating and drinking. And they love the fact that the way they eat and drink remains spectacularly unchanged by the passage of time, the arrival of advertising and the pressures of fashion. It's part of the fabric of life.

CALEM
PORTO
CALEM
PORTO

Eating and drinking in cafes, bars and restaurants is the common thread that links all of Portugal. Waking hours are punctuated both by the immediate pleasures of the table and an opportunity to share in the ancient culinary and wine making traditions that inspire pride. It all starts with breakfast. That's where you'll see healthy-looking young women, of average body shape and size, tucking into the biggest, sweetest, richest-looking pastries you've ever seen. And smiling, laughing, and – it seems – enjoying every mouthful. How many countries can you go to and see *that*? It's pure joy, and nowhere near the neurotic alternative of pretending none of us has an appetite.

Now the funny thing is that women seem to hang out a lot in **pastelarias** (pastry shops) and cafes eating pastries and drinking coffee and tea (and smoking), while men are seen separately in cafes, **tascas** (cheap eateries) and other eating places, drinking quite a lot of alcohol and catching up with mates (and smoking). It seems that ne'er the twain shall meet. Why? This is a most Catholic country, and conservative at that, with only a generation between dictatorship and democracy. This means that good girls live at home with their parents until they meet a man they'd like to marry. They are most definitely not hanging around alone in places of potential ill repute, such as those offering food and alcohol. And that's a little sad because it's quite an imbalance and there aren't a lot of public places for a woman alone to eat and drink. Unless, of course, she's a crazy foreigner ...

Eating out anywhere in Portugal means choosing between three rock or hard place scenarios. First there's the smoking. Everyone (or so it seems) does it, and it usually includes a charming hacking cough just as you're about to take the first bite of your meal. There's nothing you can do about it. If you're a non-smoker this could be a big problem, since many eating places have shared tables and they're often packed out. Just swallow, and wait for the day when the EU directive on passive smoking comes down.

Second, the TV. Yep, these are in every place you come across, even in some of the more expensive places, and most definitely if there's any football on. It's bizarre. You can be watching the box at breakfast, lunch and dinner. Often it's angled so that everyone in the room has the possibility of seeing it, which is less than a joy if you actually want to talk to the people you're with. Some places have two TVs. Even if you're the only diner in the place you're outnumbered. The box stays on.

The third joy, which may confront you if you've cleverly positioned yourself away from smoking and television, is the toilets. Most likely the only table in the place that doesn't have a view of the TV is the worst in the house, which means you're looking straight into the toilets. Sometimes they only have swinging doors, and sometimes the washbasin will actually be right beside your table. Again: take a deep breath and choose. The smoke? The TV? The toilet? If you've only struck two out of three, you're doing OK.

A reflective moment at Café Avenida Diogo Leite, Porto

But a definite joy that awaits you is the possibility of seeing your food cooked in the corner of the dining room. This may be over a char grill, or directly over the coals of an open fire. The informality and immediacy will send you to heaven. It's almost like camping. Glassware is usually pretty basic, regardless of the price bracket you're in, so don't go getting huffy about how much better the wine would taste in Riedel. You should be grateful if it's clean and unchipped. Actually, lots of people routinely give their cutlery a wipe with a napkin when they sit down. But never fear. Portugal is a country that loves a bottle of bleach and is none too shy about splashing it around. It's all pretty spotless to the naked eye. Don't make any assumptions about credit cards because lots of places will be cash only. And making a fuss about getting a printed receipt will (from most places) only result in a great deal of turmoil and nothing useful anyway. Forget it.

A tip of 5% to 10% is reasonable to pay if you've enjoyed yourself, but better restaurants may already include a **serviço** (service charge) so check the bill. Suffice to say that if your bill has been handwritten on the paper tablecloth before you, it's unlikely there's a service charge, so use your discretion. Mobile phones have recently caught on in Portugal and it's common to see and hear far more about what's going on in someone else's life than you'll ever need to know. However, it's best to be discreet, and excuse yourself from the table if yours should ring during a meal. Better still, leave it off.

One of the more amusing pastimes is watching people attempt to get rubbish into a bin. If you enter a place at the beginning of service it will be spotless. But over the course of the hours ahead you'll see just about everyone, both staff and customers, throw their papers, cigarette butts, food and whatever else in the general direction of the bin. So walk in at the end of service and you may well be wading through rubbish that won't be cleaned up until the end. Also don't be surprised, in some of the more casual eateries, to see the family cat or dog wandering around in the dining area or kitchen. Get over it or you'll end up very hungry. Be polite when you walk into an eatery and start off on the right foot with a heartfelt "Bom dia!" (Good day!), or if you've already been to the place before and you recognise the staff, use the less formal "Olá!" (Hi!).

Look on a business card to see exactly what a place offers: it may be a mix of establishments such as snack-bar pastelaria or cafe-restaurante, or it may indicate exactly what type of food is offered: lunch, savoury snacks and char grills; regional pastries; conventual sweets; or regional cooking. Or the reverse of the card may indicate which special dishes are served on which days. In the front door or window of any eatery there will be a clear indication of the hours of business as well as the licensed operator. Many places are closed on Sunday (or at least Sunday afternoon and evening). This is when it's best to get yourself invited to someone's home.

Where to Eat & Drink

Heaven awaits. But leave any preconceptions at home about what kind of place might serve good food and drink. Portugal does not have a fine dining tradition and although there are now plenty of hospitality schools teaching new recruits about the finer points of service, this training may take a while to filter through the industry. Use the listings in this chapter to give you an indication of the price and style of different outlets. For the best overall experience, including value for money and quality of food, choose modest establishments offering traditional Portuguese food in simple surroundings.

There is a disturbing trend in Portugal of trying to compensate for a lack of fine dining by trying to 'internationalise' the food. So if you see a place offering **cozinha regional e internacional**, you'll get both local and generic international food. It's unlikely to please because it will possibly do neither well. This is largely an attempt to please foreign palates that are not brave enough to eat local. What ever local food is prepared tends to be a watered-down version.

Most restaurants are first come first served. Only the more expensive restaurants take bookings, and it's advisable to make one during peak season in tourist areas or on weekends. Mind you, if you're swanning about in expensive restaurants you haven't been paying attention at all.

Adega (Cellar)

In addition to selling wine produced on an estate, an adega may also have a restaurant or bar. The best adegas will use the opportunity to offer the other produce of the property (if there is any – some adegas are purely for wine making and have no public facilities). This produce may include fruits that have been made into liqueur, farm-pressed olive oil and preserved olives, jams and preserves, sausages and or Portuguese salami as well as wine from the barrel. There will often be traditional wine making paraphernalia or olive oil presses. The adega may only be open on weekends, or for special functions, but it's always worth finding out its opening hours because the produce will be farm fresh and simply prepared in traditional ways. At a community level, an adega co-op is sometimes where locals with an interest in the co-op may meet up after work for a glass of regional wine and a snack. So while the range of eating facilities of adegas vary, eating or snacking at one can be a delight.

Agro Turismo (Agricultural Tourism)

This is one of the best ways to get to know the produce of a region, the ways in which it is traditionally prepared, and the people who may have been doing it for generations. Working properties offering accommodation in an active agricultural environment are centrally registered, and some can be wonderfully grand. It may be as simple as staying the night at a 17th century **quinta** (farm) and eating strawberries and fresh cheese from the farm; watching with pleasure as the new season's lambs are driven by shepherds down the laneway past your door; eating fresh woodfired bread made by the village matriarch at her home; or drizzling fresh local honey over your other spoils – or your mate. Or you may opt to be involved in the workings of the farm, including participating in seasonal activities at certain times of year. Working farms are never idle, so whatever the time of year there's sure to be something to join in with, and it never feels like a touristy thing to do. Agro Turismo plus one would have to be Eco Agro Tourism, which has a register of organic or eco-friendly working properties offering farmhouse accommodation and organic produce (see the European Centre for Eco Agro Tourism Web site at **www.pz.nl/eceat/** for more information).

Bar

In Portugal you can get a drink at just about any kind of establishment anywhere in the country, so there's no special reason to go to a bar. Some bars are cafe-bars, where you can have snacks as well as drinks. Others are bars for shaking your booty until the wee hours, although it's also possible to choose from a small bar menu of a few hot dishes and sandwiches. There's plenty of nightlife, and Lisbon has a dedicated bar strip at the Docks, which is quite mad. There's even someone to coordinate the area's parking, and it can attract thousands of punters. Odd, but everyone seems to have a good time.

Cafe

The Portuguese are very particular about the quality of their coffee (see Café in the Drinks chapter) and this is where they'll go to get their fix. Open from early morning until late, cafes serve coffee around the clock. There's a price difference between standing and sitting, and many people simply drop in for **uma bica** (a short black) at the bar and a two minute pit stop. Others will hang around with the newspaper, and unless you're in a tourist area with people lining up at the door to get in, you're unlikely to be asked to leave once you've finished the coffee. It's possible to drop into other establishments for coffee also, and unless it's a restaurant during meal hours (around noon to 3pm for lunch and 7pm to 10.30pm for dinner), most places will be happy to serve you just a coffee.

Casa de Chá (Teahouse)

A teahouse will, usually in addition to excellent coffee, offer a range of herbal and black teas. They will also offer a sometimes staggering range of sweets and cakes, as it would be a wasted opportunity not to eat as well. They are unlikely to be the type of pastries offered at a **pastelaria** (pastry shop), but they may include some of the extraordinarily rich and sweet **doces regional** or **doces conventuais** (regional or conventual sweets – see Doces & Pastéis in the Staples chapter), which can also be bought to take away. While the offerings will vary from region to region, the basic ingredients will not: egg yolks and sugar, maybe with some almond and spice. Amazingly, you'll even see people happily pouring extra sugar in their tea. Teahouses are for all those between-meal sugar hits that people are so fond of, and often there are also savoury snacks for a simple lunch.

Casa de Pasto (Cheap Restaurant/Diner)

These are large dining rooms found in bigger towns and cities, offering budget, three-course meals that usually represent good value. The food is simple (entree, main, and dessert or cheese) with a house wine and coffee. While this type of eating may not inspire you, it can be a lot of fun to check out the buzz here during a busy service.

Bartender, Castelo Branco, Beiras

Cervejaria (Beer House)

A beer house is indistinguishable from some of the less expensive eateries in that there is a small, seasonal menu and simple surrounds in which to eat it. You will *not* find a thousand different beers on tap or even in bottles: it will be the same limited variety as elsewhere (see Cerveja in the Drinks chapter). But here's where you come when you really feel like a thirst-quenching beer, regardless of the time of day, and you don't want people looking askance at you because they think you should be drinking wine at meal times like they are. Mind you, you'll still find **vinho da casa** (house wine) at a cervejaria so if all in your group don't agree, there is a choice. You can drop into a cervejaria at any time of the day and far into the night, and simply stand at the bar nursing a beer and snacking on the types of foods that complement it, including roasted pig's ears, **pastéis de bacalhau** (salt cod fishcakes), olives, finely sliced **presunto** (smoked ham) and **chouriço** (a garlicky pork sausage flavoured with red pepper paste). All of these also make excellent picnic food – flavoursome, small snacks that are easy to eat and taste superb cold.

Churrasqueira/Churrascaria (Barbecue Restaurant)

Welcome to chicken land. These are family-style restaurants that specialise in **frango no churrasco**, or char-grilled chicken. It's one of the most distinctive Portuguese exports: specialist Portuguese chicken restaurants have popped up all over the globe. The reason they're popular in Portugal is because the chicken is so delicious and the bill so reasonable. Buying a fresh chicken at a supermarket is very cheap and it's likely to be miles better quality than even the fanciest, organically grown, free range expensive ones you'll search high and low for at home. And the Portuguese have a long and happy tradition of both raising and eating chickens, so when they can't here's the place to eat them. Other foods are also served grilled, but the chicken is the reason people come here. It will be simply prepared for cooking with olive oil, and perhaps paprika. All you need to do is order some **batatas fritas** (potato chips) to go with it, and splash on the **piri piri** (red hot chilli pepper sauce). Eat with your fingers, and go straight to heaven.

Fumeiro (Smokehouse)

These are family-run fun. Found in the Home of Ham belt from the Alentejo region up to the Beiras, smokehouses are where the serious business of preserving pork products through smoking and curing goes on. Apart from being able to buy the products, there may also be (and often is) a tavern area out the back with huge slabs of wood as share tables and rustic stools. And this is where you can tuck into some of the pork products *in situ*. Suspended from the ceiling will be innumerable smoked hams waiting to be

Gotta love smiling service – Restaurant Casa de Hospedes, Viseu, Beiras

pronounced cured and ready to eat, as well as strings of preserved sausages. As soon as you walk in the door – which can be just about anytime during the day or evening – you'll get one of the more wonderful slabs of cheese, deep golden **broa** (corn bread), and spicy olives. Clay jugs of **tinto** (red wine) or **branco** (white wine) will be put down in front of you, along with ceramic cups. Then you order: maybe some **salpicâo** (smoked pork fillet) slices; **farinheira** (sausages made with chunks of lard and flour); roasted spicy chouriço; slices of **morcela** (pork blood sausage); chunks of house smoked presunto, of course; and, for something completely different, a clay dish of freshly deep-fried **enguias** (baby eels). This really is the kind of food that Portugal excels at: big flavours, regional logic, and dishes that haven't changed in centuries. So wherever you see the word 'fumeiro', beg to be fed.

Grill/Grill Restaurante

This is the meat version of churrasqueira chicken-fest, where you'll get improbable quantities of all types of regional meats soundly skewered, or otherwise tied down, and deliciously grilled in front of you over leaping flames. If your idea of a good time is *not* to see the slaughtered beast from whence your dinner came, you may get squeamish. The best of the grill restaurants are likely to be very proud of the quality of meat on offer and you may well be sharing dining room space with a beautiful glass fridge filled with raw meat: various cuts, various beasts and at various stages of ageing. So take your pick, and wait for your **grelhado** (grilled food) to be brought sizzling to the table. Servings will be generous to the point of pornographic. You will not find better grilled-to-order premium cuts of meat anywhere, so take your appetite with you and tuck in. And by the way, don't bother looking for these on the coast: the hoofed beasts that make your meal live inland, not by the sea.

Marisqueira (Seafood Restaurant)

Here's where the fish in fish tanks live. Fish and all their crustacean cousins shamelessly flaunt themselves over ice in full public view. Hang on to your credit card, as these specialist seafood restaurants can be expensive. Oysters, crabs, lobsters and all the little clams etc will add up and you won't even necessarily have to eat a lot. Pick your own fish or lobster, and ask how much it will cost because it may well be more than you're prepared to pay. Prices are by the kilo. Naturally enough you'll find these places on the coast and often in a perfect location for outdoor eating. These are the best places to look for bottled **vinho verde** (light sparkling wine) from the Alvarinho grape (see Vinho Verde in the Drinks chapter), which will complement the food perfectly. This is special occasion eating, or for those lucky enough to not have budget worries.

Padaria (Bakery)

Bread was traditionally made by a village baker, who was often the only one in the village with an oven, but this practice is sadly dying out. In its place is the local padaria, which may be a commercial operation or an artisanal one. Although they are retail outlets, it's also possible to eat in some of them. What they offer depends on the region. It may be as simple as coffee and sandwiches or it could be something quite special where you can sit down and feast on bread and anything else that might go with it. There are also sweets, and especially common are **pastéis de nata** (custard tarts). A padaria can be a cross between a cafe and a **pastelaria** (pastry shop), except that the goodies may come straight from the oven in front of you. They're worth a look for simple meals.

Pastelaria (Pastry Shop)

What you should scan the place for are the magic words 'fabrico próprio' (made on the premises) – when it comes to pastry, this is definitely preferable. This is where you'll be for breakfast every day (and maybe for an afternoon sugar hit too) so you'd better get used to working your way through the infinite array on offer. If too many white breakfast rolls are binding you up, ask sweetly for a sandwich made with **pão de integral** (wholegrain bread). Or try a simple, not too sweet cake such as **bolo de laranja** (orange cake). Pastries range from flabby and dull versions of croissant (don't go there) to deliciously crisp and light fruit or almond pastries. There are also savoury pastries and pies to be had, which means you can drop in for a quick bite at meal times as well. Each establishment will offer a different selection, and you should notice differences as you cross regions. As in cafes, it will cost you less to stand at the counter with the locals, but you'd be denying yourself the theatre of watching them. Much more fun, for a marginally greater cost.

Pousada (Government Inn)

Pousadas are government-run, deluxe accommodation in castles, monasteries and palaces throughout Portugal. There are about 60 in total, and they are expensive to stay at. All have a restaurant and they are required by law to feature regional wine and food on their wine lists and menus, so even if you're not staying, it might be worthwhile booking into the restaurant. The quality and service varies, so this can be an expensive mistake, especially since the pousadas are unlikely to attract many locals. However, the buildings that have become pousadas can be gobsmackingly grand and the locations absolutely superb. So ask around about the particular restaurant's reputation. Otherwise, just go along for the other aesthetic benefits, if your credit card will stand it.

PASTELARIA ANAZU
Intruder

Restaurante (Restaurant)

This is where to go when you're up for a more formal, full two- or three-course lunch or dinner. Hours are usually from noon to 3pm for lunch and 7pm to 10.30pm for dinner, but they start packing out at about 1pm and 8pm. The dead time is from 4pm to 7pm, but if you're desperate to eat restaurant food at this hour, it's always worth asking. In more touristy areas or during peak season, hours may be extended. Not all restaurants take credit cards, but they are more likely to do so than the simpler, family-run establishments. Don't assume that a restaurant will be more expensive than some of the other eateries, or, if it is, that it will therefore offer better food. You may be surprised at the indifferent service frequently encountered, and the poor quality of linen and flatware. Remember, it will be a while before the standard that was acceptable under dictatorship fades under a greater awareness of quality. Some restaurants are terrific. Others are the pits. Try to recalibrate your expectations or you may find the experience frustrating and, whatever you do, *don't* make comparisons with France.

Restaurante Típico (Typical/Traditional Restaurant)

This type of restaurant is legally required to serve typical regional food and wine, offer traditional entertainment (such as **fado** – Portugal's tradition of melancholic singing) and display regional artefacts in its interior design. The staff are also required to wear traditional costume. Admittedly these places can have a bit of a communist feel and be a little unfashionable, but they can also offer superb food at reasonable prices. Have a look at the business card which may list regional food and wine specialities on the back. These places are definitely worth a look, and don't judge the book by its cover. You could really miss out on something special.

Ticket Restaurante (Ticket Restaurant)

As in other Western European countries with a tradition of eating out at lunch, Portugal has a 'Ticket Restaurant' system. As part of wage packages, employees are sometimes provided with ticket books that allow them a discount on dining at restaurants and cafes displaying the Ticket Restaurant sticker on their window. Lots of eateries belong to this system, and it's a good indicator for visitors that the food served is likely to be simple, traditional and inexpensive as well as probably turning over a lot of local custom. Even if you don't have a book of tickets, navigating by this system is usually a reliable way to choose where to have lunch. Often such places are only busy at lunch, and in the afternoon and evening revert to snack foods and alcoholic drinks rather than sit-down meals. Look for the sticker on an entrance door or window. There are likely to be other stickers there too, indicating which credit cards are accepted and whether the eatery belongs to any other system.

Sugar hit pleasure, Pastelaria Anazu, Tavira, Algarve

The beautiful Café Majestic, Porto

Sala de Jantar (Lunch Hall)

If you see people streaming upstairs from a tiny cafe, they may all be headed for the sala de jantar. So if it's lunchtime, you're in luck.

Snack Bar

You can purchase a drink, snack or sandwich here. Look for **piri piri amendoims** (chilli peanuts), **broas** (in this case, small sweet potato cakes – not corn bread), pistachios, **amêndoas** (almonds) or **cajus** (cashews) or more substantial **pastéis de bacalhau** (salt cod fishcakes, delicious hot or cold) and **pataniscas** (salt cod fritters). In the north look for the wonderful **bola de carne**, an enriched bread dough (a little like brioche) that is served in slices layered with different cured meats. Simple and superb.

Street Food

While there isn't a lot of food sold on the street other than on big market days (see Markets in the Shopping chapter), on the island of Madeira it does happen on a regular basis. Driving around the island on a weekend means you're likely to run into a local man or woman making the traditional bread **bolo do caco** (hot, garlic filled griddle bread) by the roadside (see Madeira in the Regional Variations chapter). It can be bought to take home, or, joy of joys, will be hot garlic buttered to eat immediately. Sometimes the dough will be wrapped around a spicy chouriço before being cooked on the griddle, and it too is served hot with garlic butter. This alone is worth travelling to the island for. On weekends locals will also be char grilling home grown chickens (which are so sumptuous they need no adornment), or selling the extra fresh produce of their home gardens. You may have the luck to pass by pickers in a strawberry field and get to eat the fruit within minutes of picking, still warm from the sun. On the mainland, the char grills frequently seen outside homes are likely to be for sardines. Sometimes you may be able to buy the char-grilled sardines, and during independence celebrations they may be given away to revellers.

Taberna (Tavern)

A tavern, or its pipsqueak cousin the **tasquinha** (small tavern), is where locals hang out, and the clientele is likely to be made up of loyal regulars. Usually the word 'taberna' will be on the eatery's business card, but it can be confusing because sometimes there's not much difference between a tavern and a restaurant. However, look out for taverns that have one special regional dish each day (daily dishes may be so standard that they are printed on the reverse of the card) and most of the action will be at lunchtime. Decor will be simple, the service basic, fast and friendly, and the bill a bargain. The wine choice will probably be between tinto and branco, and these are likely to

Frederic the food guide, Viseu, Beiras

come direct from barrels that are somewhere in view. Tables will possibly be shared, and manual labourers, local government officials, intelligentsia and gastronomes alike will squash in to become instant friends – that is, if they don't already know one another – and enjoy the spoils of the day. This is local food prepared for locals, and there won't even be a menu. Just look at what everyone else is eating, and order the same. Serves will be huge, the place will be packed and corners will be cut to get everyone fed and kept happy. Usually open all day and until quite late, they serve only snacks and alcohol after the lunch rush. It's sheer joy when you find one you like.

Tasca (Cheap Eatery)

A tasca is not, as in Spain, a tapas bar. It is an inexpensive eatery that is often run by a husband and wife team or extended family. A good tasca is worth its weight in gold, both to the proprietors and anyone with an appetite. You'll usually find fresh, seasonal produce simply cooked, and the cuts of meat and types of fish will be at the less expensive end of the spectrum. Tascas can be tiny – just half a dozen tables. Find one you like and stick with it. You'll soon be treated as one of the family. Grilled sardines, various **bacalhau** (dried salt cod) dishes, bean soup and char-grilled chicken are some of the simple dishes on offer, and it is common to order only a main dish (as they're so filling). There is always a soup and cheese or sweets and desserts for bigger appetites.

Vegetarians & Vegans

What do you mean you don't eat meat? Everyone eats meat in Portugal. Don't you remember the bad old days when only the wealthy could afford meat? Seriously though, Portugal is actually a disaster zone from top to tail for vegetarians. Pesco-vegetarians will do OK, and ovo-lacto vegetarians will also scrape by. But vegans hoping to taste Portugal are definitely going to miss out. You'll even have to watch out for desserts whose distinctive flavour may come from quite strong tasting **toucinho** (bacon fat) or loads of neutrally flavoured lard (pig fat). But take heart. There are plenty of fresh fruits, vegetables and nuts at all the markets, and the breads and cheeses can be simply superb. So what if you have to cook your own food? At least it was grown in Portugal. You may be curious to note that most of the vegetables that look so luscious at the markets are rarer than hens' teeth in eateries. They are most likely to make their way into a soup, so eat lots of soup. **Caldo verde** (Galician kale and potato soup) is the obvious soup to try, as is **sopa de feijão** (bean soup). If it's too hot for soup, ask for **tem alguma hortaliça** (a plate of vegetables). Salad will disappoint, since it will simply be plain lettuce, tomato and onion slices that you dress with the oil and vinegar on the table. Good luck.

LUNCH AT JOÃO'S

Walking into João's has the easy familiarity of coming home after school. João, his wife, Maria, and father, José, race around in organised chaos six days a week. Located in the Baixa district of Lisbon, João's place is a minuscule **tasca** (cheap eatery) called Zé Carvoeiro, 'the coal merchant'. Why the name? Because way before you can find this tiny hole in the wall you'll see grill smoke billowing from the rooftop, carrying with it the suspended aromas of char-grilling meat and chicken.

"Olá!" is the first word out of everyone's mouth. If you arrive at noon, the tiny share-tables and equally elfin school-style stools are all neatly set: knives, forks, upside-down tumblers, paper napkins and **piri piri** (red hot chilli sauce). Arriving this early means you can take your pick of tables: half an hour later and you'll be lining up at the door, hungry and waiting with the rest. There are hooks behind every seat for jackets and bags and it's best to use them because you'll be squashed into a can of sardines by 1pm.

The questioning cry comes from across the room: "Pão?" (Bread?) followed by "Sim!" (Yes!). This is some of the finest rustic crust you'll see in a land where crisp white bread dominates. It's bread to tear into, no butter, no oil. You've got less than a minute before it's time to order and since it's Tuesday the very best dish of **entrecosto com feijão e arroz** (ribs with beans and rice) will draw people from across the city. "Tinto ou branco?" (Red or white?) comes the next cry, along with hand and eyebrow movements to suggest the options of a full or half bottle. The **vinho verde** (light sparkling wine) comes straight from the barrel, still bubbling at the neck of the bottle. The family are from Ponte de Lima in the Minho region and it influences the way they run the business, and what is offered.

Shouts and cries fly across the room as the staff behind the bar cut the bread, get the wine, make the coffee, slice the cheese and pass out dessert to João and his father on the floor. Maria works the grill in the corner of the room and shouts across to her husband who's taking a quick slug of wine as the pace heats up.

The wine is a house-blended rosé. Glasses are upturned next to us and forks poked into them: reserved for regulars on their way. We tear greedily at the bread and see people streaming into the tiny space that seats around 30 but may turn each seat over at least a few times in the next 2½ hours. Workmen walk in and head for the washbasin next to the char grill. They greet Maria, alert and with a firm grip on her tongs, as she deftly flicks long strips of ribs back and forth then piles them onto plates of beans and rice from the kitchen.

"Sentido!" (Attention!) – João comes zigzagging across the room with two huge platters of beans with rice, and strips of golden crisp ribs that stretch way beyond the platter's rim. The beans are poured straight off the platter and onto a serving plate like a thick soup. The ribs are on placed top, scattered with carrots and cauliflower preserved in vinegar and thin slices of lemon. It's food to fall on, and conversation is impossible until the first few mouthfuls are down. Cutlery is unnecessary: the ribs are torn apart and eaten with the hands. The wonderfully rich beans are scooped up with bread and maybe with the tines of a fork. A large open jar of house-made piri piri is passed from plate to plate. Nods of greeting to neighbouring diners is essential. You'll be bumping elbows with them so there's no point being aloof. This is Portuguese food at its best: substantial, social and full of flavour.

Plates will disappear fast, and if there's wine left in your glass it's time for a little **queijo picante** (strong cheese crusted with pimento powder). The rind is sliced off and the cheese sliced finely. It arrives on a small plate for nibbling at with the remaining bread, then it's time for **doces** (sweets or desserts), a small bowl of sweet custard flavoured with mango or topped with crushed biscuit crumbs. And of course, **uma bica e um aguardente** (coffee and **aguardente** – a brandy-type spirit). Here's where you show the locals how much you've learned, by sloshing some aguardente into your coffee. It tastes sweetly of burnt caramel and slips down hot and fast. If you're a woman doing this, the local men will be incredulous. So do it.

Time to leave comes around fast as the pressure of the hungry queue is felt and João or his father pulls a pen from behind his ear and tallies up your bill on the paper cloth in front of you. If you've wondered why your glasses weren't cleared, it's so there's no dispute over how many you've had. Cash only and "Obrigado!" (Thank you!) all round finish the exchange, and it's out into the sunshine to let the next diners in. A few hours later the tasca is calm enough to return to, this time for a nibble on a cold roasted pig's ear or to tear at cold cooked ribs and stand at the bar. Have a beer, chew the fat, relax. This is Portugal.

understanding the menu

Some **ementas** (menus) may scare you half to death with lots of different sections, and odd-looking dishes. But happily the majority of menus will be easy to navigate. Some will be so simple there's not even a choice, and eating that one well-practised dish may be the best meal you have.

Understanding the Menu

Portugal does not have a high restaurant tradition (see the Where to Eat & Drink chapter) so any attempt in this direction is probably aimed at tourists who will face a hodgepodge of choices, or feel forced to cop out with an **ementa turística** (tourist menu). While the dishes won't be bad, they also won't give you the full range of Portuguese potential. They aren't necessarily good value either. So first of all, if there are menus in three or more languages out the front of the place you're thinking of choosing, don't go in. Especially not if there's also a flag to match the language at the top of the menu. Be brave and instead choose a place with a menu in Portuguese, or a scrap of paper or blackboard advertising **hoje temos** (daily menu). At a stretch, take a place with menus in both Portuguese and English. Cast an eye and ear around the room. If your fellow diners look like, and speak like, locals, you'll probably eat well.

Pequeno-almoço (breakfast) usually just consists of a coffee and a breadroll, which makes it difficult to go too far wrong, so just head to a busy cafe or **pastelaria** (pastry shop). Standing will be cheaper than sitting, but neither is expensive compared to the rest of Western Europe. There are no breakfast menus so rehearse getting the coffee you want (see the Bean There boxed text in the Drinks chapter for a complete list) and decide on the full sugar hit of **pastéis** (pastries) or a **sande queijo** or **sande fiambre** (cheese or ham sandwich). Cafes will have hard-boiled **ovos** (eggs) and salt at the counter, or you can order a **tosta mista** (toasted ham and cheese sandwich), if you must. When you're done, ask for 'a conta, se faz favor' (the bill, please) and pay. Lunch and dinner require a few more navigational tools ...

Once you're safely seated either at **almoço** (lunch) or **jantar** (dinner), food you haven't ordered will instantly appear, long before a menu or wine list, and may include **pão** (bread) and **manteiga** (butter). In addition there may be fish paste, green or black olives, cheese spread, a slab of cheese, or cured beans. These are not freebies to thank you for your restaurant choice. They're covers, or as you'll see on the bill **couvert** or **pão e manteiga**, and regardless of the fact that you didn't order them, you'll pay even if you so much as nibble at the edges. So take your time and have a look at whether they might be worth eating. At worst, pappy bread, packet butter, dull and flabby olives or packet tuna spread will be slung in front of you. At best you may face gloriously rustic chunks of **pão da casa** (house bread), a slab of fresh cheese, deliciously plump olives or a freshly made carrot and coriander preserve. So use your common sense and self-control. If they look boring, send them back without touching them and if they look good, tuck in – it won't cost you much either way.

Tripas à moda do Porto (tripe in the Porto style) – tripe with beans, chicken, chouriço and cumin

Smaller establishments may separately list some of the items that turn up as a couvert when you arrive at a restaurant. These include bread, butter, olives, pastes, aged or fresh cheese and sometimes a choice of small, cold **entrada** dishes for a single price. This means you can mix and match and still stick to a budget. One of the strangest habits to get used to is that cheese is almost always eaten as a snack before the meal instead of after. You'll find **queijo fresco** (fresh cheese) won't interfere too much with what follows, but frequently the cheeses offered are aged and strong so if you want to taste the main dishes, don't start with a strong cheese. Other phrases that may crop up and confuse are **preço variável** (market price), **por pessoa** (per person), **2 pessoas** (dish is for a minimum of two people), **pratos por encomenda** (dishes ordered in advance), **especialidades da casa** (house specialities), **especialidades regionais** (regional specialities) and **ementa especial** (special set price menu). **Outros pratos** (other dishes) crops up when dishes do not happen to suit the standard menu divisions of the particular establishment. An area well known for certain dishes, such as roast suckling pig in Bairrada or snails in the Algarve, will advise that the dish is on the menu with a picture of the beast to be cooked and the word 'Há' (meaning 'here', as in 'here we serve').

Dining in Évora, Alentejo

What comes as a main will largely depend on where you've chosen to eat (see the Where to Eat chapter). Three courses are normal for lunch and dinner so unless you've opted for a simple sandwich in a cafe, you'll need to have a think about what you want. Relax about all the possible menu divisions. Many places will have a **prato do dia** (dish of the day) or offer simply soup, fish, meat and dessert. Some menus divide the dishes according to the cooking techniques, so it's useful to know what some of them are. Simpler menus will include the cooking technique in the name of the dish, while the more complex ones will divide a section, such as fish, into **cozido** (boiled and poached) or **frito e grelhado** (fried and grilled). Any dish that is listed as **à casa** means 'in the house style' and is probably not a bad choice. More reliable are the words **à moda da** (in the style of), which will be followed by the name of a region, town or style of preparation – a dish cooked in the local style is a good choice. Alternatively look for the words **da região** in a dish description, meaning 'of the region'. And don't be shy about ordering a **meia dose** (half serve). It's not a child's portion but at half the size (and up to two-thirds of the price), it's plenty. The serving sizes are routinely huge. Prices will be listed in euros, and cuts of meat or fish may be listed at a per kilo price rather than per serve.

Entradas e Acepipes (Entrees & Hors d'Oeuvres)

These are for snacking on, or, in good restaurants, they may be the starting point at which you may get to enjoy some of the house specialities. Look out for raw shredded cod, grilled blood and fat or smoked sausages, skinned whitebait, some cold calf's head, pig's ear or octopus salad, stewed giblets or a plate of snails. They're good – honest – especially snails in the Algarve.

Sopas (Soups)

Sopa do dia (soup of the day) is usually a good bet, and so is **caldo verde** (Galician kale and potato soup), especially if you're up around the Minho region where it was born. However, it's all over the country and may even be safe enough for vegetarians since it should only contain kale, potatoes, water and seasoning. If you see the rich bread soup **açorda** listed, beware: you won't be needing anything to follow. A lighter soup is often ordered as part of every meal and don't assume it's eaten before everything else: many people have soup *after* the main meal.

Ovos (Eggs)

Eggs are unlikely to be listed separately unless the menu is very long (or if it's a tourist menu). Order an omelette if you want, but there's nothing Portuguese about that choice. Or try eggs **mexidos** (scrambled), **estrelados** (fried) or **ervilhas com ovos** (poached eggs with peas).

Peixes (Fish)

Sometimes this will include seafood choices (see the following entry) as well as freshwater. **Cozido** is when the fish is boiled or poached, **frito** is fried, and **grelhado** is grilled. Another word to memorise is **espetada** (skewer or kebab), which is huge chunks of all kinds of food (including fish), grilled and served on massive metal skewers.

Marisco e Moluscos or Frutos do Mar (Shellfish or Seafood)

Clams, shrimp, cuttlefish, squid, lobster, cockles, crab and octopus may be offered. And even limpets. Take your pick.

Bacalhau (Dried Salt Cod)

There are so many imaginatively luscious ways to enjoy bacalhau (see the boxed text Bacalhau Bliss) that sometimes it has a menu section of its own.

BACALHAU BLISS

Every day's a good day for **bacalhau** (dried salt cod) and it seems there is at least one recipe for every day of the year. Here are 10 to taste:

Bacalhau com batatas à murro (grilled salt cod with baked and smashed potatoes)
Steaks or pieces of salt cod are grilled over the coals. They're served with potatoes that have been baked in their skins and split open with a blow of the fist. The whole platter is seasoned with hot olive oil and sliced garlic.

Bacalhau com natas (salt cod with cream)
Flaked salt cod is cooked with chopped garlic, chopped onion and olive oil, then baked in the oven with mashed potato and cream.

Bacalhau à cozinha velha (old kitchen style salt cod)
Finely chopped salt cod, onions and carrots are fried in olive oil. They are then cooked in a white sauce that's enriched with egg and seasoned with nutmeg, pepper and lemon juice, then covered with breadcrumbs and baked in the oven.

Bacalhau à Gomes de Sá (salt cod Gomes de Sá)
Flaked salt cod is soaked in boiling milk, then browned in the oven with olive oil, diced potatoes, onion, garlic and pepper. It is served with slices of hard-boiled eggs, olives and chopped parsley.

Bacalhau assado com pimentos (grilled cod with green capsicums)
Pieces of grilled cod and strips of grilled green pepper are mixed with

Aves e Caça (Poultry & Game)

If in doubt, look for the word **frango** (chicken) and you won't go too far wrong. In this section of the menu you'll find plenty of chicken choices and maybe even **coelho** (rabbit), **codorniz** (quail), **pombo** (pigeon) and **peru** (turkey).

Carnes (Meats)

This may include **vaca** (beef), **vitela** (veal), **cabrito** (kid), **porco** (pork), **borrego** (lamb) and **carneiro** (mutton) dishes, and look out for **bife**, which means a steak of any type of meat and not just beef. The black wild pig of the Alentejo region is called **javali**. Restaurants that specialise in meat (so-called **grill** restaurants – see the Where to Eat & Drink chapter) could offer such a range of choices that the different kinds of meat will actually have separate sections.

chopped raw onion and garlic, then seasoned with olive oil, vinegar and pepper and served with boiled potatoes.

Bacalhau à Assis (grilled salt cod Assis)
Crumbled salt cod is cooked in olive oil with thin strips of onion, red capsicum, potatoes, **presunto** (smoked ham) and carrots, then mixed with eggs and parsley and baked until golden.

Bacalhau guisado (stewed salt cod)
Salt cod steaks are stewed in the oven with olive oil between layers of sliced onion, tomatoes, potatoes, butter, garlic, bay leaf, paprika, pepper and parsley.

Bacalhau desfiado (raw shredded cod)
Fine strips of raw salt cod are dipped in water, then well squeezed and served with chopped onion and garlic and seasoned with pepper, olive oil and vinegar.

Bacalhau com grão (salt cod with chickpeas)
Grilled or baked salt cod steaks are served with hot large chickpeas strewn with onion and garlic. The whole dish is then seasoned with buckets of olive oil, vinegar and pepper.

Bacalhau à Brás (salt cod à Brás)
Flaked cod is scramble-fried with egg and chunks of cooked potato. The hot dish is then strewn with coarsely chopped parsley and green or black olives. This is one of the most substantial – and delicious – typical peasant dishes.

Acompanhamentos (Accompaniments)

These are most likely to be listed separately at a grill or fish restaurant that offers dishes at a per kilo price. The meat and fish arrive plainly cooked, and the side dishes cost extra. Expect to see rice and potato dishes offered.

Pratos Completos (Complete Plates)

This makes it easy. Here's where you'll find one-pot dishes that will make ordering simple and fill you up at the same time. If you see the words **caldeirada** (a stew usually made from fish), **açorda** (bread soup), or the many dishes that begin with either **arroz** (rice), **feijoada** (bean stew) or **favas** (broad beans), then you're one-stop shopping. Other one-pot dishes may announce themselves by style such as **migas** (side dishes with olive oil and garlic) or **ranchos** (chickpea-based stews – see Sopas & Pratos Completos in the Staples chapter). They will be substantial and cover all the main food groups, which means your only other responsibility is to leave some space for dessert.

Sobremesas or Doces (Desserts)

Want some eggs and sugar? You'd better, 'cause that's how they make their desserts around here: rich and sweet. **Arroz doce** (rice pudding) and **leite creme** (custard cream with caramelised sugar) are common, as are **fios de ovos** (sweet egg yolk threads).

Dolce de Ovos (sweet eggs), Aveiro

Fruta (Fruit)

Fresh fruit may be separately listed even in a modest eatery and may include a fruit salad, a single piece of fresh fruit such as mango or sliced pineapple, or fruit with some kind of alcohol.

Sweets to rival your grandma's, Quinta do Portal, Douro

Lista de Vinhos (Wine List)

Bottled wine has only become common over the past 30 years or so in Portugal, which means that many eating places, especially the simpler and less expensive ones, only have two choices when it comes to wine: **tinto** (red) or **branco** (white). Even where there are bottled wines, the best bet may still be **vinho do casa** (house wine). This means there's often no wine list at all. If there is, it will be proffered by a **garçon dos vinhos** (a wine waiter) and may include a distinction between whites, reds, aged or **maduro** (mature) wine and **vinhos verdes** (young and spritzy wines) See the Drinks chapter for more information on wine types.

a portuguese banquet

No pomp and ceremony. Lots of family, friends and children. Plenty of fresh, seasonal food and boundless generosity. These are the elements you must aim for when banqueting Portuguese style, for the chaos and confusion that ensue can be conducive to a good time.

If you're thinking of a banquet, set the scene for yourself by thinking grand proportions and a relaxed feel. Not complicated. Ponder the words of the English aesthete William Beckford who, on visiting the extraordinary Alcobaça monastery in 1794, called the kitchen "the most distinguished temptation of gluttony in all Europe". He described:

> *... on one side, loads of game and venison were heaped up; on the other, vegetables, fruit in endless variety ... a numerous tribe of lay brothers and their attendants were rolling out and puffing up [pastry] into a hundred different shapes, singing all the while as blithely as larks in a corn-field.*

Naturally enough, there was a river specially diverted to run through the centre of the kitchen to provide water for cooking and washing. It was filled with fish plumping up for eating. Just to give you an idea of the proportions, there were enough capacious, tile-covered chimneys to roast up to seven oxen at a time. Eating was good at Alcobaça, such that the Portuguese have a saying, "Quem passa por Alcobaça tem que voltar a Alcobaça" (Who passes Alcobaça returns to Alcobaça). Hmmm. The scale of Alcobaça may be hard to replicate at home, but if not carried out in practice then at least do it in spirit. It's a fantasy banquet, so you may as well have a fantasy or two while you do it.

Torresmos (Pork Crackling)

These are delicious and moreish, and so they should be. You're eating fat, salt and a bit of pig skin.

Ingredients

20cm to 30cm	square piece of pork rind (hair singed off), with 0.5cm of fat attached
1 tsp	good quality sea salt
2 tsp	olive oil

Chill the piece of skin in the fridge (or briefly in the freezer), which will make it easier to cut. Preheat the oven to 180°C. Using a very sharp knife and with the skin side up, cut the skin in half to make two pieces of about 10cm wide each. Cut each of the pieces into 1cm wide strips and toss them together in a bowl with the salt and the olive oil. Spread the strips on a fine wire rack over a baking tray and roast them until all the fat has melted off and the skin is curled, golden and crisp (about 20 to 30 minutes). Drain all the fat away – you can use it to baste roasting vegetables or meat – and put the pork crackling onto paper towel to drain. Serve hot or cold with icy Sagres beer as a snack or entree.

First of all, pour yourself a Sagres beer. Wonderfully fresh and not too hard to find at bottle shops around the world, beer is most definitely not what the Portuguese would have with starters, but we can't see a good reason not to enjoy it with a meal. Think of the delicious little morsels you'd find at a **cervejaria** (more officially in a restaurant the **acepipes** – hors d'oeuvres) and offer plenty to your guests. Think crisp and salty **torresmos** (pork crackling – see the recipe); wafer thin slices of **presunto** (smoked ham), with which you could offer a well-chilled glass of white port; chilled **paio**, the thinly sliced rounds of sausage made from lean and fat pork meat smoked in its intestine; olives; **queijo fresco** (fresh cheese); and bread, of course, and some less predictable choices: carrots preserved with coriander; finely sliced pig's ears pickled in vinegar and herbs; boiled broad beans ready to jump from their skins; and, if you can afford it, fresh, finely sliced truffle stirred through scrambled eggs. Just lay the lot out, and just when it looks like everyone's had a good nibble, tantalise them with your truffled egg magic.

Portuguese taste buds can detect **bacalhau** (dried salt cod) at a thousand paces, and they would surely confess to wanting to eat it as often as possible, and at least 'até do fim do mundo' (until the end of time). So your banquet should have some in it. There are more than 365 bacalhau recipes from which to choose, but perhaps few are as popular and useful at a banquet as the moreish little **pastéis de bacalhau** (salt cod cakes) or their cousins **pataniscas de bacalhau** (salt cod fritters). Hot or cold, they're delicious.

Since you've inevitably employed some idle monks to help you with the banquet, there's no question that after all this grazing material comes shellfish, and plenty of it. Try oysters, crabs and crayfish, the former chilled and just shucked, and the latter simply boiled up and offered with more bread, and perhaps a few lashings of Alvarinho **vinho verde** (light sparkling wine). If you've offered lots of different morsels to eat with the fingers, followed by lots of fresh shellfish, also to eat with the hands, you'll save yourself some washing up. You've stuffed your guests half full and haven't even used any cutlery! This is great news, and should encourage you no end. It is quite normal for guests to stay with the same set of cutlery all through a meal, so to get this far and not even use any reflects very good planning. You could let them drink beer from the bottle or can, meaning that the vinho verde is the first sign of needing glassware. Paper napkins will be fine, and guests should keep them tucked under the side of their plates (when they get one) rather than on their laps; much easier to get to when eating with fingers. And you can throw them out afterwards. You see, people aren't judging you on the fineness of your place settings. They couldn't care less. Crockery and glasses could even be cracked. What they do care about is how fresh the food is, how wide a variety there is and whether you've been generous with your bounty. The rest – lights, action etc – is mere gloss.

Pataniscas de Bacalhau (Salt Cod Fritters)

Ingredients

¼ cup	plain flour
½ tsp	sea salt
¼ tsp	freshly ground black pepper
1	large egg, beaten
1 Tbs	olive oil
2	cloves garlic, crushed
¼ cup	very finely chopped onion
280g	desalted, reconstituted salt cod, flaked
1 Tbs	finely chopped fresh coriander or parsley
	vegetable oil for frying

To serve

wedges of lemon
black olives

In a large bowl, whisk together the flour, salt, pepper, egg and olive oil. Fold in the garlic, onion, cod and herbs. Heat enough oil in a saucepan to either deep- or shallow-fry the fritters. When the oil is at the correct temperature for frying (test by dropping a tiny amount of mix in, and if it spins, and bubbles form at the edges, the fat is ready), add a large dessertspoonful of the mix and fry on both sides until golden. If the mix seems a little thin, add a touch more flour. If it is too thick, add a little water. Continue frying in batches of 4 or 5 until all the mix is fried. Serve the fritters either warm or cold with wedges of lemon and a bowl of black olives.

Serves 4–6

Now for the mains. It's hard these days to get a domestic oven big enough to take a whole oxen for roasting, but you should be able to find one big enough for roast kid, suckling pig or lamb. What's that you say? Slaughter of innocents? Yes, yes, you're right. But this is the traditional celebratory fare, and a banquet simply wouldn't be complete without it. Papery crisp skin and succulent, melting flesh is exactly what the gods require. After all, it's not every day you'll be going to such trouble. And you may as well toss in a few splayed free range chickens, cooked over the coals and splashed with **piri piri** (red hot chilli pepper sauce). Now for the tricky bit. No rice, no beans, just lots of peeled, boiled potatoes with a drizzling of the roasting juices and brought steaming hot to the banquet table. And salad. Lots of lovely crisp leaves with a sharp, apple cider vinegar and olive oil dressing, and made with salt and freshly ground pepper. Mmmm. Not something you'd often find in Portugal, but essential to help you balance all that animal fat.

Pataniscas de bacalhau (salt cod fritters)

Grilled Chouriço
(Grilled Spicy Sausage)

There is nothing more spectacular than a dish of flaming, grilled **chouriço** arriving at your table. Down it with crusty bread, accompanied by a robust red wine. This recipe was kindly supplied by Fernando Goncalves, of the Portuguese Sagres restaurant in Elwood, Australia.

Ingredients

1 chouriço sausage
splash **aguardente** (brandy-like spirit)

Cut deep slashes into the chouriço. So that the shape is maintained, do not cut completely through the sausage. Heat a frying pan over a moderate flame. Add the chouriço, turning it every now and then to prevent burning. You will not need extra cooking fat, because the fat from the sausage is sufficient to prevent sticking.

Once the chouriço is brown and crispy on the outside, and heated through completely, add a splash of aguardente to the pan. This will combine with the fat to create a flame and a delicate flavour. Immediately turn the sausage out onto a serving dish, preferably an earthenware dish, making sure to keep the flame alight.

Serves 1

Gingas de Alcool (Cherry Liqueur)

This is similar to the **ginjinha** (cherry brandy) available all over the country.

Ingredients

2 cups	fresh cherries
250g	white sugar
500ml	**aguardente** (brandy-like spirit), or brandy

Wash the cherries well. Remove the stems and dry the fruit thoroughly with a paper towel or a cloth. Leave the stones in the fruit. Shake the sugar and aguardente together in a large, sterilised jar until the sugar dissolves. Add the cherries and ensure there is as little air in the neck of the jar as possible, seal, and put in a cool, dark place to infuse. Give the jar a shake every day for the first week, then leave to stand for a minimum of 3 months (preferably a year), tasting occasionally to see if it has the flavour you like. Serve a shot of the liqueur over a few of the cherries.

THE PORTUGUESE PANTRY

Can't be bothered worrying which region things come from? Stock up on these flavours, and start tasting Portugal at every meal:

Almonds, bay leaves, red capsicum, cinnamon (for both savoury and sweet dishes), coriander leaves, curry powder, plenty of garlic, lemons, mint, olives and olive oil, onions, oranges, oregano, flat-leaf parsley, sweet and hot paprika, saffron, **piri piri** (especially hot chillies and the sauce made from them), tomatoes, white vinegar, and red and white dry wines. Add lots of fresh fish; meat and poultry; **bacalhau** (dried salt cod); hams and sausages; bread; fresh and dried fruit; and honey; cheese; and sugary egg desserts and you're there. Look out Lisbon, here you come.

By now you should also be tucking into a sassy red vinho verde, which your slaves have hopefully managed to procure by the barrel. This is neither the time nor the place for label queens. Young and fresh is what goes best, and you can even serve it in the same glasses as the white vinho verde; just swish it all around first with the appropriate water – Pedras Salgadas is what foodies would drink with a meal, being comparable to France's chi-chi Badoit and intended for the purpose of aiding digestion. You can't argue with that. Onto the red, no change of glasses and no alternative wine choices offered. This is a dictatorship.

The red wine will also roll you over into the cheese department, whose proper place is after the mains, not to start with (unless it's a very fresh cheese, that is). Take your pick. Serra would have to be present, both young and creamy and a more aged, piquant version, as well as mild Rabaçal from near Coimbra, and pungent Azeitão – and more bread.

'Background music!' you cry? Purists may say you don't need music while you banquet; others would argue there's no better time than this for the beloved Amália and her 'fado', the hauntingly beautiful – or wrist-slashingly mournful – songs about fate that express a particularly Portuguese version of melancholy called 'saudade'. Fado is, however, depressing for some, and you sure can't dance to it. So get yourself some spunky Nelly Furtado as a backup if your party gets glum. If your party looks like turning into a dance party, try Madredeus or Dulce Pontes.

Around about now your guests should be showing signs of satiation, if not inebriation, so it's time for a shot of the best black coffee you can muster, and a slosh of **aguardente velha reserva** (old reserve brandy-like spirit). Oops – we forgot dessert (how could we?). Back up to before the

There's nothing like a home-cooked meal, Quinta de São Martino, Mateus, Douro

BOTTOMS UP!

Every country has its own way of toasting company before downing a drink. So if you want to make friends in Portugal, raise a glass and say 'Á nossa!' (To us!). But if you really want to impress your Portuguese friends, memorise this one:

Vai acima *(go to up)*
while raising your glass towards the ceiling

Vai abaixo *(go to down)*
while lowering your glass towards the floor

Vai ao centro *(go to centre)*
while stretching your glass out in front of you

Bota abaixo *(pour it down)*
while ... you can work this bit out yourself.

coffee and ask if anyone wants dessert. Does anyone want dessert? After all that? OK. Something for the sweet of tooth. Let's see. What you really want is a **toucinho do-céu** ('bacon from heaven'), which is one of the very few not overwhelmingly sweet sweets. In fact, it's an almond and cinnamon cake, perfect with a short black coffee and aguardente. And there we have it. A banquet with a running sheet that should render you as blithe as a lark in a corn-field.

fit & healthy

Eating and drinking your way around Portugal is more likely to threaten your waistband than either your wallet or your wellbeing. It's possible that the worst health risk you face is getting yourself hooked on more wine, pork meat and sweet treats than you'd normally go for at home. But by following the usual precautions and making sure you get lots of fresh fruit and vegetables, serious trouble should be averted.

Morning heat, near Estremoz, Alentejo

Portugal will comprehensively threaten your calorie count from four angles: the lavish use of animal fat, the habit of drinking alcohol with every meal, the seductive sweets, and the temptation to put your feet up and relax – but hey! You're on holiday, right? Right, but it's wrong to think that means you can let your health slide too far. So keep the honesty meter accurate on excess fat, sugar and booze and on the temptations of sloth.

Hygiene & Water

Tap water is safe in most towns and cities across the country, but it's wise to exercise caution in small villages. There are roadside fountains throughout Portugal that provide locals with fresh spring water, so if you see people filling their drinking bottles you can freely follow suit – just be sure to fill from the running water at the source and not the still pool below which could be home to just about anything. If you see a sign saying 'água non potável' (water not potable), don't drink the water.

Fluid Balance

Portugal can be overwhelmingly hot, especially in the south and on the central plains. Always make sure you have a supply of drinking water with you, and make sure you drink it. Much as you might like them, sugary drinks, alcohol and coffee won't do the same for you as water will, and you'll need even more if you drink these other liquids regularly. Water is everywhere in Portugal, so there's no excuse for not getting enough. And remember, if you feel thirsty, you're already dehydrated.

LOOK OUT! HERE COMES THE HANGOVER!

You're on holiday, your guard is down, the calorie and alcohol count are off the scale and you've marked on your map the densely populated and well-known City of Overindulgence. You're headed straight for it. So what do you do when you get there? The medieval medical School of Salerno was already on the case:

> **Si nocturna noceat potatio vini,**
> **Hoc tu mane bibas iterum, et fuerit medicina.**
>
> *(If an evening of wine does you in,*
> *More the next morning will be medicine.)*

It might work, but it's not necessarily a good thing. Too much alcohol, regardless of location and language, depresses the nervous system, leaving you hypersensitive to light and sound. During a session of overindulgence the body adjusts to a higher level of alcohol, and the higher the level achieved and the longer it stays there, the longer (and more painfully) the body takes to return to normal. The unpleasant alcohol withdrawal symptoms include – in case you've never been there yourself – headaches, a dry mouth, tiredness, malaise and perhaps an overwhelming desire to throw up. Having another drink in the morning restores the high alcohol conditions the body had adjusted itself to as well as numbing it all over again. This merely defers the inevitable, and despite the fact that it may work temporarily, it's no solution. There's no real cure for a hangover, other than time. The cause of the headache is dehydration, so it's best to drink a glass of water before bed, perhaps with a multivitamin pill. Then drink more water in the morning, possibly with a painkiller. And try to sip water when drinking alcohol the night before. Basically, you're a fool to get yourself here because it means you'll probably lose an extra day's worth of luscious meals and sensible portions of wine.

Eating the Right Stuff

Unfortunately the healthy eating pyramid arrived in Portugal upside down. So instead of fats and sugary foods being at the small, pointy, don't-eat-too-many-of-us end, they can all too easily form the broad base of the pyramid where the oh-so-healthy bread and grains and fruit and vegetables should be. So watch it. If you don't ask for salad or buy some fresh fruit you sure won't come across it any other way. And bearing in mind that salad means lettuce and tomato with a slice of onion, you may even need to start nibbling on fresh carrots and other raw vegetables in between what will mostly be a meat and fish fest.

Diarrhoea & Constipation

The latter will probably force you to seek out the dried plum department of the nearest health food store, whereupon you will undoubtedly find other healthy treats to keep you regular (or bind you up) should you need them. They may even be organic. Should you have the runs, avoid dehydration by drinking plenty of water, and stick to small amounts of plain, starchy food for a few days until the clenched fist in your stomach relents. It may just be an upset stomach related to a different diet or the nervous anticipation of a Mighty Big Adventure. If other symptoms are present, though, you may have a problem and should head off to the doctor. So rest, and keep the liquid levels up – weak black tea with a little sugar; soda water; or soft drinks allowed to go flat and diluted 50% with clean water are all good. Seek advice if you have the urgent urge more than six times in a day, or if any other symptoms strike.

Food on the Runs

Ease diarrhoea symptoms by eating plain rice, bread, or noodles, dry biscuits (salty or not too sweet) and bananas.

Avoid eating fruit and vegetables (except bananas), spicy foods, greasy foods and dairy products (including yoghurt).

Indigestion

Indigestion and his close friend, heartburn, are quite possibly intending to join you on your eating odyssey. While the former will announce his arrival by scorching your upper abdomen, the latter will be busy burning your gullet and may intend to swish a little acid around your mouth as well. Why did they come? Probably for the change in diet, the prospect of loads of delicious fatty foods, and the stress and nerves that travel sometimes stimulates. So try to eat small, regular meals of plain food and steer clear of alcohol, cigarettes and anything spicy. They'll leave soon enough.

Children

Getting married and having healthy children is considered a very fortunate thing in Portugal, so take your family along because they'll be welcome all over. Keep the children cool at the beach and warm in the mountains and follow all the same common sense precautions as you would at home. The kids can usually eat half portions for half price at restaurants, and all their other needs can be filled at the **minimercado** and **hipermercado** (see the Shopping chapter) and **farmacia** (pharmacy). For advice on breastfeeding, alternative health, pregnant travel and on-the-road children's health, as well as ideas on how to keep your kids occupied, see Lonely Planet's *Travel with Children* guide.

Heat

The heat can be blistering so precautions are essential in summer. Wear a hat and good sunglasses and use sunblock, even on cloudy days. Tempting as it may be, try very hard to avoid drinking alcohol in the sun – it's probably a bad idea. Drink lots of water instead. If anyone in your travelling party has spent too long in the sun and is suspected of suffering from heatstroke, organise professional assistance immediately and stabilise the victim by getting them out of the sun, removing clothes, covering them with a wet towel and administering fluids if they're still conscious. It can be fatal, so get help fast. Be especially cautious of allowing children to play too long in the heat.

Allergies

Shellfish, nuts and eggs are among the worst allergy offenders, and Portugal has plenty of each. If you're allergic to shellfish at home, foreign fish won't be any different. The three words to look out for are **crustáceo**, **frutos do mar** and **marisco**. Don't go near them, and be sure to ask whether there is any shellfish in your **caldeirada** (stew). **Amendoim** (peanuts) and **manteiga de amendoim** (peanut butter) are not the only problem for peanut allergy sufferers – traces of peanut may be found in all kinds of chocolates and sweets, and since so little can cause such a devastating reaction, abstinence is your best bet. This is a nation of egg lovers, such that up to six dozen egg yolks can be used to make a single special cake. So be especially cautious of any desserts and pastries if eggs are an allergen. Travellers with wheat allergies will suffer the social loss of not breaking bread with their friends, but should be able to find plenty else to eat that is wheat-free. Only health food stores sell wheat-free bread. Dairy allergies should not create too many problems, though meals sometimes start with a slab of cheese and if you're starving, it will be tricky to wait. Hog the olives instead.

Diabetics

Beware. You're entering a danger zone and you should be prepared for full combat. Short of strapping on a sugar-filled nosebag at home, there are few places on the planet that can threaten your sugar consumption like Portugal can. *Do not* be tempted to even taste the sweets, and make sure you remember to *ask* whether your food has has sugar added: you would be surprised how it can sneak into the ingredient list of the most benign dishes. It really is best to take all your own medical supplies, along with proof of your condition, and make sure you stash your booty safely during the trip.

Behind the Wheel

Try not to jump behind the wheel of a car, bus or truck after a beer or a glass of wine. Not only is this dangerous given the way most Portuguese people drive even when they're alcohol free, it's also going to put you over the limit. Portugal has the worst road fatality record in Western Europe and in an attempt to stem the flow, the blood alcohol limit is now down to 0.02. Mind you, don't be surprised to see locals flouting the law – it's just that *you'll* have a greater chance of survival with sharper wits. Oh, and try to avoid the IP5 highway. It's affectionately known across the country as 'death road'. In Portugal, a nation of high-speed tailgating and mind-bogglingly risky driving behaviour, that really means something scary. It's worse than Italy and Indonesia combined.

A Word on Mad Portuguese Cows ...

There have been officially documented instances of 'mad cow disease', or BSE, in Portugal but just about everyone you come across during your travels will tell you it simply isn't so. If pressed they may say a case was heard of in so-and-so (always distant) region but it won't really help because it's never going to be in the region whose delicacies you're about to lay into. Like the French after Chernobyl chowing down on their cheese and telling themselves (and the rest of us) that the cloud didn't reach as far as French pastures, it's a case of can't see, can't touch, can't believe it could be true. Or, in the have-another-chilled-chocolate-biscuit school of thought, why deny yourself today because there might be a health bill years down the track? After all, something else might knock you off first. So, as with other countries where mad cow disease has surfaced, use your common sense. If you like eating beef and aren't concerned about the potential risk, tuck in. But being sensible probably means avoiding beef offal – which is thought to pose the greatest risk if an animal is infected – such as brains, heart, kidney, liver, tripe, sweetbreads, tongue, cheek, tail and spleen. And try not to eat meat you can't identify, especially in the sausage department. It's likely to be pork anyway.

Food Poisoning

A nasty subject, but it's best to know the basics in order to avoid it. Symptoms may include diarrhoea, nausea, vomiting, dehydration, fever, stomach pain, a swollen abdomen and dizziness. While there's no greater risk in Portugal than in many other developed countries, it still pays to be cautious since even the bugs that pose no problems to locals can still affect unaccustomed travellers. Poor food storage, inadequate cooking or reheating techniques, cross-contamination from one person, utensil or surface to another, and an infected food handler all increase your chances of picking

Mad, or just a little annoyed? Serra do Larouco, Minho

up some kind of food-borne illness. So if you suspect any of this has been going on, eat elsewhere. Take great care with shellfish and avoid undercooked meat. You can often see, smell, touch or taste that a certain food is not at its best and, since you'd probably rather spend your time taking food in and not urgently ridding yourself of it, now's the time to play it safe. Make a mantra of freshness, and seek a doctor's advice if food poisoning is suspected. A particular consideration is eating dairy produce. *Listeria monocytogenes* is a bacteria that may or may not be present in raw (unpasteurised) milk. The cheesemakers say that raw milk makes better cheese, and flavour and other comparisons between cheeses made from pasteurised and unpasteurised milk suggest that this is true. But here's the catch. Across Europe where lots of cheese is legally made from unpasteurised milk, there were 96 deaths and 7000 reported poisonings from listeria in the 15 years from 1983 to 1997. So use your common sense. Know that eating cheese made from raw milk can pose a health risk, and act accordingly.

eat your words
language guide

Pronunciation

In Portuguese there are two gender forms: the masculine and the feminine. In the majority of cases, the masculine can be changed to the feminine by using *'a'* in the place of *'o'* at the end of a word. Adjectives generally follow the same rules as nouns. They possess the same types of endings and change, as nouns do, in gender and number. They nearly always follow the noun they modify and must agree with it in gender and number as well: *'É um homem simpático'* ('He's a nice man')/*'É uma mulher simpática'* ('She's a nice woman').

The article system is more complex than in English, since articles must reflect both gender and number. The definite articles for the singular are *'o'* (masculine) and *'a'* (feminine); for the plural they are *'os'* (masculine) and 'as' (feminine). The indefinite articles in the singular are *'um'* (masculine) and *'uma'* (feminine) and in the plural *'uns'* (masculine) and *'umas'* (feminine).

Vowels

To the visitor, Portuguese can sound like a long succession of consonants with no vowels except a conspicuous nasal *ão* sound at the end of certain words. You can be sure, though, that there *are* vowels and that most of them have more than one pronunciation.

a (stressed, open)	**ah**	as the 'a' in 'father'
a (stressed, closed; unstressed)	**uh**	as the 'u' in 'cut'
e (stressed, open)	**eh**	as the 'e' in 'bet'
e (stressed, closed)	**e**	as the 'e' in 'berry'
e (unstressed)		barely perceptible in speech, and not represented in the transliterations
i	**ee**	as the 'ee' in 'see'
o (stressed, open)	**oh**	as the 'o' in 'hot'
o (stressed, closed)	**o**	as the 'o' in 'port'
o (unstressed)	**oo**	as the 'oo' in 'tool'
u	**oo**	as the 'oo' in 'tool'

Diphthongs

Sometimes two vowel sounds are combined in the same syllable.

ai	**ai**	as the 'y' in 'fly'
au	**ow**	as the 'ow' in 'now'
ei	**ay**	as the 'ay' in 'day'
eu	**e-w**	as the 'e' in 'bet' + the 'oo' in 'too'
oi	**oy**	as the 'oy' in 'boy', but shorter
ua	**wa**	as the 'w' in 'what' + the 'a' in 'far'
ue	**we**	as the 'whe' in 'when'
ui	**wi**	as the word 'we'
uo	**wo**	as the 'wo' in 'wobble'

Nasal Vowels

When a vowel is followed by *n* or *m,* or is marked with a tilde (~), the vowel is nasal. Imagining an 'ng' at the end of the syllable, as in the word 'sing', can help you make this nasal sound. Remember, though, that the 'g' isn't actually pronounced.

ã/an	**ang**	as the 'an' in 'fan' + 'ng'
em/en	**eng**	as the 'e' in 'bet' + 'ng'
im/in	**ing**	as the 'ee' in 'see' + 'ng'
õ/om/on	**ong**	as the 'o' in 'bone' + 'ng'
um/un	**oong**	as the 'oo' in 'too' + 'ng'

Nasal Diphthongs

Almost all transliterations of diphthongs include a 'w' or 'y', depending on the sound. A very common word, muito (much/very), is pronounced as a nasal diphthong, even though the letter combination 'ui' isn't normally nasalised.

ão	**õw**	as the 'oun' in 'ounce'
am	**õw**	like **ão**, but unstressed
ãe/em/en	**ãy**	at the end of a word, as the 'i' in 'wine' + 'ng'
õe	**õy**	as the 'oy' in 'boy' + 'ng'

Consonants

The pronunciation of many consonants is the same as in English, but there are a few you should learn.

c	**k**	as the 'k' in 'kite' before *a*, *o* and *u*; as the 's' in 'sin' before *e* and *i*
ç	**s**	as the 'c' in 'celery'. This letter's known as 'c-cedilha'.
ch	**sh**	as the 'sh' in 'ship'
g	**g**	as the 'g' in 'game' before *a*, *o*, and *u*
	zh	as the 's' in 'pleasure' before *e* and *i*
h		always silent
j	**zh**	as the 's' in 'pleasure'
lh	**ly**	as the 'li' in 'million'
nh	**ny**	as the 'ny' in 'canyon'
qu	**k**	as the 'k' in 'kite' before *e* or *i*
	kw	as the 'qu' in 'quit' before *a* or *o*
r	**rr**	at the beginning of a word or when written as *rr*, this is a very guttural, raspy sound
	r	elsewhere, as the 'tt' in 'butter' when pronounced quickly
s	**s**	as the 's' in 'sin' at the beginning of a word or when written as *ss*
	sh	as the 'sh' in 'ship' at the end of a phrase or before *p*, *t*, *c(k)* or *f*
	z	as the 'z' in 'zebra' between vowels
	zh	as the 's' in 'pleasure' before *b*, *d*, *g*, *m*, *n*, *r* or *x*
	sh	elsewhere, as the 'sh' in 'ship'
z	**zh**	as the 's' in 'pleasure' at the end of a word or phrase
	z	as the 'z' in 'zebra' between two vowels

Useful Phrases

Eating Out

restaurant	**rreshtowrangt**	*restaurante*
local eatery	**tahshkuh**	*tasca*
seafood restaurant	**muhreeshkayruh**	*marisqueira*
beer house (food also served)	**servzhuhreeuh**	*cervejaria*
fado house (food also served)	**kahzuh d fahdoozh**	*casa de fados*
restaurant selling local and international food	**koozeenyuh rrezhiwnahl ee ingternuhsiwnahl**	*cozina regional e internacional*
pastry shop; cafe	**puhshtluhreeuh**	*pastelaria*
cafe	**kuhfeh**	*café*
ice cream shop	**zhluhduhreeuh**	*geladaria*
pizzeria (other foods and snacks also served)	**peezuhreeuh**	*pizzaria*
bar	**bahr**	*bar*

Do you speak English?
fahluh ing-glezh? — *Fala inglês?*

Table for ..., please.
oomuh mezuh puhruh ..., s fahsh fuhvor — *Uma mesa para ..., se faz favor.*

Do you accept credit cards?
uhsaytuh kuhrtõyzh d krehdeetoo? — *Aceita cartões de crédito?*

Do you have a highchair for the baby?
tãy oomuh kuhdayruh d behbeh? — *Tem uma cadeira de bebé?*

Can I pay by credit card?
pohsoo puhgahr kong oong kuhrtõw de krehdeetoo? — *Posso pagar com um cartão de crédito?*

Just Try It!

What's that? **oo k eh eesoo?** — *O que é isso?*

What are the ingredients in this dish?
k ing-grdee-engtsh tãy esht prahtoo? — *Que ingredientes tem este prato?*

What's the speciality of this region?
kwal eh uh shpeseeuhleedahd dehshtuh rrzheeõw? — *Qual é a especialidade desta região?*

What do you recommend?
oo k eh k rrkoomengduh? — *O que é que recomenda?*

What are today's specials?
kwahl eh oo prahtoo doo deeuh? — *Qual é o prato do dia?*

The Menu

Can I see the menu please?
pohsoo ver oo menoo; uh eemengtuh, poor fuhvor? — *Posso ver o menu; a ementa, por favor?*

Do you have a menu in English?
tãy oomuh eemengtuh ãy ing-glezh? — *Tem uma ementa em inglês?*

daily menu	**ozh temoosh**	*hoje temos*
tourist menu	**eemengtuh tooreeshteekuh**	*ementa turística*
variable price (market price)	**presoo vuhreeahvehl**	*preço variável*
dish is for a minimum of two people	**dwuhsh psouhsh**	*duas pessoas*
per person	**poor psouh**	*por pessoa*
house specialities	**shpeseeuhleedahdesh duh kahzuh**	*especialidades da casa*
regional specialities	**shpeseeuhleedahdesh rrzhiwnaish**	*especialidades regionais*
special set price menu	**eemengtuh shpeseeahl**	*ementa especial*
I'd like ...	**kreeuh ...**	*Queria ...*
What does it include?	**oo k eh k ingklwi?**	*O que é que inclui?*

Is service included in the bill?
oo serveesoo ingklooeedoo nuh kongtuh? *O serviço está incluído na conta?*
Does it come with salad?
vãy kong suhlahduh? *Vem com salada?*
What's the soup of the day?
kwal eh uh sopuh doo deeuh? *Qual é a sopa do dia?*
Will this dish feed two people?
esht prahtoo dah puhruh doeesh? *Este prato dá para dois?*
Could I please have a half serve?
poodeeuh serveerm mayuh dohz poor fuhvor? *Podia servir-me meia dose, por favor?*
What's in this dish?
oo k eh k lehvuh esht prahtoo? *O que é que leva este prato?*
Not too spicy please.
pokoo peekangt, poor fuhvor *Pouco picante, por favor.*
Is that dish spicy?
es prahtoo eh mwingto peekangt? *Esse prato é muito picante?*
I like it hot and spicy.
kreeuhoo peekangt *Queria-o picante.*

Throughout the Meal

Do you have sauce?	**tãy molyoo**	*Tem molho?*
It's not hot (temperature).	**nõw shtah kengt**	*Não está quente.*
It's not hot (spicy).	**nõw shtah peekangt**	*Não está picante.*
I didn't order this.	**nõw pdee eeshtoo**	*Não pedi isto.*
I'd like ...	**kreeuh ...**	*Queria ...*
I'd like something to drink.	**kreeuh b-ber ahlgoomuh koyzuh**	*Queria beber alguma coisa.*

Can I have (a beer) please?
(oomuh servuhzhuh), poor fuhvor? *(Uma cerveja), por favor?*
Is the water OK to drink?
pohds b-ber ehshtuh ahgwuh? *Pode-se beber esta água?*
Will it take much longer?
uhingduh dmohruh mwingtoo tengpoo? *Ainda demora muito tempo?*

We're in a rush.
eh k shtuhmoosh kong prehsuh — *É que estamos com pressa.*

Can you please bring me some more ...?
truhzeeuhm maizh ...? — *Trazia-me mais ...?*

Please bring me ...	**truhzeeuhm ...**	*Trazia-me ...*
an ashtray	**oong zingzayroo**	*um cinzeiro*
some more bread	**maish põw**	*mais pão*
a cup	**oomuh shahvnuh**	*uma chávena*
a fork	**oong gahrfoo**	*um garfo*
a glass	**oong kohpoo**	*um copo*
a knife	**oomuh fahkuh**	*uma faca*
a napkin	**oong gwuhrduhnahpoo**	*um guardanapo*
some pepper	**peemengtuh**	*pimenta*
a plate	**oong prahtoo**	*um prato*
some salt	**sahl**	*sal*
a spoon	**oomuh koolyehr**	*uma colher*
a teaspoon	**oomuh koolyehr de shah**	*uma colher de chá*
a toothpick	**oong puhleetoo**	*um palito*
sparkling/still water	**ahgwuh kong/sãy gahzh**	*água com/sem gás*
carbonated water	**kong gahsh**	*com gás*
some red/white wine	**veenyoo tingtoo/brangkoo**	*vinho tinto/branco*
beer	**servuhzhuh**	*cerveja*

This food is ...	**ehshtuh koomeeduh shtah ...**	*Esta comida está*
cold	**freeuh**	*fria*
lukewarm	**mohrnuh**	*morna*
brilliant	**ohteemuh**	*óptima*
delicious	**dleeseeohzuh**	*deliciosa*
burnt	**kaymahduh**	*queimada*
spoiled	**shtruhgahduh**	*estragada*
not fresh	**puhsahduh**	*passada*
undercooked	**pokoo koozeenyahduh; mahl puhsahduh**	*pouco cozinhada; mal passada*
rare	**mwingtoo mahl puhsahdoo**	*muito mal passado*
raw	**krwuh**	*crua*
very oily	**mwingtoo uhzaytahduh**	*muito azeitada*
too salty	**mwingtoo sahlgahduh**	*muito salgada*
bland; not salty enough	**ingsosuh**	*insossa*

Thank you, that was delicious.
obreegahdoo, shtahvuh dleeseeozoo/ohteemoo — *Obrigado, estava delicioso/óptimo.*

Please pass on our compliments to the chef.
de oozh me-wsh puhruhbãyz ow shehf — *Dê os meus parabéns ao chefe.*

The bill, please.
uh kongtuh, s fahsh fuhvor — *A conta, se faz favor.*

Children

Is there a children's menu?
tãyãy menoo puhruh kreeangsuhzh? *Têm menu para crianças?*

Do you have a highchair for the baby?
tãy kuhdayruh d behbeh? *Tem cadeira de bebé?*

You May Hear

Já foi atendido?
zhah foy uhtengdeedoo? Have you been served?

Mais alguma coisa?
maiz ahlgoomuh koyzuh? Anything else?

Hoje, não temos ...
ozh, nõw temoozh ... We have no ... today.

Bom apetite!
bong uhpteet Enjoy your meal!

E para beber?
ee puhruh b-ber? Do you want anything to drink?

Deseja ... ?	**dzuhzhuh ...?**	Would you like ...?
sobremesa	**soobrmezuh**	a dessert
um café	**oong kuhfeh**	a coffee
um apéritif	**oong uhpreeteevoo**	an aperitif
São ... euros.	**sõw ... e-wroozh**	It's ... euros.
Com licença.	**kong leesengsuh**	Excuse me.
Está quase pronto.	**shtah kwaz prongtoo**	It's almost ready.

Family Meals

Can I bring anything?
pohsoo lvahr ahlgoomuh koyzuh? *Posso levar alguma coisa?*

Let me help you. **dayshm uhzhoodahr** *Delxe-me ajudar.*

Can I watch you make this?
pohsoo ver komoo eh k fahz eeshtoo? *Posso ver como é que faz isto?*

You're a great cook! [to a woman]
uh snyoruh eh oomuh grangd koozeenyayruh! *A senhora é uma grande cozinheira!*

You're a great cook! [to a man]
oo snyor eh oong grangd koozeenyayroo! *O senhor é um grande cozinheiro!*

This is brilliant! **eeshtoo eh ohteemoo!** *Isto é óptimo!*

Do you have the recipe for this?
tãy uh rresaytuh? *Tem a receita?*

Is this a family recipe?
eh oomuh rresaytuh d fuhmeelyuh *É uma receita de família?*

Are the ingredients local?
ooz ing-gredee-engtsh sõw kah duh zonuh? *Os ingredientes são cá da zona?*

I've never had a meal like this before.
noongkuh koomee oomuh rrefaysõw komoo ehshtuh *Nunca comi uma refeição como esta.*

I've never eaten food like this before.
noongkuh teenyuh proovahdoo koomeeduh komoo ehshtuh *Nunca tinha provado comida como esta.*

If you ever come to (Australia), I'll cook you a local dish.
s ahlgoomuh vezh vee-ehr uh (owshtrahlyuh), fahsooly oong prahtoo rrezhiwnahl *Se alguma vez vier a (Austrália), faço-lhe um prato regional.*

Could you pass the (salt) please?
poodeeuh puhsahrm (oo sahl), poor fuhvor? *Podia passar-me (o sal), por favor?*

One is enough, thank you.
soh oong/oomuh, obreegahdoo *Só um/uma, obrigado.*

Do you use ... in this? **põy ... nesht prahtoo?** *Põe ... neste prato?*

Yes, please; the meal is great.
sing, obreegahdoo; eeshtoo shtah ohteemoo *Sim, obrigado; isto está óptimo.*

No thank you, I'm full.
nõw, obreegahdoo, shto shayoo/uh *Não, obrigado, estou cheio/a.*

I've already eaten. **zhah koomee** *Já comi.*

Thanks very much for ... **mwingtoo obreegahdoo/uh peloo ...** *Muito obrigado/a pelo ...*
the lunch **ahlmosoo** *almoço*
the dinner **zhangtahr** *jantar*

Vegetarian & Special Meals

I'm a vegetarian. **so vzhetuhreeuhnoo/uh** *Sou vegetariano/a.*

I'm a vegan; I don't eat meat, fish or dairy products.
so vzhetuhreeuhnoo/uh uh sehriw; nõw komoo kahrn, nãy paysh, nãy luhkteeseeniwzh *Sou vegetariano/a a sério; não como carne, nem peixe, nem lacticínios.*

Is it cooked with pork lard or chicken stock?
eeshtoo foy koozeenyahdoo kong buhnyuh o kong kahldoo d guhleenyuh? *Isto foi cozinhado com banha ou caldo de galinha?*

I only eat vegetables. **soh komoo vzhetaizh** *Só como vegetais.*

I don't want any meat at all.
nõw komoo n-nyoomuh kahrn *Não como nenhuma carne.*

Don't add ...	**nõw ly ponyuh ...**	*Não lhe ponha ...*
I don't eat ...	**nõw komoo ...**	*Não como ...*
egg	**ovoo**	*ovo*
chicken	**frang-goo**	*frango*
cured/processed meats	**kahrn foomahduh/ engluhtahduh**	*carne fumada/ enlatada*
cold cuts	**kahrnsh freeuhzh**	*carnes frias*
fish	**paysh**	*peixe*
meat	**kahrn**	*carne*
pork	**kahrn d porkoo**	*carne de porco*
beef	**kahrn d vahkuh**	*carne de vaca*
poultry	**ahvzh**	*aves*
game	**kahsuh**	*caça*
seafood	**muhreeshkoo**	*marisco*

Do you have any vegetarian dishes?
tãy prahtoosh vzhetuhreeuhnoozh? *Tem pratos vegetarianos?*

Can you recommend a vegetarian dish, please?
pohd rrkoomengdahrm ahlgoong prahtoo vzhetuhreeuhnoo? *Pode recomendar-me algum prato vegetariano?*

Does this dish have meat?
esht prahtoo tãy kahrn? *Este prato tem carne?*

Can I get this without the meat?
esht prahtoo pohd veer sãy kahrn? *Este prato pode vir sem carne?*

Is the sauce meat-based?
oo molyoo eh faytoo ah bahz d kahrn? *O molho é feito à base de carne?*

Does it contain eggs/dairy products?
lehvuh ohvoozh/luhkteeseeniwzh? *Leva ovos/lacticínios?*

Does this dish have gelatine?
esht prahtoo tãy zhluhteenuh? *Este prato tem gelatina?*

I follow a ... diet.	**shto uh fuhzer oomuh dee-ehtuh ...**	*Estou a fazer uma dieta ...*
carbohydrate	**ah bahz d eedrahtoozh d kuhrbonoo**	*à base de hidratos de carbono*
fat	**ah bahz d goordooruhzh**	*à base de gorduras*
high fibre	**rreekuh ãy feebruhzh**	*rica em fibras*
low fat	**kong oong teeor baishoo d goordooruh**	*com um teor baixo de gordura*

Is it free of ...?	**nõw kongtãy ... ?**	*Não contém ... ?*
gluten	**glooten**	*glúten*
lactose	**luhktohz**	*lactose*
salt	**sahl**	*sal*
sugar	**uhsookahr**	*açúcar*
wheat	**treegoo**	*trigo*
yeast	**fermengtoo**	*fermento*

I'm allergic to (peanuts).
so uhlehrzheekoo/uh uh (uhmengdooingsh) — *Sou alérgico/a a (amendoins).*

I'd like a kosher meal.
kreeuh oomuh rrfaysõw zhoodaikuh — *Queria uma refeição judaica.*

Is this kosher?
eeshtoo eh koomeeduh zhoodaikuh? — *Isto é comida judaica?*

Is this organic?
eh oong proodootoo biwlohzheekoo? — *É um produto biológico?*

organically grown produce
proodootoosh biwlohzheekoozh — *produtos biológicos*

protein	**prootuheenuh**	*proteína*
sodium	**sohdiw**	*sódio*

I am a diabetic.
so deeuhbehteekoo/uh — *Sou diabético/a.*

At the Market/Self Catering

Where's the nearest (market)?
ongd feekuh (oo merkahdoo) maish prohseemoo? — *Onde fica (o mercado) mais próximo?*

Where can I find the (sugar)?
ongd eh k pohsoo engkongtrahr (oo uhsookahr)? — *Onde é que posso encontrar (o açúcar)?*

Where can I buy ...?	**ongd pohsoo kongprahr ...?**	*Onde posso comprar ... ?*
I am looking for ...	**shto ah prohkooruh d ...**	*Estou à procura de ...*
I'd like to buy ...	**kreeuh kongprahr ...**	*Queria comprar ...*
I'd like some ...	**kreeuh ...**	*Queria ...*
Can I have a ...	**kreeuh ...**	*Queria ...*
bottle	**oomuh guhrrahfuh**	*uma garrafa*
box	**oomuh kaishuh**	*uma caixa*
can	**oomuh lahtuh**	*uma lata*
packet	**oong puhkoht**	*um pacote*
bag	**oong sahkoo**	*um saco*
tin	**oomuh lahtuh**	*uma lata*
How much?	**kwangtoo eh?**	*Quanto é?*
How much for ...?	**kwangtoo eh ...?**	*Quanto é ... ?*
both	**uhzh dwuhz; oozh doyzh**	*as duas; os dois*
per fruit	**oomuh pehsuh d frootuh**	*uma peça de fruta*
per piece	**uh ooneedahd**	*a unidade*
per dozen	**uh doozeeuh**	*a dúzia*

How much is (a kilo of cheese)?
kwangtoo kooshtuh (oong keeloo d kayzhoo)? — *Quanto custa (um quilo de queijo)?*

How much altogether?
kwangtoo eh toodoo? *Quanto é tudo?*
Do you have anything cheaper?
tãy ahlgoomuh koyzuh maizh buhrahtuh? *Tem alguma coisa mais barata?*
Give me (half) a kilo, please.
dem (mayoo) keeloo, s fahsh fuhvor *Dê-me (meio) quilo, se faz favor.*
I'd like (six) slices of (ham).
kreeuh (sayzh) fuhteeuhzh d (feeangbr) *Queria (seis) fatias de (fiambre).*
I don't want to buy anything.
nõw kehroo kongprahr nahduh *Não quero comprar nada.*

I'm just looking.	**shto soh uh ver**	*Estou só a ver.*
No, thank you!	**nõw, obreegahdo/uh!**	*Não, obrigado/a!*
Who's next?	**kãy shtah uh sgeer?**	*Quem está a seguir?*
Best before ...	**kongsoomeer angtezh d ...**	*Consumir antes de ...*

I'd like some ...	**kreeuh ...**	*Queria ...*
bread	**põw**	*pão*
butter	**mangtayguh**	*manteiga*
cheese	**kayzhoo**	*queijo*
chocolate	**shookoolaht**	*chocolate*
(half a dozen) eggs	**(mayuh doozeeuh d) ohvoozh**	*(meia dúzia de) ovos*
(one kilo of) flour	**(oong keeloo d) fuhreenyuh**	*(um quilo de) farinha*
fruit and vegetables	**frootuh e lgoomzh**	*fruta e legumes*
ham	**feeangbr**	*fiambre*
prosciutto	**prezoongtoo**	*presunto*
honey	**mehl**	*mel*
jam	**kongpohtuh**	*compota*
juice	**soomoo**	*sumo*
quince jam	**oomuh engbuhlahzhãy d muhrmlahduh**	*uma embalagem de marmelada*
(a carton/litre of) milk	**(oong puhkoht/ leetroo d) layt**	*(um pacote/ litro de) leite*
mineral water	**ahgwuh meenrahl**	*água mineral*
olive oil	**uhzayt**	*azeite*
pasta	**mahsuh**	*massa*
pepper	**peemengtuh**	*pimenta*
(a kilo of) rice	**(oong keeloo d) uhrrozh**	*(um quilo de) arroz*
salt	**sahl**	*sal*
sugar	**uhsookahr**	*açúcar*
vegetable oil	**ohliw vzhetahl**	*óleo vegetal*
yoghurt	**eeohgoort**	*iogurte*

... olives	**uhzaytonuhsh ...**	*azeitonas ...*
black	**pretuzh**	*pretas*
green	**verdzh**	*verdes*
stuffed	**rresheeahduhzh**	*recheadas*

This is a present for someone.
eh puhruh ofreser — *É para oferecer.*

Could you gift-wrap this?
poodeeuh engbroolyahr puhruh ofreser? — *Podia embrulhar para oferecer?*

What's the expiry date?
ongd shtah uh dahtuh d leemeet d kongsoomoo? — *Onde está a data de limite de consumo?*

Can I taste it? **pohsoo proovahr?** *Posso provar?*

Will this keep in the fridge?
eeshtoo kongsehrvuhs noo freegooreefeekoo? — *Isto conserva-se no frigorífico?*

Is this the best you have?
eh oo mlyohr k tãy? — *É o melhor que tem?*

What's the local speciality?
kwahl eh uh shpseeuhledahd duh rrzhiõw? — *Qual é a especialidade da região?*

Can you give me a discount?
pohd fuhzerm oong deshkongtoo? — *Pode fazer-me um desconto?*

When does this shop open?
uh k ohruhz eh k ahbr ehshtuh lohzhuh? — *A que horas é que abre esta loja?*

The ingredients of this recipe are ...
ooz ing-grdee-engtzh dehshtuh rresaytuh sõw ... — *Os ingredientes desta receita são ...*

At the Bar

Shall we go for a drink?
vuhmoosh toomahr oong kohpoo? — *Vamos tomar um copo?*

I'll buy you a drink.
kongveedoot uh toomahr oong kohpoo — *Convido-te a tomar um copo.*

Thanks, but I don't feel like it.
obreegahdoo, nõw m uhptehs — *Obrigado, não me apetece.*

I don't drink (alcohol).
nõw kooshtoomoo b-ber (ahlkohl) — *Não costumo beber (álcool).*

What would you like?
oo k eh k tohmuh/kehr? — *O que é que toma/quer?*

You can get the next one.
vose pahguh uh prohseemuh — *Você paga a próxima.*

I'll have ...	**kreeuh ...**	*Queria ...*
It's on me.	**pahgoo e-w/kongveedoo e-w**	*Pago/Convido eu.*
It's my round.	**eh uh meenyuh vezh**	*É a minha vez.*
OK.	**okay; shtah bãy**	*OK/Está bem.*
Let's go Dutch.	**puhguhmooz uh mayuhzh**	*Pagamos a meias.*
I'm next.	**so uh sgeer**	*Sou a seguir.*

Can I buy you a coffee?
pohsoo ofreserly/konveedahloo uh oong kuhfeh? *Posso oferecer-lhe/convidá-lo a um café?*
Excuse me.
deshkoolpe/kong leesengsuh *Desculpe/Com licença.*
I was here before this lady/gentleman.
e-w shtahvuh angtsh dehshtuh snyoruh/desht snyor *Eu estava antes desta senhora/deste senhor.*

I'll have ...	**vo toomahr ...**	*Vou tomar ...*
a beer	**oomuh servuhzhuh**	*uma cerveja*
a 200ml beer	**oomuh ingpreeahl**	*uma imperial*
a 330ml beer	**oong pringsep**	*um príncipe*
a 500ml beer	**oomuh kuhnehkuh**	*uma caneca*
a 1L beer	**oomuh zheerahfuh**	*uma girafa*
a brandy	**oong brangdee**	*um brandy*
a champagne	**shangpuhny**	*champanhe*
a cocktail	**oong kohktayl**	*um cocktail*
a gin and tonic	**oong dzheen tohneek**	*um gin tónico*
a liqueur	**oong leekor**	*um licor*
a rum	**rroong**	*rum*
a shot	**oomuh oonyuh/oong shoht**	*uma unha/um shot*
a vodka and orange	**oong vohdkuh kong soomoo d luhrangzhuh**	*um vodka com sumo de laranja*
a whisky	**oong wiskee**	*um whisky*
a mineral water	**oomuh ahgwuh meenrahl**	*uma água mineral*
an orange juice	**oong soomoo d luhrangzhuh**	*um sumo de laranja*

Cheers! (informal) **ah twuh/ah vohsuh!** *À tua! (sg); À vossa! (pl)*
Good health! **ah twuh/swuh suhood!** *À tua/sua saúde!*

No ice. **sãy zheloo** *Sem gelo.*

Can I have ice, please?
pohd porm zheloo, poor fuhvor? *Pode pôr-me gelo, por favor?*
Same again, please.
oo mezhmoo, s fahsh fuhvor *O mesmo, se faz favor.*

Is food available here? **sehrvãy koomeeduh uhkee?** *Servem comida aqui?*

This is hitting the spot.
eeshtoo shtahm uh suhber mezhmoo bãy *Isto está-me a saber mesmo bem.*
Where's the toilet?
ongd feekuh uh kahzuh d buhnyoo? *Onde fica a casa de banho?*
I'm a bit tired; I'd better get home.
shto oong bookahdoo kangsahdoo/uh; eh mlyohr eer puhruh kahzuh *Estou um bocado cansado/a; é melhor ir para casa.*

I'm feeling drunk. **shto kong oosh kohpoozh** *Estou com os copos.*

I'm never, ever drinking again.
noongkuh maizh vohltoo uh b-ber *Nunca mais volto a beber.*
I want to throw up.
tuhnyoo vongtahd d voomeetahr *Tenho vontade de vomitar.*
So, do you come here often?
engtõw, vãy uhkee mwingtuhsh vezezh? *Então, vem aqui muitas vezes?*
I really, really like you.
gohshtoo mwingtoo, mwingtoo d tee *Gosto muito, muito de ti.*

I'm hung over. **shto kong rrsahkuh** *Estou com ressaca*

Wine

May I see the wine list, please?
pohsoo ver uh kahrtuh d veenyoozh, poor fuhvor? *Posso ver a carta de vinhos, por favor?*

Can you recommend a good local wine?
pohd rrkoomengdahrm oong bong veenyoo duh rrzheeõw? *Pode recomendar-me um bom vinho da região?*

What is a good year? **oo k eh oong bong uhnoo?** *O que é um bom ano?*
May I taste it? **pohsoo proovahloo?** *Posso prová-lo?*

Which wine would you recommend with this dish?
k veenyoo eh k m rrkoomengduh puhruh esht prahtoo? *Que vinho é que me recomenda para este prato?*

I'd like a glass/bottle of ... wine **kreeuh oong kohpoo/oomuh guhrrahfuh d veenyoo ...** *Queria um copo/uma garrafa de vinho ...*
house **duh kahzuh** *da casa*
green **verd** *verde*
red **tingtoo** *tinto*
rosé **rroze** *rosé*
sparkling **shpoomangt** *espumante*
white **brangkoo** *branco*

This wine has a nice/bad taste.
esht veenyoo tãy oong bong/mow suhbor *Este vinho tem um bom/mau sabor.*
This wine has a nice/bad colour.
esht veenyoo tãy oomuh bouh/mah kor *Este vinho tem uma boa/má cor.*
This wine is corked.
esht veenyoo sahb uh rrolyuh *Este vinho sabe a rolha.*

English–Portuguese Glossary

The following notation is used throughout the Eat Your Words section:

- / forward slash indicates when single words on either side of the slash are interchangeable. It also separates two (or more) alternatives where they consist of one word only. These could be synonyms or different forms of the same word.
- ; semicolon separates two (or more) alternatives where one (or more) consists of more than one word

A

advocaat	*uhvookaht; leekor d zhemuh*	avocaat; licor de gema
afternoon tea	*langsh*	lanche
allspice	*peemengtuh duh zhuhmaikuh*	pimenta da Jamaica
almond	*uhmengdwuh*	amêndoa
almond liqueur	*uhmengdwuh uhmahrguh*	amêndoa amarga
amaretto	*uhmuhretoo; leekor d uhmengdwa uhmahrguh*	amareto; licor de amêndoa amarga
anchovy	*angshovuh*	anchova
angelica	*angzhehleekuh*	angélica
anise	*uhneezh*	anis
aniseed	*ehrvuhdos*	erva-doce
aperitif	*uhpreeteevoo*	aperitivo
apple	*muhsang*	maçã
apricot	*duhmahshkoo/ahlpehrs*	damasco/alperce
artichoke	*ahlkuhshohfruh*	alcachofra
asparagus	*shpahrgoozh*	espargos
au gratin	*gruhteenahdoo*	gratinado
aubergine	*bringzhehluh*	beringela
avocado	*uhbuhkaht*	abacate

B

bacon	*baykong/toseenyoo*	bacon/toucinho
bacon, smoked	*toseenyoo foomahdoo*	toucinho fumado
bake	*koozeenyahr noo fornoo*	cozinhar no forno
baked	*uhsahdoo/uh*	assado/a
bakery	*pahduhreeuh*	padaria
baking powder	*fermengtoo ãy poh*	fermento em pó
baking soda	*beekuhrboonahtoo d sohdiw*	bicarbonato de sódio
balsamic vinegar	*veenahgr bahlsuhmeekoo*	vinagre balsâmico
bamboo shoot	*rrbengtoozh d bangboo*	rebentos de bambú
banana	*buhnuhnuh*	banana
bar	*bahr*	bar
barbecue	*noo/oong shoorrashkoo*	no/um churrasco
barley	*svahduh*	cevada
barley coffee	*kuhfeh de svahduh*	café de cevada

English	Pronunciation	Portuguese
barnacles	*persehvzh*	perceves
basil, sweet	*buhzeeleeshkoo*	basilisco
bass	*rroobahloo*	robalo
large mouth	*uhsheegang*	achigã
sea	*rroobahloo*	robalo
stone	*shehrn*	cherne
baste, to	*oongtahr*	untar
batter	*mahsuh/polm*	massa/polme
bay leaf	*loroo*	louro
bean	*fayzhõw*	feijão
black	*pretoo*	preto
black-eyed pea	*frahd*	frade
broad	*fahvuh*	fava
butter	*d mangtayguh*	de manteiga
garbanzo	*grõw (d beekoo)*	grão (de bico)
kidney	*vermelyoo*	vermelho
pinto	*kuhtuhreenoo*	catarino
red	*engkuhrnahdoo*	encarnado
runner	*verd*	verde
soy	*sohzhuh*	soja
–sprout	*rrbengtoozh d sohzhuh*	rebentos de soja
white	*brangkoo*	branco
beat, to	*buhter*	bater
beef	*kahrn d vahkuh*	carne de vaca
beef, ground	*kahrn peekahduh*	carne picada
beef stock	*kahldoo d kahrn*	caldo de carne
beefsteak	*beef d vahkuh*	bife de vaca
beer	*servuhzhuh*	cerveja
blonde	*loruh*	loura
dark	*pretuh*	preta
regular	*loruh*	loura
stout	*pretuh*	preta
beetroot	*btrrahbuh*	beterraba
berries	*frootoozh/bahgos*	frutos/bagos
best before ...	*kongsoomeer angtzh d*	consumir antes de ...
beverage	*bebeeduh*	bebida
bicarbonate of soda	*beekuhrboonahtoo d sohdiw*	bicarbonato de sódio
bill	*kongtuh*	conta
bird	*pahsuhroo/ahv*	pássaro/ave
birthday	*uhneeversahriw*	aniversário
birthday cake	*boloo d uhnoozh*	bolo de anos
biscuits	*boolahshuhzh/beeshkoytozh/ booleenyoozh*	bolachas/biscoitos/ bolinhos
bitter	*uhmahrgoo/uh*	amargo/a
bitters	*anggooshtooruh*	angostura
black bean	*fayzhõw pretoo*	feijão preto
blackberry	*uhmohruh*	amora
black-eyed pea	*fayzhõw frahd*	feijão frade

bland (taste)	*ingsosoo*	insosso
blender	*buhtdayruh*	batedeira
blueberry	*meerteeloo*	mirtilo
boar, wild	*zhuhvuhlee*	javalí
boil, to	*koozer/ferver*	cozer/ferver
boiled	*koozeeduh/koozeedoo*	cozida/cozido
bone	*osoo*	osso
bonito	*booneetoo*	bonito
bottle	*guhrrahfuh*	garrafa
bottle opener	*ahbr guhrrahfuhzh*	abre-garrafas
bourbon	*boorbong*	bourbon
bowl	*teezhehluh*	tigela
brains	*meeohloozh*	miolos
braise, to	*shtoofahr*	estufar
braised	*geezahdoo/uh*	guisado/a
bran	*semyuh/fuhrehloo*	sêmea/farelo
brandy	*ahgwahrdengt*	aguardente
bratwurst	*sahlseeshuh uhlmang*	salsicha alemã
Brazil nut	*kuhshtuhnyuh doo bruhzeel*	castanha do Brasil
bread	*pōw*	pão
light rye	*d sengtayoo*	de centeio
wheat and barley	*d meeshtooruh*	de mistura
wheat-flour	*d treegoo*	de trigo
whole-grain	*ingtegrahl*	integral
breadcrumbs	*pōw rroolahdoo*	pão rolado
breakfast	*pkenoo ahlmosoo*	pequeno-almoço
breakfast cereal	*sreeahl*	cereal
bream, gilt head	*dorahduh*	dourada
sea	*goorahzh/bzoogoo/pahrgoo*	goraz/besugo/pargo
white	*sahrgoo*	sargo
breast	*paytoo*	peito
brisket	*kahrn d vahkuh geezahduh*	carne de vaca guisada
broad bean	*fahvuh*	fava
broccoli	*brohkooloozh*	bróculos
broth	*sopuh/kahldoo*	sopa/caldo
Brussels sprouts	*kovzh d broosheheluhzh*	couves de bruxelas
buckwheat	*treegoo srruhsenoo*	trigo serraceno
butter	*mangtayguh*	manteiga
–bean	*fayzhōw mangtayguh*	feijão manteiga
cocoa	*mangtayguh d kuhkow*	manteiga de cacau
–sauce	*molyoo d mangtayguh*	molho de manteiga

C

cabbage	*kov*	couve
Chinese	*sheenezuh*	chinesa
purple	*rroshuh*	roxa
red	*rroshuh*	roxa
savoy	*kooruhsōw d boy*	coração de boi
white	*longbahrduh*	lombarda

cafeteria	*kuhftuhreeuh*	cafetaria
cafe	*puhshtluhreeuh*	pastelaria
cake	*boloo*	bolo
can	*lahtuh*	lata
can opener	*ahbr lahtuhzh*	abre-latas
candy (lolly, sweet)	*rrboosahdoo/dos*	rebuçado/doce
cantaloupe	*mlouh*	meloa
capers	*ahlkuhpahrruh*	alcaparra
capon	*kuhpõw*	capão
capsicum	*peemengtoo*	pimento
green	*verd*	verde
red	*vermelyoo*	vermelho
yellow	*uhmuhrehloo*	amarelo
caramel	*kuhruhmehloo; uhsookahr āy kahlduh*	caramelo; açúcar em calda
caraway seed	*smengt d koomeenyoo*	semente de cominho
cardamom	*kuhrduhmomoo*	cardamomo
cardoon	*kahrdoo; kahrdoo d kwalyoo*	cardo; cardo de coalho
carrot	*snoruh*	cenoura
cashew	*kahzhoo*	cajú
cauliflower	*kov flor*	couve-flor
caviar	*kuhveeahr*	caviar
cayenne	*peemengtuh kaiehn*	pimenta cayenne
celery	*aipoo*	aipo
seed	*smengt d aipoo*	semente de aipo
cereal	*sreeahl*	cereal
champagne	*shangpuhny*	champanhe
chargrilled	*nuh brahzuh; noo shoorrahshkoo; grelyahdoo/uh*	na brasa; no churrasco; grelhado/a
chayote	*shooshoo/kayohtuh/p-peenehluh*	chuchu/caiota/pepinela
cheese	*kayzhoo*	queijo
aged	*sekoo/koorahdoo*	seco/curado
blue	*rrohkfohr*	Roquefort
cottage	*rrkayzhõw*	requeijão
cow's milk	*d vahkuh*	de vaca
cream	*krehm*	creme
goat's milk	*d kahbruh*	de cabra
hard	*sekoo*	seco
processed	*foongdeedoo*	fundido
semi-aged	*mayoo koorahdoo*	meio curado
sheep's milk	*d ovelyuh*	de ovelha
soft	*uhmangtaygahdoo*	amanteigado
chef	*shehf*	chef
cherry	*sruhzhuh*	cereja
–liqueur	*leekor d sruhzhuh; zhingzhinyuh*	licor de cereja; ginginha
sour	*zhingzhuh*	ginja
sweet	*sruhzhuh*	cereja

cherry tomato	*toomaht sruhzhuh*	tomate cereja
chestnut	*kuhshtuhnyuh*	castanha
chicken	*frang-goo*	frango
chicken stock	*kahldoo d guhleenyuh*	caldo de galinha
chickpea	*grōw; gōw d beekoo*	grão; grão de bico
chicory	*sheekohryuh*	chicória
chilli	*peereepeeree*	piri-piri
red hot	*muhluhgetuh/peereepeeree*	malagueta/piri piri
chips	*buhtahtuhsh freetuhzh*	batatas fritas
chive	*shooleenyoo*	cebollnho
chocolate	*shookoolaht*	chocolate
dark	*shookoolaht pretoo*	chocolate preto
white	*shookoolaht brangkoo*	chocolate branco
chop (cut of meat)	*kooshtletuh*	costeleta
chopping board	*tahbwuh d koortahr*	tábua de cortar
chopsticks	*powzeenyoozh*	pauzinhos
chump	*muhshteegahr*	mastigar
cider	*seedruh*	sidra
cilantro	*kooengtroozh*	coentros
cinnamon	*kuhnehluh*	canela
citrus fruit	*frootuh seetreenuh*	fruta citrina
clam	*uhmayzhoouh*	ameijoa
clove (of garlic)	*dengt (d ahlyoo)*	dente (de alho)
clove (spice)	*kruhveenyoo*	cravinho
cockle	*berbeegōw/kongkeelyuh*	berbigão/conquilha
cocktail	*kohktayl*	cocktail
cocoa	*kuhkow*	cacau
cocoa butter	*mangtayguh d kuhkow*	manteiga de cacau
coconut	*kokoo*	coco
cod	*buhkuhlyow*	bacalhau
coffee	*kuhfeh*	café
barley	*kuhfeh de svahduh*	café de cevada
–beans	*kuhfeh āy grão*	café em grão
black	*beekuh/kuhfeh*	bica/café
decaffeinated	*deshkuhfuheenahdoo*	descafeinado
espresso	*kuhfeh*	café
–grinder	*mooeenyoo d kuhfeh*	moinho de café
ground	*kuhfeh mooeedoo*	café moído
instant	*kuhfeh ingshtangtuhniw*	café instantâneo
–milk	*mayuh d layt; guhlōw*	meia de leite; galão
machine	*mahkeenuh d kuhfeh*	máquina de café
coffee pot/maker	*kuhfiayruh*	cafeteira
coffee shop	*kuhftuhreeuh*	cafetaria
cold	*freeoo/uh*	frio/a
condiment	*tengperoo*	tempero
conserve	*kongpohtuh*	compota
consommé	*kongsome*	consomé
cook, to	*koozer*	cozer

GLOSSARY

cooked	*koozeeduh/koozeedoo*	cozida/cozido
cookies	*boolahshuhzh/beeshkoytozh/ booleenyoozh*	bolachas/biscoitos/ bolinhos
cool	*freshkoo/uh*	fresco/a
coriander	*kooengtroozh*	coentros
corn	*meelyoo dos*	milho doce
corn flakes	*kohrnflayks; flohkoosh d meelyoo*	cornflakes; flocos de milho
cornbread	*pōw d meelyoo*	pão de milho
cornmeal	*fuhreenyuh d meelyoo*	farinha de milho
cornstarch	*uhmeedoo d meelyoo*	amido de milho
courgette	*koorzheht*	corgete
couscous	*kooskoos*	cuscus
crab	*suhpuhtayruh*	sapateira
crackers	*boolahshuhzh*	bolachas
crackling	*toorrezhmoozh*	torresmos
cranberry	*uhrangdoo*	arando
crayfish	*luhgooshting*	lagostim
cream	*nahtuhzh*	natas
sour	*nahtuhz uhzeduuhzh*	natas azedas
whipped	*shangteelyee*	chantilly
whipping	*puhruh buhter*	para bater
crepe	*krehp*	crepe
cress	*uhgreeōw*	agrião
croaker fish	*koorveenuh*	corvina
croissant	*krwasang*	croissant
croquette	*krohkeht*	croquete
cruet	*guhlytayroo*	galheteiro
cucumber	*p-peenoo*	pepino
cumin	*koomeenyoozh*	cominhos
cup	*shahvnuh*	chávena
curd	*kwuhlyahduh/rrkayzhōw*	coalhada/requeijão
cure, to	*koorahr*	curar
currant	*pahsuhsh d kooringtoo*	passas de corinto
curry	*kuhreel*	caril
paste	*pahshtuh d kuhreel*	pasta de caril
powder	*kuhreel āy poh*	caril em pó
custard apple	*uhnonuh*	anona
cutlery	*tuhlyehrzh*	talheres
cuttlefish	*shohkoozh*	chocos

D

dairy	*luhkteeseeniwzh*	lacticínios
dates	*tuhmuhruhzh*	tâmaras
deep-fried	*freetoo/uh*	frito/a
delicatessen	*shuhrkootuhreeuh*	charcutaria

dessert	*dos/soobrmezuh*	doce/sobremesa
dice, to	*koortahr ãy kooboozh*	cortar em cubos
dill	*foongshoo*	funcho
dinner	*zhangtahr*	jantar
dogfish	*kuhsõw*	cação
dough	*mahsuh*	massa
dressing	*molyoo*	molho
dried	*sekoo/uh*	seco/a
drink	*bebeeduh*	bebida
soft	*rrefreezhrangt*	refrigerante
duck	*pahtoo*	pato

E

eel	*eng-geeuh*	enguia
conger	*suhfeeoo*	safio
moray	*moorayuh*	moreia
egg	*ovoo*	ovo
boiled	*ovoo koozeedoo*	ovo cozido
fried	*ovoo shtrlahdoo*	ovo estrelado
poached	*ovoo shkahlfahdoo*	ovo escalfado
scrambled	*ovoo msheedoo*	ovo mexido
–white	*klahruh d ohvoo*	claras de ovo
–yolk	*zhemuh*	gema
eggplant	*beringzhehluh*	beringela
endive	*engdeevyuh*	endívia
entree	*engtrahduh*	entrada
etiquette	*eteeketuh*	etiqueta

F

fast food	*rrefaysõw rrahpeeduh*	refeição rápida
fatty	*kong mwingtuh goordooruh*	com muita gordura
fennel	*ehrvuh dos; uhneezh*	erva-doce; anis
fennel seed	*smengt d ehrvuh dos*	semente de erva-doce
fenugreek	*fenoo gregoo*	feno-grego
fig	*feegoo*	figo
fillet	*longboo*	lombo
filling (stuffing)	*rreshayoo*	recheio
fish	*paysh*	peixe
bass	*rroobahloo*	robalo
–bone	*shpeenyuh*	espinha
bonito	*booneetoo*	bonito
croaker	*koorveenuh*	corvina
cuttlefish	*shohkoozh*	chocos
dogfish	*kuhsõw*	cação
dory	*dorahduh*	dourada

–fillet (hake)	*feelehtzh (d peshkahduh)*	filetes (de pescada)
flounder	*solyuh*	solha
gilt head bream	*dorahduh*	dourada
grayling	*paysh songbruh*	peixe-sombra
grouper	*guhropuh*	garoupa
haddock	*uhringkuh*	arinca
halibut	*uhluhboht*	alabote
herring	*uhrengk/sahvehl*	arenque/sável
John Dory	*dorahduh*	dourada
kipper	*uhrengk foomahdoo*	arenque fumado
lamprey	*langprayuh*	lampreia
large mouth bass	*uhsheegang*	achigã
monkfish	*tangbooreel*	tamboril
–paste	*pashtuh d paysh*	pasta de peixe
perch	*pehrkuh*	perca
pike	*loosiw*	lúcio
plaice	*solyuh*	solha
ray	*raiuh*	raia
red mullet	*sahlmoonet*	salmonete
redfish	*ingpruhdor*	imperador
–roe	*ohvuhzh d paysh*	ovas de peixe
salmon	*sahlmōw*	salmão
salt cod	*buhkuhlyow*	bacalhau
sardine	*suhrdeenyuh*	sardinha
sauce	*molyoo d paysh*	molho de peixe
scabbard	*paysh shpahduh*	peixe-espada
sea bass	*rroobahloo*	robalo
sea bream	*bzoogoo/goorahzh/pahrgoo*	besugo/goraz/pargo
sole	*ling-gwadoo*	linguado
–soup	*sopuh d paysh*	sopa de peixe
–stock	*kahldoo d paysh*	caldo de peixe
stone bass	*shehrn*	cherne
sturgeon	*shtoorzhōw*	esturjão
swordfish	*shpuhdahrt*	espadarte
trout	*trootuh*	truta
tuna	*uhtoong*	atum
turbot	*prgahdoo/rroodoovahlyoo*	pregado/rodovalho
white bream	*sahrgoo*	sargo
whiting	*pshkahduh*	pescada
whiting, small	*pshkuhdeenyuh*	pescadinha
flan	*pooding flang*	pudim flan
flank	*ahbuh*	aba
flavour	*suhbor/uhromuh*	sabor/aroma
flounder	*solyuh*	solha
flour	*fuhreenyuh*	farinha
plain	*fuhreenyuh*	farinha
wholewheat	*d treegoo ingtegrahl*	de trigo integral

fork	*gahrfoo*	garfo
free range	*doo kangpoo*	do campo
–chicken	*frang-goo doo kangpoo*	frango do campo
–range eggs	*ohvoozh doo kangpoo*	ovos do campo
fresh	*freshkoo/nuhtoorahl*	fresco/natural
fried	*freetoo/uh*	frito/a
frozen	*kongzhlahdoo/uh*	congelado/a
fruit	*frootuh*	fruta
–preserve	*kongpohtuh*	compota
–salad	*suhlahduh d frootuhzh*	salada de frutas
–shake	*buhteedoo*	batido
–shop/stall	*frootuhreeuh; poshtoo d frootuh*	frutaria; posto de fruta
fry, to	*freetahr*	fritar

G

game	*kahsuh*	caça
garbanzo beans	*grōw (d beekoo)*	grão (de bico)
garlic	*ahlyoo*	alho
gelatine	*zheluhteenuh*	gelatina
gherkin	*p-peenoo āy veenahgr*	pepino em vinagre
giblets	*miwdezuhzh*	miudezas
gin	*dzheen*	gin
ginger	*zhengzheebr*	gengibre
glass	*kohpoo/kahlees*	copo/cálice
goat	*kahbruh/kuhbreetoo*	cabra/cabrito
goose	*gangsoo*	ganso
gooseberry	*grozuhlyuh*	groselha
grains	*sreeahl*	cereal
gram	*gruhmuh*	grama
grapefruit	*torangzhuh*	toranja
grapes	*oovuhzh*	uvas
grate, to	*rruhlahr*	ralar
grater	*rruhluhdor*	ralador
gravy	*molyoo*	molho
grayling	*paysh songbruh*	peixe-sombra
grease	*goordooruh*	gordura
greens	*ortuhleesuh*	hortaliça
grill, to	*grlyahr*	grelhar
grouper	*guhropuh*	garoupa
guava	*goyahbuh*	goiaba

H

haddock	*uhringkuh*	arinca
halibut	*uhluhboht*	alabote
ham	*feeangbr*	fiambre

GLOSSARY

ham, Parma	*prezoongtoo*	presunto
hamburger	*angboorgehr*	hambúrguer
handle (of a pot)	*pehguh*	pega
hare	*lehbr*	lebre
hazelnut	*uhvlang*	avelã
heart	*kooruhsõw*	coração
hen	*guhleenyuh*	galinha
herring	*uhrengk/sahvehl*	arenque/sável
hominy	*pahpuhzh d meelyoo*	papas de milho
honey	*mehl*	mel
cane syrup	*mehl d kuhnuh*	mel de cana
honeydew melon	*mlõw*	melão
hors d'oeuvres	*uhspeepzh*	acepipes
horse	*kuhvahloo*	cavalo
horseradish	*rrahbuhnoo peekangt*	rábano picante
hot (temperature/spicy)	*kengt/peekangt*	quente/picante

I

ice	*zheloo*	gelo
ice cream	*zhlahdoo*	gelado
ice cube	*kooboo d zheloo*	cubo de gelo
icing	*koobertooruh*	cobertura
icing sugar	*uhsookuhr peeleh*	açúcar pilé
ingredient	*ing-grdee-engt*	ingrediente

J

jam	*dos*	doce
guava	*goeeuhbahduh*	goiabada
quince	*muhrmlahduh*	marmelada
jelly	*zhlayuh*	geleia
John Dory	*dorahduh*	dourada
jug	*guhrruhfõw*	garrafão
juice	*soomoo*	sumo
apple	*soomoo d muhsang*	sumo de maçã
fruit	*soomoo nuhtoorahl*	sumo natural
lemon	*soomoo d leemõw*	sumo de limão
orange	*soomoo d luhrangzhuh*	sumo de laranja
pineapple	*soomoo d uhnuhnahzh*	sumo de ananás
juniper berry	*bahgoo d zingbroo*	bago de zimbro

K

kebab	*shpetahduh*	espetada
kettle	*shuhlayruh*	chaleira
kid (goat)	*kuhbreetoo*	cabrito
kidney	*rreng*	rim
kidney bean	*fayzhõw vermelyoo*	feijão vermelho

kilo(gram)	*keeloo*	quilo
kipper	*uhrengk foomahdoo*	arenque fumado
kitchen	*koozeenyuh*	cozinha
kiwi(fruit)	*keevee*	kiwi
knife	*fahkuh*	faca
boning	*fahkuh d dzosahr*	faca de desossar
butter	*fahkuh d mangtayguh*	faca de manteiga
carving	*fahkuh d tringzhahr*	faca de trinchar
serrated	*fahkuh d sehrruh*	faca de serra
knuckle	*mõw*	mão
kosher	*kuhsher*	cacher
kumquat	*koongkooaht*	cumquat

L

lager	*srvuhzhuh loruh*	cerveja loura
lamb	*uhnyoo/boorregoo/koordayroo*	anho/borrego/cordeiro
lamprey	*langprayuh*	lampreia
lard	*buhnyuh*	banha
leavening	*fermengtoo*	fermento
leek	*ahlyoo frangsezh/porroo*	alho francês/porro
leg	*pehrnuh*	perna
legumes	*lgoomeenohzuhzh*	leguminosas
lemon	*leemõw*	limão
–balm	*ehrvuh seedrayruh; mleesuh*	erva-cidreira; melissa
lemonade	*leemoonahduh*	limonada
lentil	*lengteelyuh*	lentilha
lettuce	*ahlfahs*	alface
lime	*leemuh*	lima
liqueur	*leekor*	licor
cherry	*leekor d sruhzhuh; zhingzhinyuh*	licor de cereja; ginginha
almond	*uhmengdwuh uhmahrguh*	amêndoa amarga
liquorice	*ahlkuhsoozh*	alcaçuz
litre	*leetroo*	litro
liver	*feeguhdoo*	fígado
loaf (of bread)	*põw d formuh*	pão de forma
lobster	*luhgoshtuh*	lagosta
loin	*longboo*	lombo
lolly (sweet candy)	*rrboosahdoo/dos*	rebuçado/doce
loquat	*neshpruh*	nêspera
lounge	*bahr*	bar
lunch	*ahlmosoo*	almoço
lychee	*leeshyuh*	líchia

M

macadamia	*muhkuhduhmyuh*	macadamia
mackerel	*kuhruhpow/kuhvahluhzh/sahrduh*	carapau/cavalas/sarda
mackerel, small	*sheeshahrroozh*	chicharros

GLOSSARY

macrobiotic	*mahkrohbeeohteekoo/uh*	macrobiótico/a
main course	*prahtoo pringseepahl*	prato principal
maître d'	*shehf d mezuh*	chefe de mesa
malt	*mahlt*	malte
mandarin	*tangzhreenuh*	tangerina
mango	*mang-guh*	manga
margarine	*muhrguhreenuh*	margarina
marinate, to	*muhreenahr*	marinar
market	*merkahdoo*	mercado
marjoram	*mangzheronuh*	manjerona
marmalade	*dos d luhrangzhuh*	doce de laranja
marrow	*tootuhnoo*	tutano
marzipan	*muhsuhpōw; booleenyoozh d uhmengdwuh*	maçapão; bolinhos de amêndoa
mature (wine)	*muhdooroo/uh*	maduro/a
mayonnaise	*maiohnehz*	maionese
meal	*rrefaysōw*	refeição
meat	*kahrn*	carne
medium (cooked)	*nāy bāy nāy mahl puhsahdoo*	nem bem nem mal passado
melon	*mlōw*	melão
menu	*eemengtuh/kahrtuh/menoo*	ementa/carta/menú
meringue	*mreng-g*	merengue
milk	*layt*	leite
condensed	*layt kongdengsahdoo*	leite condensado
powdered	*layt āy poh*	leite em pó
–shake	*buhteedoo*	batido
skim	*layt mahgroo*	leite magro
soy	*layt d sohzhuh*	leite de soja
millet	*meelyoo meeoodoo; meelyoo puhingsoo*	milho miúdo; milho painço
mince	*peekahr*	picar
mincer	*mahkeenuh d peekahr*	máquina de picar
mineral water	*ahgwuh meenrahl*	água mineral
mint	*ortlang*	hortelã
mix, to	*meeshtoorahr*	misturar
molasses	*mlahsoo*	melaço
monkfish	*tangbooreel*	tamboril
moray	*moorayuh*	moreia
mortar	*ahlmoofuhreezh*	almofariz
mousse	*moos*	mousse
muesli	*moozhlee*	muesli
mulberry	*uhmohruh*	amora
mullet, red	*sahlmoonet*	salmonete
mushroom	*koogoomehloozh*	cogumelos
mussels	*msheelyōyzh*	mexilhões
mustard	*mooshtahrduh*	mostarda
mutton	*kurnayroo/koordayroo*	carneiro/cordeiro

N

napkin	*gwuhrduhnahpoo*	guardanapo
neck	*peshkosoo*	pescoço
noodles	*mahsuh grohsuh*	massa grossa
nougat	*noogaht/noogahdoo*	nougat/nogado
nut	*frootoo sekoo*	fruto seco
almond	*uhmengdwuh*	amêndoa
Brazil	*kuhshtuhnyuh doo bruhzeel*	castanha do Brasil
cashew	*kahzhoo*	cajú
chestnut	*kuhshtuhnyuh*	castanha
hazelnut	*uhvlang*	avelã
peanut	*uhmengdooing*	amendoim
pine nut	*peenyõw*	pinhão
pistachio	*peeshtahshoo*	pistacho
walnut	*nozh*	noz
nutcracker	*kehbruh-nohzezh*	quebra-nozes
nutmeg	*nozh mooshkahduh*	noz moscada

O

oatmeal	*flohkoosh d uhvayuh*	flocos de aveia
oats, rolled	*flohkoozh d uhvayuh*	flocos de aveia
octopus	*polvoo*	polvo
oil	*ohliw*	óleo
cooking	*ohliw uhleemengtahr*	óleo alimentar
corn	*ohliw d meelyoo*	óleo de milho
olive	*uhzayt*	azeite
peanut	*ohliw d uhmengdooing*	óleo de amendoim
sesame	*ohliw d sehzuhmoo*	óleo de sésamo
sunflower	*ohliw d zheeruhsohl*	óleo de girassol
vegetable	*ohliw vzhetahl*	óleo vegetal
okra	*keeahboo*	quiabo
olive	*uhzaytonuh*	azeitona
black	*uhsaytonuh pretuh*	azeitona preta
green	*uhzaytonuh verd*	azeitona verde
–oil	*uhzayt*	azeite
stuffed	*uhzaytonuh rrsheeahduh*	azeitona recheada
omelette	*ohmleht*	omelete
onion	*sboluh*	cebola
pickling	*sboluh ãy veenahgr*	cebola em vinagre
red	*sboluh vermelyuh*	cebola vermelha
spring	*sbooleenyuhzh*	cebolinhas
orange	*luhrangzhuh*	laranja
oregano	*orehgõwzh*	orégãos
organic	*biwlohzheekoo*	biológico
ostrich	*uhveshtroozh*	avestruz
oven	*fornoo*	forno
oxtail	*rrahboo d boy*	rabo de boi
oyster	*oshtruh*	ostra

GLOSSARY

P

pan, frying	*freezheedayruh*	frigideira
papaya	*puhpaiuh*	papaia
paprika	*kooloorow*	colorau
parsley	*sahlsuh*	salsa
parsnip	*puhshteenahguh*	pastinaga
partridge	*perdeezh*	perdiz
passionfruit	*muhruhkoozhah*	maracujá
pasta	*mahsuh*	massa
pastry	*boloozh/puhshtehl*	bolos/pastel
–shop	*puhshtluhreeuh*	pastelaria
pâté, goose liver	*fwagrah*	foie-gras
peach	*pesgoo*	pêssego
peanut	*uhmengdooing*	amendoim
pear	*peruh*	pêra
peas	*eerveelyuhzh*	ervilhas
peeler	*deshkuhshkuhdor*	descascador
pepper	*peemengtuh*	pimenta
black	*peemengtuh pretuh*	pimenta preta
white	*peemengtuh brangkuh*	pimenta branca
peppermint	*ortlang peemengtuh*	hortelã pimenta
perch	*pehrkuh*	perca
persimmon	*diwshpeeroo*	diospiro
pestle	*pehguh do ahlmoofuhreezh*	pega do almofariz
pheasant	*faizōw*	faisão
pickle	*peekls*	picles
pickled	*kongsehrvuh āy veenahgr*	conserva em vinagre
picnic	*peekneek*	piquenique
pie	*tahrt*	tarte
apple	*tahrt d muhsang*	tarte de maçã
shepherd's	*engpuhdōw*	empadão
pig, sucking	*laytōw*	leitão
pigeon	*pongboo*	pombo
pike	*loosiw*	lúcio
pine nut	*peenyōw*	pinhão
pineapple	*uhnuhnahzh*	ananás
pinto bean	*fayzhōw kuhtuhreenoo*	feijão catarino
pip	*kuhrosoo*	caroço
pistachio	*peeshtahshoo*	pistacho
plaice	*solyuh*	solha
plain	*singplezh*	simples
plate	*prahtoo*	prato
plum	*uhmayshuh*	ameixa
poach, to	*shkahlfahr*	escalfar
polenta	*pahpuhzh d meelyoo*	papas de milho
pomegranate	*rromang*	romã
popcorn	*peepohkuhzh*	pipocas
poppy	*puhpoyluh*	papoila

pork	*porkoo*	porco
port	*portoo; veenyoo doo portoo*	porto; vinho do Porto
dry white	*portoo brangkoo*	porto branco
ruby	*portoo rroobee*	porto ruby
pot	*tahshoo*	tacho
potato	*buhtahtuh*	batata
baked	*buhtahtuh uhsahduh*	batata assada
boiled	*buhtahtuh koozeeduh*	batata cozida
–chips	*buhtahtuhzh freetuhzh*	batatas fritas
mashed	*pooreh d buhtahtuh*	puré de batata
sweet	*buhtahtuh dose*	batata doce
poultry	*ahvzh*	aves
prawn	*kuhmuhrõw/gangbuhzh*	camarão/gambas
tiger	*kuhmuhrõw teegr*	camarão tigre
preservative	*kongservangt*	conservante
preserve of	*kongsehrvuh d*	conserva de ...
pressure cooker	*puhnehluh d prsõw*	panela de pressão
prosciutto	*prezoongtoo*	presunto
prune	*uhmayshuh sekuh*	ameixa seca
pudding	*pooding*	pudim
pulses	*lgoomsh sekoozh*	legumes secos
pumpkin	*uhbohbooruh*	abóbora
puree	*pooreh*	puré

Q

quail	*koodoorneezh*	codorniz
quality, good/bad	*kwuhleedahd bouh/mah*	qualidade boa/má
quiche	*tahrt*	tarte
mushroom	*tahrt d koogoomehloozh*	tarte de cogumelos
spinach	*tahrt d shpeenahfrezh*	tarte de espinafres
vegetable	*tahrt d lgoomzh*	tarte de legumes
quince	*muhrmehloo*	marmelo

R

rabbit	*koouhlyoo*	coelho
radish	*rrahbuhnoo*	rábano
raisins	*pahsuhzh/sooltuhnuhzh*	passas/sultanas
rare (cooked)	*mahl puhsahdoo*	mal passado
raspberry	*frangbwezuh*	framboesa
ray	*raiuh*	raia
receipt	*fahtooruh*	factura
redfish	*ingpruhdor*	imperador
refrigerator	*freegooreefeekoo*	frigorífico
reservation	*rrzehrvuh*	reserva
restaurant	*rreshtowrangt*	restaurante
rhubarb	*rrwibahrboo*	ruibarbo
ribs	*engtrkoshtoo*	entrecosto

GLOSSARY

English	Pronunciation	Portuguese
rice	*uhrrozh*	arroz
arborio	*kuhrooleenoo*	carolino
basmati	*bahzhmahtee*	basmati
brown	*ingtgrahl*	integral
glutinous	*glooteenozoo*	glutinoso
jasmine	*kong suhbor uh zhuhzhming*	com sabor a jasmim
long grain	*uhgoolyuh*	agulha
short grain	*kuhrooleenoo*	carolino
ripe (fruit)	*muhdooroo/uh*	maduro/a
roast	*uhsahdoo/uh*	assado/a
rockmelon	*mlouh*	meloa
rolling pin	*rroloo duh mahsuh*	rolo da massa
rosemary	*uhlkring*	alecrim
rosé	*veenyoo rroze*	vinho rosé
rum	*rroong*	rum
rump	*beef d ahlkahtruh*	bife de alcatra
runner bean	*fayzhõw verd*	feijão verde

S

English	Pronunciation	Portuguese
saffron	*uhsuhfrõw*	açafrão
sago	*sahlvuh (plangtuh mdeeseenahl)*	salva (planta medicinal)
salad	*suhlahduh*	salada
fruit	*d frootuhzh*	de frutas
lettuce	*d ahlfahs*	de alface
salami	*sahlseeshõw eetuhlyuhnoo*	salsichão italiano
salmon	*sahlmõw*	salmão
salt	*sahl*	sal
salt & pepper mills	*mooeenyoozh d sahl ee peemengtuh*	moinhos de sal e pimenta
salty	*sahlgahdoo/uh*	salgado/a
sandwich	*sangdzh/sangdwish*	sandes/sanduiche
sardine	*suhrdeenyuh*	sardinha
sauce	*molyoo*	molho
apple	*pooreh d muhsang*	puré de maçã
butter	*molyoo d mangtayguh*	molho de manteiga
caramel	*molyoo d kuhruhmehloo*	molho de caramelo
cranberry	*uhrangdoo molyoo*	arando molho
fish	*molyoo d paysh*	molho de peixe
hot (spicy)	*peekangt*	picante
white	*molyoo brangkoo*	molho branco
Worcestershire	*molyoo ing-glezh*	molho inglês
saucepan	*tahshoo pkenoo*	tacho pequeno
saucer	*peerzh*	pires
sausage	*sahlseeshuh*	salsicha
sauteed	*freetoo/uh*	frito/a; salteado/a
savoury	*sahlgahdoo/uh*	salgado/a
scabbard	*paysh shpahduh*	peixe-espada
scallop	*veeayruh*	vieira

scampi	*gangbuhzh*	gambas
scissors	*tzoruh*	tesoura
sea vegetables	*vzhetaizh muhreenyoozh*	vegetais marinhos
seafood	*frootoozh doo mahr*	frutos do mar
season, to	*tengprahr*	temperar
seasoning	*tengperoo*	tempero
semolina	*semooluh*	sêmola
serve, to	*serveer*	servir
service	*serveesoo*	serviço
serving, large/small	*dohz oomuh/mayuh*	dose uma/meia
sesame	*sehzuhmoo*	sésamo
sesame seed	*smengtezh d zherzheling*	sementes de gergelim
shad	*sahvehl*	sável
shallot	*shuhlohtuh*	chalota
shallow fry	*freetoo nuh freezheedayruh (kong pokoo ohliw)*	frito na frigideira (com pouco óleo)
shandy	*servuhzhuh kong guhzohzuh*	cerveja com gasosa
sharpening stone	*pehdruh d uhmoolahr*	pedra de amolar
shellfish	*muhreeshkoo*	marisco
shepherd's pie	*engpuhdõw*	empadão
sherry	*shrezh*	Xerez
shoulder	*pah*	pá
shrimp	*kuhmuhrõw/gangbuhzh*	camarão/gambas
sieve	*kreevoo/pnayruh*	crivo/peneira
sifter	*pnayruh*	peneira
simmer	*ferveelyahr*	fervilhar
sirloin	*engtrkot*	entrecôte
skewer	*shpetoo*	espeto
slice	*fuhteeuh*	fatia
slice, to	*tringshahr*	trinchar
smoke, to	*foomahr*	fumar
snap peas	*eerveelyuhsh tohrtuhzh*	ervilhas tortas
soak	*dmoolyahr; por d molyoo*	demolhar; pôr de molho
soda water	*sohduh; ahgwuh kong gahzh*	soda; água com gás
soft drink	*rrefreezherangt*	refrigerante
sole	*ling-gwahdoo*	linguado
soup	*sopuh/kahldoo*	sopa/caldo
sour	*uhzedoo/uh*	azedo/a
sour cherry	*zhingzhuh*	ginja
soy bean	*sohzhuh*	soja
spaghetti	*shpahrgeht*	esparguete
spaghetti squash	*sheeluh/zheeluh*	chila/gila
sparerib	*engtrkoshtoo*	entrecosto
spatula	*shpahtooluh*	espátula
spices	*shpeseeuhreeuhzh*	especiarias
spicy	*peekangt*	picante
spinach	*shpeenahfrezh*	espinafres
spirits	*b-beeduhz shpeereetoo-ohzuhzh*	bebidas espirituosas
split pea, green	*eerveelyuhsh sekuhzh*	ervilhas secas

GLOSSARY

spoon	*koolyehr*	colher
spring onion	*shooleenyuhzh*	cebolinhas
sprinkle, to	*polveelyahr*	polvilhar
squash	*uhbohbooruh*	abóbora
squid	*looluhzh*	lulas
stale	*dooroo/uh; vehlyoo/uh*	duro/a; velho/a
star anise	*uhneezh shtrlahdoo*	anis estrelado
steak	*beef/pohshtuh*	bife/posta
beef	*beef d vahkuh*	bife de vaca
steam, to	*koozeenyahr uh vuhpor*	cozinhar a vapor
steamer	*vuhpooreezuhdor*	vaporizador
stew	*geezahdoo/uh*	guisado/a
stew, to	*shtoofahr*	estufar
stock	*kahldoo*	caldo
stone	*kuhrosoo*	caroço
stout	*servuhzhuh pretuh*	cerveja preta
stove	*foogōw*	fogão
strawberry	*moorang-goo*	morango
stuffing	*rreshayoo*	recheio
sturgeon	*shtoorzhōw*	esturjão
sugar	*uhsookuhr*	açúcar
brown	*uhmuhrehloo*	amarelo
caster	*gruhnoolahdoo*	granulado
icing	*peeleh*	pilé
sultanas	*sooltuhnuhzh*	sultanas
sun-dried	*sekoo ow sohl*	seco ao sol
sweet (dessert)	*dos/soobrmezuh*	doce/sobremesa
sweet (lolly, candy)	*rrboosahdoo/dos*	rebuçado/doce
sweet (taste)	*dose*	doce
sweet potato	*buhtahtuh dose*	batata doce
sweetcorn	*meelyoo dos*	milho doce
swordfish	*shpuhdahrt*	espadarte
syrup	*kahlduh (d uhsookahr)*	calda (de açúcar)

T

table	*mezuh*	mesa
tablecloth	*twalyuh*	toalha
tarragon	*shtruhgōw*	estragão
tart	*tahrt*	tarte
tart (taste)	*uhzedoo*	azedo
tea	*shah*	chá
black	*pretoo*	preto
chamomile	*kuhmoomeeluh*	camomila
decaffeinated	*deshkuhfuheenahdoo*	descafeinado
green	*verd*	verde
herbal	*d ehrvuhzh*	de ervas
jasmine	*d zhuzhming*	de jasmim
lemon	*kong leemōw*	com limão

milk	*kong layt*	com leite
peppermint	*d ortlang peemengtuh*	de hortelã-pimenta
rose hip	*d rroozayruh brahvuh*	de roseira brava
tender	*muhseeoo/uh*	macio/a
tequila	*tekeeluh*	tequila
thyme	*toomeelyoo*	tomilho
tip	*goorzhetuh*	gorjeta
toast	*toorrahduh*	torrada
toast, to	*bringd*	brinde
toaster	*toorrahdayruh*	torradeira
tofu	*toofoo*	tofu
tomato	*toomaht*	tomate
tongs	*tnahzh/pingsuh*	tenaz/pinça
tongue	*lIng-gwuh*	língua
tonic water	*ahgwuh tohneekuh*	água tónica
toothpick	*puhleetoo*	palito
torte	*tohrtuh*	torta
tough	*dooroo/uh*	duro/a
tray	*truhvehsuh*	travessa
tripe	*doobrahduh/treepuh*	dobrada/tripa
trout	*trootuh*	truta
tuna	*uhtoong*	atum
turbot	*prgahdoo/rroodoovahlyoo*	pregado/rodovalho
turkey	*peroo*	peru
turmeric	*uhsuhfrooayruh*	açafroeira
turnip	*nahboo*	nabo
turnip greens	*nuhbeesuh*	nabiça

U

unripe (fruit)	*verd*	verde

V

vanilla	*bowneelyuh*	baunilha
veal	*nooveelyoo*	novilho
vegetable	*lgoome*	legume
vegetable stock	*kahldoo d lgoomezh*	caldo de legumes
vegetarian	*vzhetuhreeuhnoo/uh*	vegetariano/a
venison	*veeahdoo*	veado
vinegar	*veenahgr*	vinagre
balsamic	*bahlsuhmeekoo*	balsâmico
wine	*d veenyoo*	de vinho
vodka	*vohdkuh*	vodka

W

waiter/waitress	*engpregahdoo/uh d mezuh*	empregado/a de mesa
walnut	*nozh*	noz
warm	*mornoo/uh*	morno/a

water	*ahgwuh*	água
bottled	*ahgwuh eng-guhrruhahduh*	água engarrafada
fresh	*ahgwuh freeuh/ freshkuh*	água fria/fresca
mineral	*ahgwuh meenrahl*	água mineral
soda	*sohduh; ahgwuh kong gahzh*	soda; água com gas
still	*ahgwuh sãy gahzh*	água sem gás
tap	*ahgwuh duh toornayruh*	água da torneira
tonic	*ahgwuh tohneekuh*	água tónica
watermelon	*mlangseeuh*	melancia
well done (cooked)	*bãy puhsahdoo/uh; koozeenyahdoo/uh*	bem passado/a; cozinhado/a
wheat	*treegoo*	trigo
buckwheat	*treegoo srruhsenoo*	trigo serraceno
whelk	*booziw*	búzio
whisk	*buhtdayruh*	batedeira
whisk, to	*buhter*	bater
whisky	*ooeeskee*	whisky
whiting	*pshkahduh*	pescada
small	*pshkuhdeenyuh*	pescadinha
wild	*sehlvahzhãy*	selvagem
wine	*veenyoo*	vinho
aged	*veenyoo engvelyseedoo*	vinho envelhecido
–cellar	*uhdehguh*	adega
dry	*veenyoo sekoo*	vinho seco
green	*veenyoo verd*	vinho verde
house	*veenyoo duh kahzuh*	vinho da casa
local	*veenyoo duh rrezheeõw*	vinho da região
–list	*kahrtuh d veenyoozh*	carta de vinhos
medium dry	*veenyoo mayoo sekoo*	vinho meio seco
–producer	*uhdehguh*	adega
red	*veenyoo tingtoo*	vinho tinto
rosé	*veenyoo rroze*	vinho rosé
sparkling	*veenyoo shpoomangt*	vinho espumante
white	*veenyoo brangkoo*	vinho branco
wing	*ahzuh*	asa

Y

yams	*eenyuhm*	inhame
yeast	*fermengtoo d pahdayroo*	fermento de padeiro
yoghurt	*eeohgoort*	iogurte
yolk	*zhemuh*	gema

Z

zest	*rrahshpuh d leemõw*	raspa de limão
zucchini	*koorzheht*	corgete

Portuguese Culinary Dictionary

The following notation is used throughout the Eat Your Words section:

/ forward slash indicates when single words on either side of the slash are interchangeable. It also separates two (or more) alternatives where they consist of one word only. These could be synonyms or different forms of the same word.

; semicolon separates two (or more) alternatives where one (or more) consists of more than one word

bolded words within the English definintion denotes that the word has its own entry within the dictionary

italicised words within the English definintion denotes that the word is neither English or Portuguese

A

abacate *uhbuhkaht* avocado
abóbora *uhbohbooruh* pumpkin
açafrão *uhsuhfrõw* saffron
acepipes *uhspeepzh* hors d'oeuvres, titbits or delicacies; smaller than an entree but grander than a snack
achigã *uhsheegang* large mouth bass
ácido *ahseedoo* sour
acompanhamentos *uhkongpuhnyuhmengtoosh* accompaniments
açorda *uhsorduh* bread-based thick soup the consistency of porridge, often but not always flavoured with garlic, coriander and olive oil
–à Alentejana *–ah uhlengtzhuhnuh* an **açorda** made with garlic, olive oil, broth, greens, poached eggs and aromatic herbs like coriander or pennyroyal (Alentejo)
–de bacalhau *–d buhkuhlyow* **açorda** with shredded salt cod
–de gambas *–d gangbuhzh* **açorda** containing prawns
–de marisco *–d muhreeshkoo* **açorda** with prawns, mussels and baby clams
–de sável *–d sahvehl* spicy **açorda** flavoured with herring broth; fried herring fillets served separately (Ribatejo)
açúcar *uhsookahr* sugar
–amarelo *–uhmuhrehloo* brown sugar
–granulado *–gruhnoolahdoo* granulated or refined sugar
adega *uhdehguh* wine producer or wine cellar
adoçante *uhdoosangt* artificial sweetener; also called **edulcorante**
agriões *uhgreeõyzh* watercress
água *ahgwuh* water
–da nascente *–duh nuhshsengt* spring water
–da torneira *–duh toornayruh* tap water
–mineral com/sem gás *–meenrahl kong/sãy gahzh* mineral water (with/without carbonation)
água-pé *ahgwuh-peh* wine with a low alcohol content made by adding water to the pressed wine dregs and letting it ferment for a short time. Considered a harvest drink, água-pé is served almost exclusively at local fairs and in small taverns.
aguardente *ahgwahrdengt* a brandy-like spirit
–de cana *–d kuhnuh* sugar cane **aguardente** (Madeira)
–de figo *–d feegoo* fig **aguardente**
–de medronho *–d mdronyoo* brandy made from the fruit of the wild strawberry tree found in the Algarve and parts of the Alentejo
–velha *–vehlyuh* fine brandy

aipo *aipoo* celery
alcachofra *ahlkuhshohfruh* artichoke
alecrim *uhlkring* rosemary
Alentejana, à *ah uhlengtzhuhnuh* Alentejo style; a dish made with garlic, olive oil, paprika, most probably pork, and usually small clams
aletria *uhltreeuh* 'angel-hair pasta'; name of dessert of cooked angel-hair pasta mixed into custard-like pudding and topped with cinnamon (Minho)
alface *ahlfahs* lettuce
alheiras *uhlyayruhzh* sausage of bread, garlic and chilli mixed with small amounts of pork and even smaller amounts of chicken, turkey or veal
alho *ahlyoo* garlic
–francês/porro *–frangsezh/porroo* leek
almoço *ahlmosoo* lunch
almôndegas *ahlmongdguhzh* meatballs, usually made of ground beef or pork; served in a tomato-based sauce
alperce *ahlpehrs* apricot
amanteigado *uhmangtaygahdoo* 'buttery'; term used to describe creamy cheeses often scooped out of their rind with a spoon
amarguinha *uhmuhrgeenyuh* almond flavoured liqueur; also called **licor de amêndoa amarga**
ameijoas *uhmayzhoouhz* clams
–à Bulhão Pato *–ah boolyõw pahtoo* broth of small clams in coriander, white wine and garlic sauce
–ao natural *–ow nuhtoorahl* steamed clams
–na cataplana *–nuh kuhtuhpluhnuh* small clams cooked in a **cataplana** with onion, chopped **chouriço**, ham and red and green capsicum (Algarve)
ameixa *uhmayshuh* plum
ameixas de Elvas *uhmayshuhzh d ehlvuhsh* (plums of Elvas) sweet dessert plums preserved in sugar and served as a sweet snack or part of a dessert
amêndoa *uhmengdwuh* almond
amendoim *uhmengdooing* peanut
amora *uhmohruh* blackberry
ananás *uhnuhnahzh* pineapple
anho *uhnyoo* lamb (*see also* **borrego**)
anona *uhnonuh* custard apple
apéritif *uhpereeteef* before-dinner drink
aperitivo *uhpreeteevoo* accompaniment to an **apéritif**; can be nuts, dried fruit, pretzels, crisps
areias *uhrayuhzh* sweet biscuit flavoured with lemon, sometimes with an almond on top
arjamolho *uhrjuhmolyoo* Algarve name for **gaspacho**
arrepiadas *uhrrpeeahduhzh* clusters of sliced almonds, held together with a bit of meringue
arroz *uhrrozh* rice
–à valenciana *–ah vuhlengseeuhnuh* a saffron-flavoured rice dish similar to paella with chicken, pork, a bit of beef, peas, carrots, red capsicum, shellfish and whole prawns
–árabe *–ahruhb* rice with raisins, nuts and sometimes chopped dried fruit
–cozido *–koozeedoo* boiled rice
–de bacalhau *–d buhkuhlyow* tomato-flavoured rice with shredded salt cod (Minho)
–de berbigão *–d berbeegõw* rice with cockles, seasoned with coriander (Algarve)
–de bucho *–d booshoo* creamy rice cooked in pork broth; served with slices of pork, chopped turnips and turnip greens (Ribatejo)
–de cabidela *–d kuhbeedehluh* chicken and rice casserole with fresh chicken blood (Beiras)
–de ervilhas *–d eerveelyuhzh* rice with peas
–de espigos *–d shpeegozh* rice with cabbage (Beiras, Minho)
–de feijão *–d fayzhõw* rice with red beans
–de forno *–d fornoo* baked rice with onion and prosciutto or **salpicão**; can include **chouriço**, chicken, thyme or saffron

–de grelos *–d greloozh* rice with cabbage
–de lampreia *–d langprayuh* lamprey and rice stew with onion, parsley, white wine, **chouriço** and lamprey blood (Minho)
–de langueirão *–d langayrõw* rice with razor clams and onion, seasoned with garlic and parsley (Algarve)
–de lapas *–d lahpuhzh* rice with limpets (Azores)
–de marisco *–d muhreeshkoo* casserole of seafood and rice in tomato sauce
–de pato *–d pahtoo* baked or braised casserole of rice with shredded duck and sausage slices
–de polvo *–d polvoo* chunks of octopus and onion in a tomato-rice stew flavoured with garlic, white wine and coriander or parsley
–de tamboril *–d tangbooreel* tomato-rice stew with chunks of monkfish
–de tomate *–d toomaht* rice cooked in a tomato broth seasoned with garlic and onion, often served with fried fish
–doce *–dos* creamy rice pudding with cinnamon; the Alentejan/Ribatejan version is made without eggs
–integral *–ingtgrahl* brown rice
–sarrabulho *–suhrruhboolyoo* stew with rice, cuts of pork, beef and chicken, and sauce made of onion and pig's blood (Minho)
arrufadas de Coimbra *uhrroofahduhzh d kooingbruh* dome-shaped, cinnamon flavoured bread
asa *ahzuh* wing
–de frango *–d frang-goo* chicken wing
–de perú *–d proo* turkey wing
assada/o *uhsahduh/oo* roast
assada de peixe *uhsahduh d paysh* mixture of different roasted/baked fish served with a sauce of olive oil, chilli and garlic
assadeira *uhsuhdayruh* large, shallow roasting pan for big birds or joints of meat
atum *uhtoong* tuna
–de escabeche *–d shkuhbehsh* raw tuna 'pickled' or 'cooked' in vinegar (Madeira)
avelã *uhvlang* hazelnut
aves *ahvzh* poultry
avestruz *uhveshtroozh* ostrich
azeite *uhzayt* olive oil
azeitonas *uhzaytonuhzh* olives
–pretas *–pretuhzh* black olives
–recheadas *–rrsheeahduhzh* stuffed olives
–sem caroço *–sãy kuhrosoo* pitted olives
–verdes *–verdzh* green olives
azevias *uhzveeuhzh* fried puff pastry with a sweet chickpea filling (Alentejo, Ribatejo)

B

baba de camelo *bahbuh d kuhmeloo* 'camel drool'; caramel mousse made with condensed milk
bacalhau *buhkuhlyow* dried salt cod
–à Assis *–ah uhseesh* crumbled salt cod cooked in olive oil with thin strips of onion, **presunto**, potatoes, carrots and red capsicum, then mixed with eggs and parsley and baked until golden
–à Brás *–ah brahzh* flaked cod scramble-fried with egg and chunks of cooked potato, then strewn with chopped parsley and green or black olives (Estremadura)
–à cozinha velha *–ah koozeenhyuh vehlyuh* finely chopped salt cod, onions and carrots fried in olive oil, then cooked in a white sauce that includes egg, nutmeg, pepper and lemon juice, covered with breadcrumbs and baked in the oven
–à Gomes de Sá *–ah gomzh d sah* flaked salt cod soaked in boiling milk, then browned in the oven with olive oil, diced potatoes, onion, garlic and pepper, and served with olives, slices of hard-boiled eggs and chopped parsley (Minho)

–**à lagareiro** *–ah luhguhrayroo* thick piece of salt cod garnished with thinly sliced onion and baked in abundant amounts of olive oil; served with **batatas à murro** (Beiras)

–**à Margarida da praça** *–ah muhrguhree-duh duh prahsuh* grilled salt cod steak served on sliced boiled potatoes topped with a generous amount of sauteed onion slices and garlic (Minho)

–**à Zé do Pipo** *–ah zeh doo peepoo* baked casserole of flaked salt cod covered with a layer of sauteed onion, topped with mayonnaise and mashed potatoes (Porto)

–**albardado** *–ahlbuhrdahdoo* salt cod fried in a doughy batter (Alentejo)

–**assado com batatas à murro** *–uhsah-doo kong buhtahtuhz ah moorroo* baked/roasted salt cod with smashed baked potatoes (skin on), garlic and olive oil

–**assado com pão de centeio** *–uhsahdoo kong pōw de sengtayoo* baked salt cod steak sprinkled with crushed garlic, olive oil and a layer of crumbled, light rye bread (Trás-os-Montes)

–**assado com pimentos** *–uhsahdoo kong peemengtoosh* pieces of grilled cod and strips of grilled green pepper mixed with chopped raw onion and garlic, seasoned with olive oil, vinegar and pepper and served with boiled potatoes

–**com batatas à murro** *–kong buhtahtuhz ah moorroo* steaks or pieces of salt cod grilled over the coals and served with potatoes that have been baked in their skins and smashed open, all seasoned with hot olive oil and sliced garlic

–**com grão** *–kong grōw* grilled or baked salt cod steaks served with hot large chickpeas strewn with onion and garlic, then seasoned with buckets of olive oil, vinegar and pepper

–**com migas de pão de milho** *–kong meeguhzh d pōw d meelyoo* baked salt cod steak brushed with olive oil and garlic and topped with crumbled corn bread; can also be baked on a bed of sliced onion (Minho)

–**com natas** *–kong nahtuhzh* flaked salt cod cooked with chopped garlic, chopped onion and olive oil, then baked in the oven with mashed potato and cream

–**com todos** *–kong todoozh* boiled salt cod served with a boiled egg and boiled vegetables

–**cozido** *–koozeedoo* boiled salt cod

–**cru desfiado** *–kroo deshfeeahdoo* shredded raw salt cod in an olive oil and vinegar dressing, garnished with finely chopped onion and garlic

–**desfiado** *–deshfeeahdoo* fine strips of raw salt cod dipped in water, then well squeezed and served with chopped onion and garlic and seasoned with pepper, vinegar and olive oil

–**espiritual** *–shpeereetwal* shredded salt cod, onion, and carrots baked into a casserole with a bechamel sauce; sprinkled with parmesan (Estremadura)

–**guisado** *–geezahdoo* salt cod steaks stewed in the oven with olive oil between layers of sliced tomatoes, onion, potatoes, butter, garlic, bay leaf, paprika, pepper and parsley

–**no borralho** *–noo boorrahlyoo* salt cod steak wrapped in bacon, cabbage leaves and greaseproof paper, cooked in burning embers (Trás-os-Montes)

–**no forno** *–noo fornoo* baked salt cod, often served smothered in an onion-olive oil sauce

–**roupa-velha** *–rropuh-vehlyuh* 'old clothes'; mixture of cut up cabbage, salt cod and potatoes, sauteed in olive oil and garlic (Minho)

bagaçeira *buhguhsayruh* **aguardente** mixed with distilled wine lees (Trás-os-Montes)

bagaço *buhgahsoo* eau de vie, often drunk with an espresso coffee

banha *buhnyuh* lard

DICTIONARY

bar *bahr* bar or lounge
barriga-de-freira *buhrreeguh-d-frayruh* sponge cake or bread covered in a sugary syrup containing eggs and a hint of lemon
barrinhas de pescada *buhrreenyuhzh d pshkahduh* fish sticks
batata doce *buhtahtuh dos* sweet potato
batatas *buhtahtush* potatoes
–**à murro** *–ah moorroo* the 'punched potatoes'; new, baked potatoes, with the skin on, that have been smashed and seasoned with olive oil and garlic
–**cozidas** *–koozeeduhzh* boiled potatoes
–**fritas** *–freetuhzh* potato chips or crisps
bater *buhter* to beat or whisk
batido *buhteedoo* milk or fruit shake
baunilha *bowneelyuh* vanilla
bavaroise *bahvuhrwaz* whipped gelatinous dessert made with cream and pieces of fruit such as strawberries or pineapple
bebida *bebeeduh* beverage
–**(não) alcoólica** *–(nõw) ahlkoo-ohleekuh* (non) alcoholic beverage
–**espirituosa** *–shpeereetoo-ohzuh* spirits
–**fria** *–freeuh* cold beverage
–**quente** *–kengt* hot beverage
berbigão *berbeegõw* cockle
beringela *bringzhehluh* aubergine/eggplant
besugo *bzoogoo* sea bream
bica *beekuh* Lisbon term for espresso coffee; small, spicy blood sausages made with cumin and maize flour (upper Minho)
–**cheia** *shayuh* short black/espresso topped with hot water (Lisbon and the south)
–**com uma pinga** *kong oomuh ping-guh* short black/espresso topped with **aguardente**; known as a digestive
bicarbonato de sódio *beekuhrboonahtoo d sohdiw* baking soda or bicarbonate of soda
bifana no pão *beefuhnuh noo põw* thin pork steak sandwich
bifana no prato *beefuhnuh noo prahtoo* thin pork steak (not in a sandwich)
bife *beef* steak of beef, other meats, poultry or fish; fillet
–**à café** *–ah kuhfeh* thick rump steak served with sauce of milk, lemon juice and mustard
–**à casa** *–ah kahzuh* 'house-style'; thin, pan-fried steak with a fried egg on top. Served with chips, rice and salad.
–**à cerveja** *–ah servuhzhuh* steak with beer-based, buttery sauce
–**à Marrare** *–ah mahrrahreh* thick rump steak served with cream sauce and ground pepper (Estremadura)
–**à pimenta** *–ah peemengtuh* steak with whole peppercorns
–**alto** *–altoo* thick steak
–**bem passado** *–bãy puhsahdoo* well-done steak
–**com ovo a cavalo** *–kong ovoo uh kuhvahloo* fried steak marinated with fresh garlic, served with a fried egg on top
–**da alcatra** *–duh ahlkahtruh* rump steak
–**da vazia** *–duh vuhzeeuh* sirloin steak
–**de atum** *–d uhtoong* tuna steak
–**de atum com tomate** *–d uhtoong kong toomaht* tuna steak served in a tomato and onion sauce, flavoured with garlic and bay leaf (Madeira, Algarve)
–**de atum em cebolada** *–d uhtoong ãy sboolahduh* tuna steak with onion sauce (Algarve)
–**de frango** *–d frang-goo* chicken cutlet
–**de perú** *–d proo* turkey cutlet
–**de vaca** *–d vahkuh* beef steak
–**do lombo** *–doo longboo* fillet steak
–**mal passado** *–mahl puhsahdoo* steak that is medium cooked
–**na frigideira** *–nuh freezheedayruh* thin, lightly pan-fried beef steak, usually served with chips
bifinho *beefeenyoo* thin, small, boneless slices of meat
biscoitos *beeshkoytoozh* biscuits/cookies
–**de azeite/alcanena** *–d uhzaytlahlkuhnenuh* light and airy biscuit made with olive oil (Beiras)

bitoque *beetohk* small steak or fillet usually served with a fried egg on top

boião *boyõw* jar

bola *bohluh* breadroll usually made from a combination of wheat and rye flour

–**de Berlim com/sem creme** *–d berling kong/sãy krehm* plain doughnut with/without custard filling

–**de carne** *–d kahrn* baked pie made of meat filling sandwiched between two layers of bread dough; filling usually includes chunks of seasoned veal, chicken, prosciutto and smoked pork tenderloin; can also include rabbit and partridge (Minho)

–**de presunto/sardinhas** *–d prezoongtoo/suhrdeenyuhzh* **bola de carne** that includes a layer of prosciutto or sardines (Trás-os-Montes, Douro)

bolachas *boolahshuhzh* crackers; biscuits

bolachos *boolahshoosh* pig's blood made into a dumpling, served with the fatty cooking juices of **rojões**

bolas de ovos (gemas) *bohluhzh d ohvoozh (zhemuhzh)* threads of sweetened egg yolk wrapped in almond marzipan with an icing glaze (Algarve)

boleima *boolaymuh* small cakes made of bread dough filled with apple slices or chopped walnuts (Alentejo)

bolinhos *booleenyoozh* biscuits

–**de amêndoa** *–d uhmengdwuh* almond marzipan moulded into different shapes: vegetables, fruit, animals (Algarve)

–**de Jerimu** *–d zhreemoo* pumpkin cakes flavoured with cinnamon (Minho)

–**de pinhão** *–d peenyõw* pine nut cakes (Estremadura)

bolo *boloo* sweet or savoury cake; pastry

–**de amêndoa** *–d uhmengdwuh* two-layer cake made of ground almonds with **ovos moles** filling

–**de anos** *–d uhnoozh* birthday cake

–**de arroz** *–d uhrrozh* cake made with rice and wheat flour topped with sugar

–**de bolacha** *–d boolahshuh* biscuits layered with sweetened butter-cream frosting to form a cake

–**de caco** *–d kahkoo* griddle bread served hot with garlic butter (Madeira); sometimes cooked with a spicy **chouriço** inside

–**de casamento** *–d kuhzuhmengtoo* wedding cake

–**de chocolate** *–d shookoolaht* chocolate cake

–**de coco** *–d kokoo* coconut custard filled pastry tart; coconut macaroon

–**de Dom Rodrigo** *–d dong rroodreegoo* small, candy-like, moist, soft, confection made of **ovos reais**, **ovos moles** and ground almonds, wrapped in festive silver paper (Algarve)

–**de família** *–d fameelyuh* spice cake made with Madeira wine and glazed fruit (Madeira)

–**de laranja** *–d luhrangzhuh* orange cake

–**de mel** *–d mehl* rich, dense, molasses and spice cake studded with candied fruit and almonds (Madeira); light, fluffy molasses cake (Ribatejo)

–**de noz** *–d nohzh* walnut cake

–**de sertã** *–de sertang* corn biscuits cooked in a **sertã** (Azores)

–**do caco** *–doo kahkoo* flat breadrolls baked on a stone or cement slab (Madeira)

–**inglês** *–ing-glezh* 'English cake'; loaf cake with walnuts, almonds and dried fruit

–**lêvedos** *–levdoozh* light scone cooked in a **sertã** (Azores)

–**podre** *–podr* 'rotten cake'; lightly spiced honey cake (Alentejo)

–**príncipe** *–pringsep* 'prince's cake'; egg yolk and almond base covered with layers of **ovos reais**, pumpkin jam, **trouxas de ovos** and a layer of marzipan (Alentejo)

–**real** *–rreeahl* dense, moist cake made with lots of eggs, grated almonds, pumpkin jam; flavoured with cinnamon and lemon; decorated with **ovos reais** (Alentejo)

–rei *–rray* a favourite Christmas bread in the shape of a large ring, studded with walnuts, pine nuts, almonds and raisins, and decorated with glazed fruit, with a fava bean or lucky charm cooked into the dough

bombons *bongbongzh* bonbons

bonito *booneetoo* bonito

borrachões *boorruhshõyzh* fried ring-shaped biscuits flavoured with brandy or white wine and cinnamon (Alentejo)

borrachos *boorrahshoozh* breadcrumb fritters in a syrup of white **vinho verde**, lemon and cinnamon (Minho)

borrego *boorregoo* lamb; also called **anho**

–assado *–uhsahdoo* roast lamb, often flavoured with garlic, bay leaf and white wine

broa *brouh* bite sized sweet potato and almond 'cakes', halfway between a cake and a biscuit; corn bread common in the north of the country; also referred to as **broa de milho**, but more commonly just **broa**.

–de milho *–d meelyoo* corn bread (Minho)

–serrana *–serruhnuh* highland bread (Beiras)

broainhas (de natal) *brouheenyuhzh (d nuhtahl)* muffin-like pastry studded with raisins, pine nuts and walnuts, flavoured with cinnamon and aniseed; sold year round but associated with Christmas (Beiras)

broas castelares *brouhzh kuhshtlahrezh* soft, dense almond-shaped biscuit made of pureed almonds and sweet potatoes, lemon and orange (Estremadura)

broas de espécie *brouhzh d shpehsee-e* almond-shaped biscuit made of sweet potato, almond, coconut and coloured sprinkles

broas de mel *brouhzh d mehl* soft dense almond-shaped biscuit made of honey and flour, flavoured with lemon and cinnamon (Madeira)

bróculos *brohkooloozh* broccoli

bucho de porco *booshoo d porkoo* pig stomach

bucho doce *booshoo dos* dessert of **bucho de porco** stuffed with eggs, bread, sugar and cinnamon

bucho recheado *booshoo rresheeahdoo* pig's belly stuffed with pork, bread or rice and cloves or cumin; served sliced (Beiras, Ribatejo)

bufet de pratos quentes *boofe d prahtoosh kengtezh* hot buffet, usually found in upscale and hotel restaurants

bufet de saladas frias *boofe d suhlahduhsh freeuhzh* cold salad buffet often with vegetable, pasta and bean salads

bum-bum *boong-boong* tequila slammer; can be made with other spirits

burras *boorruhzh* roast pig cheeks

búzio *booziw* periwinkle; whelk

–com feijão *–kong fayzhõw* a dish of whelks cooked with kidney beans

C

cabeça de xara *kuhbesuh d shahruh* pig's head cooked with garlic, herbs and white wine; served sliced (Alentejo)

cabidela, à *ah kuhbeedehluh* any dish made with blood

cabrito *kuhbreetoo* kid (goat)

–à moda da Serra de Montezinho *–ah mohduh duh sehrruh de mongtzeenyoo* whole kid rubbed with a garlic and chilli paste, then wrapped in kale, cabbage or pumpkin leaves and cooked in an underground wood-burning pit (Trás-os-Montes)

–assado *–uhsahdoo* roast kid, usually with garlic, onion, bay leaf, parsley, white wine and paprika. In Alentejo it includes cloves; in Ribatejo it includes dried red chillies and **chouriço**; in the Minho it includes wine vinegar and is served with saffron rice.

–**com arroz à moda de Monção** *-kong uhrrozh ah mohduh d mongsõw* **cabrito assado** with beef, spicy sausage and saffron rice with ham

cacau *kuhkow* cocoa

–**magro em pó** *–mahgroo ãy poh* unsweetened cocoa powder

–**quente** *–kent* hot cocoa (beverage)

caça *kahsuh* game

cação *kuhsõw* dogfish

cacholeira *kuhshoolayruh* pork liver sausage

cachorro *kuhshorroo* small canned frankfurter served on a roll

cachucho *kuhshooshoo* Portuguese variety of a medium sized bream

café *kuhfeh* coffee (north); espresso coffee; cafe

–**cheio** *–shayoo* short black/espresso topped with hot water (north)

–**com leite** *–kong layt* medium sized cup of half milk and half filter coffee (north)

–**descafeinado** *–deshkuhfuheenahdoo* decaffeinated espresso coffee

–**duplo** *–dooploo* double espresso

–**em grão** *–ãy grão* coffee beans

–**instantâneo** *–ingshtangtuhniw* instant coffee

–**moído** *–mooeedoo* ground coffee

–**pingado** *–ping-gahdoo* short black/ espresso with a dash of cold milk

–**torrado** *–toorrahdoo* roast coffee

cafetaria *kuhftuhreeuh* coffee shop or cafeteria

cajú *kahzhoo* cashew

calda (de açúcar) *kahlduh (d uhsookahr)* syrup

caldeirada *kahldayrahduh* soup-like stew, usually but not always made with fish

–**à pescador** *–ah peshkuhdor* fisherman's stew, made by baking different types of fish in an earthenware dish with onions, tomatoes and other flavourings and served with hard or toasted bread

–**de feijão verde** *–d fayzhõw verd* soup or stew made with green beans, onion, tomatoes and potatoes; served over bread and with poached eggs (Ribatejo)

–**de peixe** *–d paysh* stew of fish and seafood in tomato and wine sauce

–**rica** *–rreekuh* rich fish stew, containing up to eight types of fish (Lisbon coast)

caldo *kahldoo* soup; broth

–**de castanhas piladas** *–d kuhshtuhnyuhsh peelahdas* soup of white beans, crushed chestnuts, rice and onion (Minho)

–**verde** *–verd* potato-based soup with shredded Galician kale and usually containing slices of garlic sausage

camarão *kuhmuhrõw* prawn

–**tigre** *–teegr* tiger prawn

campo *kangpoo* country

–**do ...** *–doo ...* free range; usually applied to chicken or turkey

caneca *kuhnehkuh* large glass of draught beer

canela *kuhnehluh* cinnamon

canja (caldo) de galinha *kangzhuh (kahldoo) d guhleenyuh* chicken broth

canja (sopa) de conquilhas *kangzhuh (sopuh) d kongkeelyuhzh* cockle soup

caracóis *kuhruhkoyzh* snails; usually simmered in broth, seasoned with oregano, bay leaf and parsley, and customarily eaten by removing the snail with a pin

caracol *kuhruhkohl* similar to a Danish pastry but with raisins or candied fruit

caramelo *kuhruhmehloo* caramel; hard candy

carapau *kuhruhpow* mackerel

–**limado** *–leemahdoo* skinned mackerel in olive oil and vinegar (or lemon) dressing; can be served with sliced onion, garlic and parsley (Alentejo)

carcaça *kuhrkahsuh* common type of breadroll made from refined wheat flour; also called **papo-seco**

caril *kuhreel* curry (powder)

–**de frango** *–d frang-goo* mild curry chicken
carioca *kuhreeohkuh* weak short black/espresso
–**de café** *–d kuhfeh* small sized weak café au lait
–**de limão** *–d leemõw* small sized lemon infusion
carne *kahrn* meat
–**assada** *–uhsahduh* roast meat, usually pork
–**de cavalo** *–d kuhvahloo* horse meat
–**de porco** *–d porkoo* pork
–**de porco à Alentejana** *–d porkoo ah alengtzhuhnuh* pork cubes marinated in a sweet pepper/capsicum paste, bay leaf, garlic and white wine, and simmered with onion and baby clams; served with deep-fried potato cubes
–**de porco à Portuguesa** *–d porkoo ah poortoogezuh* **carne de porco à Alentejana** without baby clams
–**de vaca** *–d vahkuh* beef
–**do alguidar** *–doo ahlgeedahr* chunks of pork cooked in a sweet pepper/capsicum paste and preserved in pork lard; served as an appetiser (Alentejo)
–**do alguidar com migas** *–doo ahlgeedahr kong meeguhzh* sauteed pork cutlets seasoned with sweet pepper/capsicum paste; served with **migas** made of bread and wild asparagus (Alentejo)
–**picada/passada** *–peekahduh/puhsahduh* ground meat
carneiro *kurnayroo* mutton
–**assado** *–uhsahdoo* roast mutton, seasoned with garlic, parsley, onion, bay leaves, garlic, sweet pepper/capsicum paste, paprika and white wine (Alentejo)
carnes frias *kahrnesh freeuhzh* cold cuts of meat
carta *kahrtuh* menu
–**de vinhos** *–d veenyoozh* wine list
carvão, no *kuhrvõw, noo* char-broiled
casa, à *ah kahzuh* house style; meat accompanied by rice, chips, salad and a fried egg
casa de chá *kahzuh d shah* teahouse selling pastries, sweets, coffee, and herbal and black teas
casa de pasto *kahzuh d pahshtoo* large dining rooms offering budget, three-course set menus
caseiro *kuhzayroo* home style
casta *kahshtuh* the type of grape used in wine making
castanhas *kuhshtuhnyuhzh* chestnuts
cataplana *kuhtuhpluhnuh* cooking pot that resembles two copper saute pans joined with a hinge and a lock to form an enclosed vessel; also the term for the classic seafood and sausage dish cooked in the vessel
cavacas *kuhvahkuhzh* large, dry, hollow, air-filled sweet biscuit with white sugar-icing (Caldas da Rainha)
cavalas *kuhvahluhzh* mackerel
cebola *sboluh* onion
cebolada, à *ah sboolahduh* basic saute of onion, garlic, olive oil and sometimes a bay leaf
celestes de Santa Clara *slehshtezh d sangtuh klahruh* petit four made of grated almonds and egg yolks baked in a thin wafer (Ribatejo)
cenoura *snoruh* carrot
cereal *sreeahl* cereal, grains or breakfast cereal
cereja *sruhzhuh* cherry (sweet)
cerveja *servuhzhuh* beer
–**à pressão** *–ah prsõw* on tap
–**loura** *–loruh* 'blonde beer'; regular beer, as opposed to stout
–**mista** *–meeshtuh* half dark beer and half regular beer
–**preta** *–pretuh* dark beer; stout
cervejaria *servzhuhreeuh* beer house (food also served)
chá *shah* tea
–**com limão** *–kong leemõw* black tea with thick strip of lemon peel
–**de camomila** *–d kuhmoomeeluh* chamomile tea
–**de ervas** *–d ehrvuhzh* herbal tea

–de jasmim *–d zhuzhming* jasmine tea
–de limão *–d leemõw* glass or cup of boiling water with a generous twist of lemon rind
–preto *–pretoo* black tea
–verde *–verd* green tea
champanhe *shangpuhny* champagne
chamuça *shumoosuh* samosa: triangular Indian pastry with spicy filling
chanfana *shangfuhnuh* hearty stew with goat or mutton in heavy red wine sauce
chantilly *shangteelyee* whipped cream; also called **natas batidas**
charcutaria *shuhrkootuhreeuh* delicatessen; food found in a delicatessen
charros alimados *shahrrooz uhleemahdoosh* skinned mackerel in olive oil and vinegar (or lemon) dressing; served with sliced onion, garlic and parsley (Alentejo)
chef *shehf* chef
chefe de mesa *shehf d mezuh* maître d'
chicharros *sheeshahrroozh* Azores term for small mackerel
chícharros *sheeshuhrroozh* Trás-os-Montes term for black-eyed peas
chila *sheeluh* spaghetti squash
chispe com feijão branco *sheeshp kong fayzhõw brangkoo* trotters with white beans, **chouriço**, pig's ear, kale and potatoes (Ribatejo)
chocolate *shookoolaht* chocolate
–branco *–brangkoo* white chocolate
–de leite *–d layt* milk chocolate
–preto *–pretoo* dark chocolate
chocos com/sem tinta *shohkoosh kong/sãy tingtuh* cuttlefish with/without ink
choquinhos *shookeenyoozh* a small type of cuttlefish
chouriço *shoreesoo* garlicky pork sausage flavoured with red pepper paste
–assado *–uhsahdoo* grilled sausage
–de sangue *–d sang-g* blood sausage
churrasco *shoorrahshkoo* grilled on a spit or skewer over hot coals, or barbecued
churrasqueira/churrascaria *shoorruhshkayruh/shoorruhshkuhreeuh* family style barbecue restaurant specialising in **frango no churrasco**
cimbalino *singbuhleenoo* term used in northern Portugal for espresso coffee
cinzeiro *singzayroo* ashtray
claras de ovos *klahruhzh d ohvoozh* egg whites
cobertura *koobertooruh* icing or topping
coco *kokoo* coconut
codorniz *koodoorneezh* quail
coelho *koouhlyoo* rabbit
–à caçador *–ah kuhsuhdor* 'hunter's style rabbit'; rabbit stewed with red and white wine and tomato
–em vinha d'alho *–ãy veenyuh d ahlyoo* baked rabbit set atop slices of fried bread, covered with onion slices and drizzled with port or white wine
coentrada *kooengtrahduh* sauce containing abundant amounts of coriander (Alentejo)
coentros *kooengtroozh* coriander
cogumelos *koogoomehloozh* mushrooms
colheita *koolyaytuh* vintage; harvest
colorau *kooloorow* sweet paprika
com todos *kong todoozh* 'with everything' (a dish with the lot)
cominhos *koomeenyoozh* cumin
compota *kongpohtuh* fruit preserve
confeitaria *kongfaytuhreeuh* patisserie
congelado/a *kongzhlahdoo/uh* frozen
conquilha *kongkeelyuh* cockle
conserva *kongsehrvuh* tinned/canned goods
conservante *kongservangt* preservatives of food
consomé *kongsome* consommé
corante *kohrangt* food colouring
cordeiro *koordayroo* mutton
corvina *koorveenuh* croaker fish; usually served as a fish steak
coscoréis *kooshkoorayzh* orange and brandy flavoured biscuit made in a biscuit iron (Beiras)
costeleta *kooshtletuh* chop

–de borrego *–d boorregoo* lamb chop
couve *kov* cabbage
–coração de boi *–kooruhsõw d boy* savoy cabbage
–de Bruxelas *–d brooshehluhzh* Brussels sprout
–flor *–flor* cauliflower
–galega *–guhleguh* a variety of kale from Galicia
–lombarda *–longbahrduh* white cabbage
–repolho *–rrpolyoo* variety of cabbage with crinkly leaves
–roxa *–rroshuh* purple cabbage
coxa de galinha *koshuh d guhleenyuh* fried, savoury chicken mixture, in the form of a drumstick
cozer *koozer* to cook or boil
cozida *koozeeduh* cooked/boiled
–de grão com vagens à Alentejana *–d grõw kong vahzhãyz ah uhlengtzhuhnuh* dinner of lamb, sausages, chickpeas, green beans, pumpkin squash and potatoes. The vegetables are served separately from the meats and the broth is served over slices of bread and flavoured with mint (Alentejo). In the Algarve version it is served with pasta instead of bread.
–de Lagoa das Furnas *–d luhgouh duhsh foornuhzh* **cozido à Portuguesa** cooked in a small volcanic crater, located in Lagoa das Furnas on São Miguel island (Azores)
cozido *koozeedoo* cooked/boiled
–à Portuguesa *–ah poortoogezuh* a hearty one dish meal made with chunks of different meats and sausages, vegetables, beans and rice
cozinha *koozeenyuh* kitchen
–tradicional *–truhdeesiwnahl* traditional cooking
cozinhado *koozeenyahdoo* cooked food
cozinheiro/a *koozeenyayroo/uh* cook; chef
cravinho *kruhveenyoo* cloves
creme de ... *krehm d ...* any soup made from pureed vegetables
–camarão/marisco *–kuhmuhrõw/ muhreeshkoo* spicy shellfish soup with a hint of tomato
–pasteleiro *–puhshtlayroo* egg-based cream filling used in pastries
crepe *krehp* crepe
–de galinha *–d guhleenyuh* chicken crepe, fried to a crisp
–de legumes *–d lgoomezh* vegetable crepe, fried to a crisp
croissant *krwasang* croissant
–com chocolate *–kong shookoolaht* chocolate-filled croissant
–com creme *–kong krehm* custard-filled croissant
–com fiambre *–kong feeangbr* croissant with ham
–com queijo *–kong kayzhoo* croissant with cheese
–misto *–meeshtoo* croissant with ham and cheese
croquete *krohkeht* meat croquette

D

delícia de batata *dleeseeuh d buhtahtuh* leftover mashed potato mixed with almonds and cinnamon and turned into little cakes (Ribatejo)
Delícia do Frei João *dleeseeuh doo fray zhoo-õw* seasonal fruit jam rich with walnuts, originally made by monks from Alcobaça (Estremadura)
delícias do mar *dleeseeuhzh doo mahr* crab sticks, actually made of compressed fish
desossado *dzosahdoo* boned
digestivo *deezhesteevoo* after-dinner drink, usually a liqueur, brandy or port
dobrada *doobrahduh* tripe with white beans and rice
DOC (Denominação de Origem Controlada) *de o ce (dnoomeenuhsõw d oreezhãy kongtroolahduh)* term for official wine region – demarcated wine region (designation of origin; *see* the Drinks chapter)

doce *dos* sweet; dessert; jam
–conventuais *–kongvengtwaish* conventual sweets; egg yolk and sugar based sweets introduced by the Moors and perfected by nuns in the convents during the 17th and 18th centuries. The exact recipes are closely guarded secrets.
–de abóbora *–d uhbohbooruh* pumpkin jam; often served as dessert with a slice of **requeijão**
–de amêndoa *–d uhmengdwuh* marzipan sweets
–de avó *–d uhvoh* (*see* **doce da casa**)
–de chila *–d sheelu* candied **chila** gourd, the base of many sweets
–de goiaba *–d goyahbuh* guava jam
–de ovos *–d ohvoosh* egg yolk sweets
–de tomate *–d toomaht* tomato jam
–do Algarve *–doo ahlgahrv* almond marzipan (*see also* **bolinhos de amêndoa**)
–regionais *–rregiwnaish* regional sweets
Domingos Gastronómicos *doominggozh guhshtroonohmeekoosh* Gastronomic Sundays; traditional regional dishes offered at certain restaurants in the Minho region on Sundays from February to May each year
dose *dohz* a large single portion
dourada *dorahduh* John Dory; gilt head bream
duchesse *diwshehz* puff pastry filled with whipped cream and topped with fruit or **fios de ovos**

E

edulcorante *eedoolkoorangt* sugar substitute; also called **adoçante**
empada *engpahduh* miniature pot pie
–de carne *–d kahrn* **empada** with meat filling
–de galinha *–d guhleenyuh* **empada** with chicken filling
–de legumes *–d lgoomezh* **empada** with vegetable filling
empadão *engpuhdõw* dish similar to shepherd's pie, often made with veal and topped with mashed potatoes
empregado/a de mesa *engpregahdoo/uh d mezuh* waiter; waitress
encharcada *engshuhrkahduh* cooked egg yolks in a sugary syrup, decorated with cinnamon (Alentejo)
enchido *engsheedoo* any one of a variety of sausages
engarrafado na origem/quinta *engguhrruhfahdoo nuh oreezhãy/kingtuh* estate-bottled wine; grapes grown and bottled on the one estate
engarrafado por ... *eng-guhrruhfahdoo poor ...* wine bottled by ...
enguia *eng-geeuh* eel
ensopado de borrego *engsoopahdoo d boorregoo* lamb stew served on toasted or deep-fried bread (Alentejo)
ensopado de enguias *engsoopahdoo d eng-geeuhzh* eel stew served on toasted or deep-fried bread (Ribatejo)
entrada *engtrahduh* entree
entrecosto *engtrekoshtoo* pork ribs
–com feijão e arroz *–kong fayzhõw ee uhrrozh* pork ribs with beans and rice
entrecôte *engtrekot* sirloin steak
erva-doce *ehrvuh-dos* aniseed
ervas *ehrvuhsh* herbs
–aromáticas *–uhroomahteekuhzh* mixture of cooking herbs
ervilhas *eerveelyuhzh* peas
–com ovos escalfados *–kong ohvooz shkahlfahdoozh* peas and slices of **chouriço** cooked with lard, olive oil, onions and parsley and served with poached eggs
escabeche *shkuhbehsh* 'vinegar stew'; raw meat or fish (often sardines, tuna and baby mackerel) pickled in olive oil, vinegar, garlic and a bay leaf and left for up to two days before serving
escalfado *shkahlfahdoo* poached
escalopes *shkuhlohpezh* medallion-shaped, high quality cuts of boneless meat
espadarte *shpuhdahrt* swordfish
–fumado *–foomahdoo* smoked swordfish
espanhola, à *ah shpuhnyohluh* dish in tomato and onion sauce

espargos *shpahrgoozh* asparagus
–bravo *–brahvoo* wild asparagus
–bravos com ovos *–brahvoosh kong ohvoozh* asparagus with an egg yolk and bread mixture; served with **chouriço** or strips of fried bacon
esparguete *shpahrgeht* spaghetti
esparregado de espinafres *shpuhrrgahdoo d shpeenahfrezh* pureed spinach or other greens flavoured with garlic, onion and olive oil
especialidade da casa *shpeseeuhleedahd duh kahzuh* house speciality
especiarias *shpeseeuhreeuhzh* spices
espetada *shpetahduh* kebab
–à Madeirense *–ah muhdayrengs* thick chunks of marinated beef served on a large skewer hung upside-down, with a large knob of slowly melting herbed butter on top of the skewer (Madeira)
–de lulas *–d looluhzh* squid kebab
–de tamboril *–d tangbooreel* monkfish kebab
–mista *–meeshtuh* mixed grill kebab; chunks of veal and/or pork, separated by bacon or sausage slices, green capsicum and onion
espeto, no *shpetoo, noo* on a skewer
espinafres *shpeenahfrezh* spinach
espumante *shpoomangt* sparkling wine
estopeta de atum *shtoopetuh d uhtoong* flakes of tuna, slices of onion, tomatoes and green capsicum in an olive oil and vinegar dressing
estragão *shtruhgõw* tarragon
estufado/a *shtoofahdoo/uh* stewed
estufar *shtoofahr* to stew

F

faisão *faizõw* pheasant
faneca *fuhnehkuh* whiting; small fish that are usually fried
farinha *fuhreenyuh* flour
farinheira *fuhreenyayruh* sausage stuffed with spiced, flour-based mixture that often includes bits of pork fat
farófias *fuhrohfeeuhzh* dessert of beaten egg whites in a custard sauce
farripas de laranja *fuhrreepuhzh d luhrangzhuh* chocolate-covered strips of orange peel
farturas *fuhrtooruhzh* deep-fried dough swirls cut and rolled in sugar and cinnamon; usually found at fairs and local festivities
fataça na telha *fuhtahsuh nuh tuhlyuh* mullet seasoned with chopped onion, parsley, paprika and bacon, and cooked between two clay roof tiles buried in embers (Ribatejo)
fatias *fuhteeuhzh* slices
–da China/Tomar *–duh sheenuh/toomahr* steam-cooked loaf made of whipped egg yolks and sugar (Ribatejo)
–douradas *–dorahduhsh (rruhbuhnahduhzh)* slices of bread soaked in milk, dipped in eggs, fried, smothered in a sweet syrup and topped with cinnamon; also called **rabanadas**
–reais *–rreaizh* bread slices dipped in beaten egg yolk, cooked in sugar syrup and topped with pumpkin jam; served cold (Estremadura)
fava *fahvuh* broad bean
favada à Portuguesa *fuhvahduh ah poortoogezuh* stew of fava beans, sausage and sometimes poached eggs
fava-rica *fahvuh-rreekuh* fava bean soup with garlic and vinegar (Estremadura)
favas à Algarvia *fahvuhz ah ahlguhrveeuh* fava beans cooked with blood sausage, bacon, sometimes **chouriço** and mint (Algarve)
favas guisadas *fahvuhsh geezahduhzh* fava bean stew with **chouriço**, coriander and garlic; served over bread slices and garnished with shredded lettuce, coriander, mint, olive oil and vinegar (Alentejo)
febras *februhzh* thin pork cutlets, grilled or sauteed
feijão *fayzhõw* bean
–branco *–brangkoo* white bean

DICTIONARY

–branco com búzio *–brangkoo kong booziw* white beans cooked with dog whelk (Algarve)
–catarino *–kuhtuhreenoo* pinto bean
–de vaca *–d vahkuh* cow pea
–encarnado *–engkuhrnahdoo* red bean
–frade *–frahd* black-eyed pea
–manteiga *–mangtayguh* butter bean
–preto *–pretoo* black bean
feijoada *fayzhwaduh* hearty bean stew with sausages or other meat. Each region has its own variation.
fermento *fermengtoo* any kind of leavening agent
–de padeiro *–d pahdayroo* yeast
–em pó *–ãy poh* baking powder
ferraduras *ferruhdooruhzh* horseshoe-shaped pastry, sometimes layered with candied fruit
fiambre *feeangbr* pale, lightly smoked boiled ham used as a sliced snack or sandwich filling
fígado *feeguhdoo* liver
figo *feegoo* fig
figos cheios *feegoosh shayoosh* dried figs studded with almonds (Algarve)
filete *feeleht* fish fillet
–de pescada *–d peshkahduh* breaded and fried hake fillet
filhós *feelyohzh* a puffy fried dough, usually sprinkled with cinnamon and sugar; sometimes has pumpkin pulp mixed into the dough
Fino *feenoo* small glass of draught beer
fios de ovos *feeoozh d ohvoosh* egg yolks strained into boiling sugar syrup to make strands of sweet, bright golden egg, which is then used as a base for other sweets; also called **ovos reais**
focinho de porco *fooseenyoo d porkoo* pig's snout
folar *foolahr* brioche dough baked with chicken, spicy sausages and **presunto**; sold at Easter
–de valpaços *–d vahlpahsoosh* bread dough filled with layers of meat (such as chicken, **salpicão**, **presunto** or **chouriço**) and parsley (Trás-os-Montes)
folhado de carne *foolyahdoo d kahrn* puff pastry with meat filling or a sausage
folhado de salsicha *foolyahdoo d sahlseeshuh* puff pastry with sausage filling
formigos *foormeegoosh* sweetmeats; a thick paste of soaked hard bread or biscuit with egg yolks, sugar, honey, milk, cinnamon and wine, cooked slowly over low heat until egg just sets
forno, no *fornoo, noo* oven baked
framboesa *frangbwezuh* raspberry
francesinha *frangsezeenyuh* sandwich with ham, sausage and cheese, smothered in a tomato-cream sauce (Porto)
frango *frang-goo* chicken
–assado *–uhsahdoo* roast chicken
–no churrasco *–noo shoorrahshkoo* chargrilled chicken seasoned with garlic, bay leaf, paprika and olive oil
fresco/a *freshkoo/uh* fresh; cool; cold
fricassé, à *ah freekuhseh* dish with egg yolk and lemon juice sauce
frigideira *freezheedayruh* frying pan or skillet
frio/a *freeoo/uh* cold
frito/a *freetoo/uh* deep-fried; sauteed
fruta *frootuh* fruit
–cristalizada *–kreeshtuhleezahduh* candied/glazed fruit
–da época *–duh ehpookuh* seasonal fruit
frutos secos *frootoosh sekoozh* dried fruit and nuts
fumado *foomahdoo* smoked
fumeiro *foomayroo* smokehouse; a place where meats are smoked; often includes a small tavern at the back offering simple meals
funcho *foongshoo* dill

G

galão *guhlõw* large glass of hot milk with a dash of filter coffee
–bem escuro *–bãy shkooroo* stronger version of **galão**

–claro *–klahroo* milkier version of **galão**
–de máquina *–d mahkeenuh* espresso coffee with milk served in a glass
galinha *guhleenyuh* hen
–do campo *–doo kangpoo* free range chicken
gambas *gangbuhzh* prawns
–fritas com alho *–freetuhsh kong ahlyoo* prawns sauteed in garlic, sometimes with chilli
garoto *guhrotoo* ready-made filter coffee topped with warm or hot milk
garoupa *guhropuh* grouper
garrafa *guhrrahfuh* bottle
–de meio litro *–d mayoo leetroo* half-litre bottle
–de um litro *–d oong leetroo* litre bottle
–pequena *–pkenuh* small bottle
garrafão *guhrruhfõw* 5L vessel
garum *guhroong* fermented fish paste, probably introduced by the Romans, and used as a flavouring (Sétubal)
gaspacho *guhshpahshoo* chilled tomato and garlic bread soup flavoured with olive oil, vinegar and oregano, and which may also include cucumber and capsicum. Minced **chouriço**, **paio** or **presunto** may be added.
geladaria *zhluhduhreeuh* ice cream shop
gelado *zhlahdoo* ice cream
–copo *–kohpoo* ice cream in a cup
–uma/duas/três bolas *–oomuh/doouhzh/trezh bohluhzh* one/two/three scoops of ice cream
gelatina *zheluhteenuh* gelatine
geleia *zhelayuh* jelly
gelo *zheloo* ice
gemas *zhemuhzh* egg yolks
gengibre *zhengzheebr* ginger
gila *zheeluh* spaghetti squash
ginja *zhingzhuh* sour cherry
ginjinha *zhingzheenyuh* liqueur made from sour cherries
goiaba *goyahbuh* guava
goiabada *goyuhbahduh* guava jam
gomas *gomuhzh* gum drops
goraz *goorahzh* common sea bream
gorjeta *goorzhetuh* tip; gratuity
grão (de bico) *grõw (d beekoo)* chick-peas; garbanzo beans
gratinado *gruhteenahdoo* au gratin (a cooked dish topped with breadcrumbs and browned)
grelhado/a *grelyahdoo/uh* grilled
groselha *grozuhlyuh* gooseberry; gooseberry syrup
guardanapo *gwuhrduhnahpoo* 'napkin'; a jelly roll cake cut into squares and folded in half like a napkin, filled with **creme de pasteleiro**
guarnecido *gwuhrnseedoo* garnished with pickled cauliflower, carrots, onion and sometimes olives
guisado/a *geezahdoo/uh* braised

H

hipermercado *eepehrmerkahdoo* hypermarket, selling grocery items and larger goods
hortaliça *ortuhleesuh* vegetables
–cozida *–koozeeduh* boiled green leafy vegetables
–salteada *–sahlteeahduh* sautéed green leafy vegetables
hortelã *ortlang* mint

I

imperador *ingpruhdor* redfish
imperial *ingpreeahl* medium sized glass of draft beer
inhame *eenyuhm* yams
insosso *ingsosoo* bland; not salty enough
iogurte *eeohgoort* yoghurt
–líquido *–leekeedoo* liquid yoghurt
IPR (Indicação de Proveniênca Regulamentada) *ee pe ehrr (ingdeekuhsõw d proovnee-engseeuh rrgooluhmengtahduh* term for official wine region – indication of regulated provenance (*see* the Drinks chapter)
iscas *eeshkuhzh* pork liver
–com elas *–kong ehluhzh* pork liver marinated in white wine, vinegar, garlic

DICTIONARY

and bay leaf, then sliced, fried and served with sliced boiled potatoes (Estremadura)

Italiana *eetuhleeuhnuh* short shot of espresso coffee

J

jantar *zhangtahr* dinner

jardineira *zhuhrdeenayruh* hearty beef and vegetable stew

jardineira, à *ah zhuhrdeenayruh* a type of vegetable stew

javali *zhuhvuhlee* wild boar

jesuítas *zhezooeetuhzh* triangular-shaped puff pastry with baked meringue icing

joaquinzinhos *zhoouhkingzeenyoozh* term used for small fried mackerel

joelho no forno *zhwelyoo noo fornoo* 'knee'; roast leg of pork (Beiras)

K

kiwi *keevee* kiwi(fruit)

L

lagosta *luhgoshtuh* lobster

–suada à moda de Peniche *–swaduh ah mohduh d pneesh* lobster steamed in a casserole, layered with onion, parsley, tomatoes and garlic; flavoured with nutmeg, paprika, chilli, brandy, white wine and port (Estremadura)

lagostim *luhgooshting* crayfish

lampreia *langprayuh* lamprey

–à moda do Minho *–ah mohduh doo meenyoo* lamprey cooked in a sauce of red wine, diced **presunto** and lamprey blood; flavoured with parsley, bay leaf and garlic; served over slices of toast (Minho)

–de ovos *–d ohvoozh* rich egg-almond paste shaped like a lamprey and surrounded by swirls of **ovos reais**

lanche *langsh* afternoon snack

lapas *lahpuhsh* limpets, an intensely marine flavoured shellfish popular on the island archipelagos, often grilled with garlic butter and served on the half shell

laranja *luhrangzhuh* orange

lata *lahtuh* can

Late Bottled Vintage (LBV) *layt bohtl vangtahzh (ehl be ve)* port of a single year that's ready for immediate consumption. LBV is aged longer in wood than vintage port.

lavagante *luhvuhgangt* rock lobster

lebre *lehbr* hare

–com feijão branco *–kong fayzhõw brangkoo* hare and white bean stew flavoured with garlic, onion and coriander

legumes *lgoomezh* vegetables

leitão *laytõw* suckling pig roasted in a woodfired oven; can be served hot or cold

leite *layt* milk

–condensado *–kongdengsahdoo* condensed milk

–creme *–krehm* custard cream, sometimes flavoured with lemon, topped with caramelised sugar (similar to crème brûlée but not as rich)

–gordo *–gordoo* whole milk

–magro *–mahgroo* skim milk

–meio gordo *–mayoo gordoo* reduced fat milk

levedura *lvedooruh* yeast

licor *leekor* liqueur

–Beirão *–bayrõw* brand of well-known liqueur made of mountain herbs and seeds (Beiras)

–de amêndoa amarga *–d uhmengdwuh uhmahrguh* almond flavoured liqueur; also called **amarguinha**

–de gemas *–d zhemuhzh* egg-based liqueur

–de ginja *–d zhingzhuh* cherry liqueur

–de maçã *–d muhsang* apple flavoured liqueur

–de maracuja *–d muhruhkoozhah* passionfruit liquor (Madeira)

–de mel *–d mehl* honey flavoured liqueur

DICTIONARY

lima *leemuh* lime
limão *leemõw* lemon
língua *ling-gwuh* tongue
–de bacalhau *–d buhkuhlyow* deep-fried, thin strips of salt cod served in vinaigrette dressing with chopped boiled egg and parsley (Beiras)
–de gato *–d gahtoo* very small, hard vanilla biscuit
–de veado *–d veeahdoo* a wafer thin vanilla biscuit
linguado *ling-gwahdoo* sole
–à (la) Meunière *–ah (lah) muhnee-ehrr* lightly pan-fried sole sprinkled with parsley and lemon juice; served with clarified butter
linguiça *ling-gwisuh* thin, long garlicky sausage
–com inhame *–kong eenyuhm* thin, long garlicky sausage with yams (Azores)
lombinhos de porco *longbeenyoozh d porkoo* thinly sliced pork tenderloin
lombo de porco assado *longboo d porkoo uhsahdoo* roast pork loin
louro *loroo* bay leaf
lulas *looluhzh* squid
–à Sevilhana *–ah sveelyuhnuh* fried squid rings served with mayonnaise
–cheias *–shayuhzh* small squid stuffed with a mixture of rice, tomatoes, **presunto** and parsley
–recheadas *–rrsheeahduhzh* (*see* **lulas cheias**)

M

maçã *muhsang* apple
–assada *–uhsahduh* baked apple
Madeirense, à *ah muhdayrengs* Madeira style; a dish cooked with tomatoes, onion and garlic. Bananas or Madeira wine are sometimes added.
maduro/a *muhdooroo/uh* ripe (fruit); mature (wine)
magusto com bacalhau assado *muhgooshtoo kong buhkuhlyow uhsahdoo* **açorda** mixed with red or pinto beans and cabbage, served with roasted salt cod (Ribatejo)
maionese *maiohnehz* mayonnaise
malagueta *muhluhgetuh* red hot chilli peppers; also called **piri piri**
malandrinho *muhlangdreenyoo* soupy rice
mandioca *mangdeeohkuh* manioc
maneira, à *muhnayruh, ah* in the manner of
manga *mang-guh* mango
manjar branco *mangzhahr brangkoo* clove flavoured pudding, originating from a very traditional recipe for roast chicken coated in egg and fried, served atop bread that has been dipped in egg and fried, with cinnamon and sugar syrup poured over the top
manjerona *mangzheronuh* marjoram
manteiga *mangtayguh* butter
mão de vaca guisada *mõw d vahkuh geezahduh* stew of cow's feet, chickpeas, tomatoes, onion, garlic **chouriço**, parsley and white wine (Estremadura)
maracujá *muhruhkoozhah* passionfruit
maranhos *muhruhnyoozh* pork belly stuffed with lamb, **presunto**, **chouriço**, wine and rice; similar to haggis but with rice (Beiras)
margarina *muhrguhreenuh* margarine
marinar *muhreenahr* to marinate
marisco *muhreeshkoo* shellfish
marmelada *muhrmlahduh* firm quince paste
marmota *muhrmohtuh* European hake (type of small hake)
marisqueira *muhreeshkayruh* seafood restaurant
Massa *mahsuh* pasta or dough
–de amêndoa *–d uhmengdwuh* almond marzipan that is undecorated
–de doce regional *–d dos rrzhiwnahl* (*see* **massa de amêndoa**)
–de pimentão *–d peemengtõw* marinating and basting paste of roasted sweet red capsicums, crushed with garlic and olive oil (Alentejo)

–**folhada** *–foolyahduh* flaky pastry
–**obreia** *–obrayuh* thin, unleavened dough used for making pastries
–**quebrada** *–kbrahduh* dough made from flour, water and margarine
–**sovada** *–soovahduh* Portuguese sweet bread (Azores)
–**frita** *–freetuh* doughnut-type mix squirted in huge spirals into hot oil and deep-fried, then rolled, still hot, in cinnamon and sugar (Alentejo)
massapão *muhsuhpõw* flattened balls of almond marzipan cooked into little wafers and topped with an almond (Minho)
medalhão *mduhlyõw* medallion of meat/fish
medronho *mdronyoo* (*see* **aguardente de medronho**)
medronheira *medroonyayruh* honey-sweetened **medronho** (Algarve)
meia de leite *mayuh d layt* medium sized cup of half milk and half filter coffee (south)
–**de máquina** *–d mahkeenuh* medium sized cup of half espresso coffee and half milk (south)
–**directa** *–deerehtuh* medium sized cup of half milk and half espresso coffee (north)
meia dose *mayuh dohz* half serve/portion
meia garrafa *mayuh guhrrahfuh* half bottle of wine (375ml)
mel *mehl* honey
–**de abelha** *–d uhbelyuh* honey from bees
–**de cana** *–d kuhnuh* 'honey' from cane sugar (ie, like molasses)
melaço *mlahsoo* molasses
melancia *mlangseeuh* watermelon
melão *mlõw* melon; honeydew melon
–**com presunto** *–kong prezoongtoo* slices of honeydew melon topped with thin slices of **presunto**
meloa *mlouh* cantaloupe/rockmelon
–**com vinho do porto** *–kong veenyoo doo portoo* cantaloupe/rockmelon with port
melosa *melohzuh* mixed drink of brandy and honey (Algarve)
mercado *merkahdoo* market
merenda *mrengduh* snack; light lunch; picnic lunch; sweet tasting bread containing melted cheese and a slice of ham
merengue *mreng-g* meringue
mexilhões *msheelyõyzh* mussels
migas *meeguhzh* a side dish with many varieties, most including some form of bread flavoured with olive oil, garlic and spices, and fried
–**à Manuel Pescador** *–ah muhnwel peshkuhdor* (*see* **migas de bacalhau**)
–**de bacalhau** *–d buhkuhlyow* **migas** made with white bread, corn bread, shredded salt cod, onion, tomatoes, garlic, red sweet pepper/capsicum paste and coriander; traditionally served with grilled eels
–**de batata** *–d buhtahtuh* side dish made of mashed potatoes flavoured with bacon, sausage and garlic, shaped into round balls. Tomato puree may be added. (Alentejo)
mil folhas *meel folyuhzh* layers of flaky pastry with custard filling
milho doce *meelyoo dos* sweet corn
milho frito *meelyoo freetoo* cubes of fried white cornmeal served with skewers of grilled meat or poultry (Madeira)
Minhota, à *ah meenyotuh* Minho style; a dish with plenty of ham, and possibly **vinho verde**
Mini *meenee* 100ml bottle of beer
minimercado *meeneemerkahdoo* small convenience store
mini-prato *meenee-prahtoo* very small serving
miolos (**de porco**) *meeohloozh (d porkoo)* (pork) brains
míscaros *meeshkuhroosh* shiitake-like mushrooms

–com ovos *–kong ohvoozh* **míscaros** sauteed in olive oil with onion, diced pork, paprika and beaten eggs (Beiras)
miudezas *miwdezuhzh* giblets
moda, à *ah mohduh* in the style of
moda da casa, à *ah mohduh duh kahzuh* house-style; meat dish accompanied by rice, chips, salad and a fried egg
moelas *mweluhzh* chicken gizzards
molho *molyoo* sauce; gravy; dressing
–branco *–brangkoo* white sauce
–de caramelo *–d kuhruhmehloo* caramel sauce
–de cocktail *–d kohktayl* sauce made from mayonnaise, tomato sauce and a dash of whisky
–de manteiga *–d mangtayguh* butter sauce
–inglês *–ing-glezh* Worcestershire sauce
–verde *–verd* sauce for fish or octopus made with chopped onion, garlic, red capsicum, parsley, vinegar and lots of olive oil; whisked with a fork
Monte *mongt* cheese made from the milk of cows and ewes (Trás-os-Montes)
morangos *moorang-goozh* strawberries
morcela *moorsehluh* blood sausage
–de arroz *–d uhrrozh* blood sausage with rice (Ribatejo)
–de sangue *–d sang-g* blood sausage
–de São Miguel com ananás *–d sõw meegehl kong uhnuhnahzh* blood sausage served with a slice of pineapple (Azores)
moreia *moorayuh* moray
morgadinhos de amêndoa *moorguhdeenyoozh d uhmengdwuh* almond marzipan that is moulded into elaborate shapes, larger than the **bolinhos de amêndoa**; can depict, among other creations, a sow surrounded by piglets or birds in a nest (Algarve)
morgadinhos de figo *moorguhdeenyoozh d feegoo* **morgadinhos de amêndoa** made from finely chopped figs and chocolate and flavoured with lemon and aniseed (Algarve)
morgados *mohrgahdoosh* sweetmeats made with almonds and figs (Algarve)
moscatel *mooshkuhtehl* topaz-coloured, sweet dessert wine
mostarda *mooshtahrduh* mustard
mousse *moos* mousse
–de ananás *–d uhnuhnahzh* pineapple mousse
–de chocolate *–d shookoolaht* chocolate mousse
–de morango *–d moorang-goo* strawberry mousse

N

na brasa *nuh brahzuh* char-grilled
na chapa *nuh shahpuh* cooked on a hot steel plate
na pedra *nuh pehdruh* meat or fish grilled on a hot stone at the table
na púcara *nuh pookuhruh* chicken or duck cooked in a clay pot with **presunto**, tomatoes, onion, port, brandy, white wine, bay leaves and garlic
nabiça *nuhbeesuh* turnip greens
nabo *nahboo* turnip
naco *nahkoo* thick cut of meat
–na pedra *–nuh pehdruh* thick cut of meat grilled on a hot stone at the table
natas *nahtuhzh* cream
–batidas *–buhteeduhzh* whipped cream; also called **chantilly**
néctar de ... *nehktahr d ...* fruit juice with added water and sugar
negro *negroo* type of sausage made from blood rather than meat (Ribatejo)
nêspera *neshpruh* loquat
novilho *nooveelyoo* veal
noz *nozh* walnut
noz moscada *nozh mooshkahduh* nutmeg

O

óleo *ohliw* oil
–alimentar *–uhleemengtahr* cooking oil
–de amendoim *–d uhmengdooing* peanut oil

–de girassol *–d zheeruhsohl* sunflower seed oil
–de milho *–d meelyoo* corn oil
–de soja *–d sohzhuh* soybean oil
–vegetal *–vzhetahl* vegetable
omelete *ohmleht* omelette
orégãos *orehgõwzh* oregano
orelha de porco de coentrada *oorelyuh d porkoo d koengtrahduh* sliced pig's ear seasoned with garlic and lots of coriander, tossed in olive oil and vinegar dressing; served cold (Alentejo)
ostra *oshtruh* oyster
ovas (de pescada) *ohvuhzh (d peshkahduh)* fish eggs, usually hake
ovo *ovoo* egg
–cozido *–koozeedoo* boiled egg
–de chocolate *–d shookoolaht* chocolate Easter egg
–escalfado *–shkahlfahdoo* poached egg
–estrelado *–shtrelahdoo* fried egg
–mexido *–msheedoo* scrambled egg
ovos moles *ohvoozh mohlezh* sweetened egg yolks thickened to a soft creamy texture; can be eaten plain or used in desserts
ovos reais *ohvoozh rreaizh* cooked egg threads; also called **fios de ovos**
ovos verdes *ohvoosh verdzh* boiled and halved eggs stuffed with a mixture of egg yolks, butter and parsley, coated in flour and fried

P

pá *pah* front leg of an animal
padaria *pahduhreeuh* bakery
padeira, à *ah pahdayruh* dish baked in an earthenware casserole and served with roast potatoes
padeira/o *ah pahdayruh/oh* person who bakes bread
paio *paioo* smoked pork tenderloin sausage
palmier *pahlmee-e* flat, palm-shaped puff pastry
–coberto *–koobehrtoo* **palmier** with icing
–recheado *–rresheeahdoo* two **palmiers** sandwiched with egg-based filling
–simples *–singplezh* plain **palmier**
panado/a *puhnahdoo/uh* breaded; pork cutlets that are breaded
panela do forno *punehluh doo fornoo* casserole of tripe, trotters, pig's ear, bacon, **presunto** and rice, garnished with slices of **chouriço** and **farinheira** (Beiras)
pão *põw* bread
–caseiro *–kuhzayroo* bread that may or may not have been baked on the premises of an eatery
–centeio do sabugueiro *–d sengtayoo doo suhboogayroo* type of rye bread particular to the town of Sabugueiro (Beiras)
–com chouriço *–kong shoreesoo* bread-roll baked with **chouriço** slices
–da casa *–duh kahzuh* 'house bread'; bread that may or may not have been baked on the premises of an eatery
–de Alfeizerão *–d ahlfayzrõw* moist sponge cake with a rich, runny egg filling in the middle; looks like a caved-in cake (Estremadura)
–de centeio *–d sengtayoo* light rye bread
–de Deus *–d de-wzh* dome-shaped sweet bread with a coconut topping
–de forma *–d formuh* loaf of bread; cake pan/mould
–de leite *–d layt* sweet roll made with wheat flour, eggs and milk
–de milho *–d meelyoo* corn bread
–de mistura *–d meeshtooruh* wheat and barley bread
–de rala *–d rrahluh* round bread made of dough with crushed almonds and filled with pumpkin jam, **ovos reais** and **ovos moles**; can include grated chocolate (Alentejo)
–de trigo *–d treegoo* wheat-flour bread
–de-ló *–d-loh* collapsed sponge cake, runny in the centre
–doce *–dos* cinnamon and saffron flavoured biscuit rings (Minho)

–integral *–ingtegrahl* wholegrain bread
–rolado *–rroolahdoo* breadcrumbs
papaia *puhpaiuh* papaya
papas *pahpuhzh* gruel
–de milho *–d meelyoo* cornmeal porridge; can be served with shellfish, **chouriço** or other meat
–de sarrabulho *–d suhrruhboolyoo* porridge made of chicken, pig's liver, heart and blood (Minho)
papos-de-anjo *pahpoozh-d-angzhoo* little egg-based puffs in a sugar syrup
papo-seco *pahpoo-sekoo* most common type of breadroll made from refined wheat flour; also called **carcaça**
pargo *pahrgoo* sea bream
passas *pahsuhzh* raisins
pastéis *puhshtayzh* pastries (plural); can also refer to small savoury fritters such as **pastéis de bacalhau**) or something that looks more like a pie
–de bacalhau *–d buhkuhlyow* deep-fried, oval-shaped savouries made of mashed potato, onion, parsley and salt cod
–de feijão *–d fayzhõw* rich lima bean and almond mixture in flaky pastry shells, with a caramelised sugar crust on top
–de massa tenra *–d mahsuh tengrruh* moon-shaped, meat-filled pastries that are fried
–de molho *–d molyoo* baked pastry filled with ground beef and onion; served in a saffron and vinegar flavoured broth (Beiras)
–de nata/Belém *–d nahtuh/ blãy* egg custard tarts with flaky pastry shell, famously made by Lisbon's Antiga Confeitaria de Belém **confeitaria**, and all over the country
–de Santa Clara (do Convento de Coimbra) *–d sangtuh klahruh (doo kongvengtoo d kooingbruh)* moon-shaped pastry crusts filled with grated almonds in an egg yolk and sugar paste (Beiras)
–de Tentúgal *–d tengtoogahl* crepe-shaped flaky pastries with a filling of creamy egg yolk and sugar paste
–de toucinho *–d toseenyoo* small flaky pastry tarts filled with a mixture of ground almonds, egg yolks and a piece of bacon (Alentejo)
pastel *puhshtehl* pastry (singular)
–de Molho da Covilhã *d molyoo duh kooveelyang* soupy meal in a bowl; flaky layers of crisp lard pastry covered in a saffron broth soured with vinegar (Covilhã)
pastelaria *puhshtluhreeuh* pastry shop; coffee shop; pastries
pataniscas de bacalhau *puhtuhneeshkuhzh d buhkuhlyow* seasoned salt cod fritters
pato *pahtoo* duck
pé de porco com feijão branco *peh d porkoo kong fayzhõw brangkoo* stew made from pig's feet with white beans, onion, parsley, bay leaf and **massa de pimentão**
peito de frango *paytoo d frang-goo* breast of chicken
peixe *paysh* fish
–assado no forno *–uhsahdoo noo fornoo* baked fish
–espada *–shpahduh* scabbard fish
–frito *–freetoo* fried fish
–na cataplana *–nuh kuhtuhpluhnuh* fish cooked in a **cataplana**
peixinhos da horta *paysheenyoozh duh ohrtuh* green beans fried in a light batter (Estremadura)
pepino *p-peenoo* cucumber
pequeno-almoço *pkenoo ahlmosoo* breakfast
pêra *peruh* pear
–bêbeda *–bebuhduh* 'drunken pear'; fresh whole pear stewed in a red wine and syrup sauce
perceves *persehvzh* barnacles
perdiz *perdeezh* partridge
–à vapor *–ah vuhpor* braised partridge cooked with wine, vinegar, parsley, cloves and lots of garlic (Algarve)

–estufada *–shtoofahduh* stewed partridge cooked with wine, vinegar, parsley, cloves and lots of garlic (Algarve)
perna de ... *pehrnuh d ...* leg of ...
pernil no forno *perneel noo fornoo* roast leg of pork (Beiras)
peru *peroo* turkey
pescada *peshkahduh* whiting
pescadinhas de rabo na boca *pehskuhdeenyuhzh d rrahboo nuh bokuh* small whiting fried with their tails in their mouths
pêssego *pesgoo* peach
petingas *pting-guhzh* small sardines
petiscos *pteeshkoozh* appetisers including sausages, cheese and **presunto**; also includes a variety of small meat dishes
pezinhos de porco *pzeenyoozh d porkoo* pig's feet flavoured with coriander, garlic and onion (Alentejo)
picanha *peekuhnyuh* Brazil-style thin cut of rump steak accompanied by chips, black beans, boiled white rice, garnished with manioc (fried in bacon fat) and sometimes fried banana
picante *peekangt* spicy or hot; any spicy or hot sauce
pimenta *peemengtuh* pepper
–branca *–brangkuh* white pepper
–cayenne *–kaiehn* cayenne
–da Jamaica *–duh zhuhmaikuh* allspice
–preta *–pretuh* black pepper
pimento *peemengtoo* (sweet) pepper/capsicum
–verde *–verd* green capsicum
–vermelho *–vermuhlyoo* red capsicum
pimentos assados *peemengtooz uhsahdoozh* roast capsicum
pinhão *peenyõw* pine nut
pipis *peepeezh* stewed chicken giblets; flavoured with garlic, onion, paprika, white wine and chilli; served as a snack or appetiser (Estremadura)
piri piri *peereepeeree* red hot chilli peppers; sauce made from red hot chilli peppers; also called **malagueta**
–amendoims *–uhmengdooingsh* chilli peanuts, sold at snack bars
pito de Santa Luzia *peetoo d sangtuh loozeeuh* sweet made from rich yeast dough filled with sugar, cinnamon and pumpkin; women offer them to their husbands and lovers on 13 December in anticipation of either a good time, or fertile results
polme *polm* batter
polpa *polpuh* fruit or vegetable pulp
–de fruta *–d frootuh* fruit pulp
–de tomate *–d toomaht* tomato pulp
polvilhar *polveelyahr* to sprinkle
polvo *polvoo* octopus
porco *porkoo* pork
–preto/ruivo *–pretoo/rrwivoo* type of pork that's more flavourful, more tender, juicier and darker in colour. The pig was originally a cross between a domesticated pig and a wild boar. Traditionally the pig is fed only acorns. (Alentejo, Ribatejo)
porto quente *portoo kengt* mulled port
posta *pohshtuh* steak
–à Mirandesa *–ah meerangdezuh* very thick cut of beef fillet, grilled (Trás-os-Montes)
pousada *pozahduh* type of government-run deluxe accommodation, often in a castle, monastery or palace, bound by law to offer regional specialities in their restaurant
prato de grão *prahtoo d grõw* chickpea stew flavoured with tomato, garlic, bay leaf and cumin; served with croutons (Algarve)
prato do dia *prahtoo do deeuh* a daily special
prato principal *prahtoo pringseepahl* main dish
pratos de barro cozido *prahtoozh d bahrroo koozeedoo* earthenware cooking dish

pratos completos *prahtoozh kongplehtoosh* complete plates; a dish with all the elements that would constitute a meal in itself
prego no pão *prehgoo no pōw* small steak sandwich
prego no prato *prehgoo no prahtoo* very small steak served with chips
presunto *prezoongtoo* smoked ham; prosciutto; Parma-type ham; a type of salt-cured ham
–de javali *–d zhuhvuhlee* **presunto** made from wild boar
–pata negra *–pahtuh negruh* cured ham from the leg of the **porco preto** (Alentejo)
púcara *pookuhruh* earthenware jug
pudim *pooding* pudding
–da casa *–duh kahzuh* 'house pudding'
–de café *–d kuhfeh* coffee flavoured pudding (Ribatejo)
–de leite *–d layt* custard-like pudding with lemon flavoured caramel sauce (Beiras)
–de malta *–d mahltuh* similar to flan but made with flour and cinnamon
–de maracujá *–d muhruhkoozhah* passionfruit pudding (Madeira)
–de ovos *–d ohvoozh* very eggy, baked custard-like pudding
–de queijo *–d kayzhoo* sweet pudding made with eggs beaten with soft fresh cheese and cinnamon
–do Abade de Priscos *–doo uhbahd d preeshkoozh* pudding made of egg yolks, thinly sliced smoked bacon, port, lemon and cinnamon; served in a caramel sauce (Minho)
–flan *–flang* caramel custard
–molotov *–molotohv* poached meringue with caramel sauce
puré *pooreh* puree
–de batata *–d buhtahtuh* potatoes that have been mashed
–de legumes *–d lgoomezh* vegetable puree

Q

queijada *kayzhahduh* family of small tarts with sweet, dense filling. Most varieties include fresh cheese or **requeijão** but may also have almonds or orange flavouring.
queijinho de Évora *kayzheenyoo d ehvooruh* salty hardened cheese made from the milk of sheep and goats
queijo *kayzhoo* cheese
–curado *–koorahdoo* aged cheese
–da Ilha *–duh eelyuh* cow's milk cheese, similar to sharp cheddar (Azores)
–da Serpa *–duh sehrpuh* sheep's milk cheese
–da Serra/Estrela *–duh sehrruh/shtreluh* popular cheese made from sheep's milk, so creamy it's wrapped in a cheese cloth to keep its shape; served by scooping the cheese out of its rind
–de Azeitão *–d uhzaytōw* soft, creamy, high quality cheese made from sheep's milk near the town of Azeitão (Ribatejo)
–de cabra *–d kahbruh* goat's milk cheese
–de Castelo Branco *–d kuhshtehloo brangkoo* sharp cheese made from the milk of sheep or goats
–de Nisa *–d neezuh* firm yellowish-white cured cheese with small air holes; gradually hardens as it ages
–de ovelha *–d ovelyuh* sheep's milk cheese
–de vaca *–d vahkuh* cow's milk cheese
–fresco *–freshkoo* very fine curd
–fundido *–foongdeedoo* processed cheese
–meio curado *–mayoo koorahdoo* semi-aged cheese
–picante *–peekangt* a strong cheese crusted with hot pimento powder
–saloio *–suhloyoo* firm cow's milk cheese
–seco *–sekoo* dry cheese similar in texture to parmesan
quente *kengt* hot
queque *kehk* plain yellow cupcake
quinta *kingtuh* farm or property that may produce wine

R

rabanadas *rruhbuhnahduhz* (*see* **fatias douradas**)
ralado *rruhlahdoo* grated
rancho *rranshoo* hearty stew of chickpeas, onion, potatoes, macaroni, veal trotters, pork belly, **chouriço** and beef (Minho)
raspa *rrahshpuh* grated
recheado/a *rresheeahdoo/uh* stuffed
recheio *rreshayoo* stuffing or filling
refeição *rrefaysõw* meal
–rápida *–rrahpeeduh* quick meal; fast food
refogado *rrfoogahdoo* process of making **cebolada**
refrigerante *rrefreezherangt* soft drink
região demarcada *rrzheeõw dmuhrkahduh* demarcated region (for wine)
regueifas *rrgayfuhzh* cinnamon and saffron flavoured biscuit rings (Minho)
rendinhas *rrengdeenyuhzh* almond nougat; resembles lace (Alentejo/Algarve)
requeijada *rrekayzhahduh* tart made with **requeijão**
requeijão *rrekayzhõw* fresh, ricotta style cheese made from whey
reserva *rrzehrvuh* reservation; high-quality (reserve) wine
restaurante *rreshtowrangt* restaurant
restaurante típico *rreshtowrangt teepeekoo* traditional restaurant required, by law, to serve typical regional food and wine and to offer traditional entertainment
rim *rring* kidney; a kidney-shaped eclair, with an egg custard or chocolate cream filling, topped with chocolate or vanilla icing
rissol *rreesohl* rissole; fried pasty
–de camarão *–d kuhmuhrõw* **rissol** with prawn filling
–de carne *–d kahrn* **rissol** with meat filling
–de peixe *–d paysh* **rissol** with fish filling
robalo *rroobahloo* sea bass
rocha *rrohshuh* large, soft spice biscuit
rodízio *rroodeeziw* Brazilian barbecue in which waiters come to tables serving various grilled meats on skewers; also includes cold salad buffet – this is an all-you-can-eat event
rojões *rroozhõyzh* spiced and marinated chunks of fried pork, which can be prepared in a variety of regional ways
rolo de carne *rroloo d kahrn* meatloaf
rosbife *rohzhbeef* roast beef

S

safio *suhfeeoo* conger eel
sal *sahl* salt
–fino *–feenoo* refined salt
–grosso *–grosoo* rock salt
salada *suhlahduh* salad
–de alface *–d ahlfahs* lettuce salad
–de atum *–d uhtoong* salad of tuna, potato, peas, carrots, boiled eggs in an olive oil and vinegar dressing
–de bacalhau com feijão frade *–d buhkuhlyow kong fayzhõw frahd* salad of shredded, uncooked salt cod and black-eyed peas in olive oil and vinegar dressing
–de feijão frade *–d fayzhõw frahd* black-eyed pea salad flavoured with onion, garlic, olive oil and vinegar; sprinkled with chopped boiled egg and parsley
–de frutas *–d frootuhzh* fruit salad
–de tomate *–d toomaht* tomato and onion salad, often flavoured with oregano
–mista *–meeshtuh* tomato, lettuce and onion salad
–russa *–rroosuh* potato salad with peas, carrots and lots of mayonnaise
salame de chocolate *suhluhm d shookoolaht* dense chocolate fudge roll studded with bits of biscuits made to look like salami; served sliced
salgadinho *sahlguhdeenyo* small savoury pastry

salgado/a *sahlgahdoo/uh* salty; small savoury pastry
salmão – *sahlmõw* salmon
–fumado *–foomahdoo* smoked salmon
salmonete *sahlmoonet* red mullet
salpicão *sahlpeekõw* thick smoked pork tenderloin sausage flavoured with garlic, bay leaf and sometimes wine
salsa *sahlsuh* parsley; flat-leaf parsley
salsicha *sahlseeshuh* sausage
–fresca *–freshkuh* fresh pork sausage
salteado/a *sahlteeahdoo/uh* sauteed
sálvia *sahlvyuh* sage
sandes *sangdzh* sandwich
–de atum *–d uhtoong* tuna sandwich
–de carne assada *–d kahrn uhsahduh* sliced roast meat sandwich
–de fiambre *–d feeangbr* ham sandwich
–de frango *–d frang-goo* sandwich made with chicken
–de omelete/ovo *–d ohmleht/ovoo* omelette/egg sandwich
–de panado *–d puhnahdoo* breaded pork cutlet sandwich
–de presunto *–d prezoongtoo* **presunto** sandwich
–de queijo *–d kayzhoo* cheese sandwich
–mista *–meeshtuh* a ham and cheese sandwich
sanduiche *sangdwish* sandwich (*see also* **sandes**)
santola *sangtohluh* spider crab
–recheada fria *–rresheeahduh freeuh* cooked crab mixed with chopped boiled egg, pickles, brandy and other seasonings. Then poured into the crab shell and served with butter and toast. (Estremadura)
sapateira *suhpuhtayruh* rock crab
sarda *sahrduh* mackerel
sardinha *suhrdeenyuh* sardine
sargo *sahrgoo* white bream
sarrabulho *suhrruhboolyoo* variety of meats cooked in pig's blood
sável *sahvehl* shad; herring
–na telha *–nuh tuhlyuh* **fataça na telha** made with herring
seco/a *sekoo/uh* dry; dried
semifrio *smeefreeoo* soft, ice cream-type dessert sometimes layered with a biscuit crust or cake; soft ice cream
sericá/sericaia *sreekah/sreekaiuh* very soft cake with an almost creamy texture served with a stewed plum in syrup (Alentejo)
sertã *sertang* earthenware frying pan
servir *serveer* to serve
simples *singplezh* plain; with no filling, icing or accompaniments
sobremesa *soobrmezuh* sweet; dessert; jam
solha *solyuh* flounder
sonhos *sohnyoozh* sweet fried dough, sprinkled with sugar and cinnamon
sopa *sopuh* soup
–à Alentejana *–ah uhlengtezhuhnuh* clear broth highly seasoned with coriander, garlic and olive oil; served with chunks of bread and sometimes a poached egg (Alentejo)
–azeda *–uhzeduh* soup made of beans, potatoes and sweet potatoes; flavoured with vinegar, garlic, bay leaf and cinnamon (Azores)
–de açorda *–d uhsorduh* (*see* **sopa à Alentejana**)
–de bacalhau dos campinos *–d buhkuhlyow doosh kangpeenoozh* layers of sliced onion, tomatoes, potatoes, garlic and thick salt cod steaks cooked in a casserole; served over bread that soaks up the excess cooking liquid (Ribatejo)
–de beldroegas *–d beldrweguhzh* purslane soup; served with poached eggs, fresh cheese or cured sheep's milk cheese
–de cação (or cação limado) *–d kuhsõw (kuhsõw leemahdoo)* thick pieces of dogfish cooked in a highly seasoned broth of garlic, coriander and vinegar; served over home-made bread (Alentejo)
–de castanhas piladas *–d kuhshtuhnyuhsh peelahduhsh* chestnut, bean and rice soup (Trás-os-Montes)

DICTIONARY

–de feijão *–d fayzhõw* soup made from dried pulses or beans

–de feijão frade *–d fayzhõw frahd* black-eyed pea soup flavoured with sausages; served over bread

–de feijão verde *–d fayzhõw verd* soup or stew made with green beans, onion, tomatoes and potatoes; often served over bread and with poached eggs (Ribatejo)

–de lebre *–d lehbr* hare soup with onion, parsley, bay leaf, sweet paprika and white wine. The stewed hare is served separately from the broth which is served over slices of bread. (Alentejo, Algarve)

–de legumes *–d lgoomezh* vegetable soup

–de mariscos *–d muhreeshkoosh* shellfish soup (Estremadura)

–de pedra *–d pehdruh* 'stone soup'; hearty vegetable soup with red beans, onions, potatoes, pig's ear, bacon and sausages and often served as a complete meal (Ribatejo)

–de peixe (**miga de peixe**) *–d paysh (meeguh d paysh)* variety of fish in a tomato and onion broth; served over chunks of bread

–de tomate *–d toomaht* tomato soup flavoured with sausages; served with pieces of bread. A lighter version is tomato soup served with pieces of bread and poached eggs and sometimes bits of **presunto**. (Alentejo)

–de trigo *–d treegoo* wheat soup

–do dia *–doo deeuh* soup of the day

–dourada *–dorahduh* slices of sponge cake covered with syrup of egg yolks and ground almonds (Minho)

–juliana *–zhooleeuhnuh* soup made with mixed, julienned vegetables

–rica de peixes *–rreekuh d payshezh* rich soup made of various kinds of fish, prawns and mussels

–seca *–sekuh* 'dry soup', so called because the soup is baked rather than boiled. It is similar to **cozida à Portuguesa** but has the addition of leftover pork fat.

spicy bread pudding served as a dessert

sorvete *soorvet* fruit or chocolate flavoured ice milk

sultanas *sooltuhnuhzh* sultanas; raisins

sumo *soomoo* juice

–de laranja natural *–d luhrangzhuh nuhtoorahl* freshly squeezed orange juice

supermercado *soopehrmerkahdoo* supermarket

T

taberna *tuhbehrnuh* tavern

tamboril *tangbooreel* monkfish

tarte de amêndoa *tahrt d amengdwuh* thin cake base covered with slivered almonds and caramel glaze

tarte de maçã/ananás *tahrt d muhsang/uhnuhnahzh* sliced apples or pineapple on a flaky pastry crust, topped with gelatine glaze

tasca *tahshkuh* local eatery or small local tavern (usually inexpensive)

tasquinha *tuhshkeenyuh* small tavern

tecolameco *tehkooluhmehkoo* rich and sweet orange and almond cake, well loved around Portalegre (Alentejo)

temperar *tengprahr* to season

tempero *tengperoo* flavouring

ticket restaurante *teekeht rreshtowrangt* restaurants that offer discount to ticket holders, providing simple, traditional and inexpensive food

tigela *teezhehluh* small earthenware bowl

tigelada *teezhelahduh* firm egg custard flavoured with vanilla, lemon or cinnamon, baked in a **tigela**

tomate *toomaht* tomato

tomilho *toomeelyoo* thyme

tornedó *toorndoh* thick, tender steak

torrada *toorrahduh* toast

torresmos *toorrezhmoozh* pork cracklings served hot or cold as a snack

torta *tohrtuh* torte; jelly roll with filling
–de laranja *–d luhrangzhuh* rolled orange flavoured torte made with lots of eggs and little or no flour
–de Viana *–d veeuhnuh* jelly roll filled with jam; egg yolk icing
tortulhos *toortoolyoosh* sheep's tripe stuffed with more sheep's tripe (Estremadura)
tosta *tohshtuh* pieces of toast cut into triangles and usually served with a dip or sauce
–mista *–meeshtuh* toasted ham and cheese sandwich
toucinho *toseenyoo* bacon
–do-céu *–do-sehoo* 'bacon from heaven'; a rich, cinnamon flavoured dessert cake made of eggs and pumpkin or spaghetti squash (Alentejo)
–fumado *–foomahdoo* smoked bacon
–rançoso *–rrangsozoo* cake made with almonds and lots of egg yolks; sprinkled with sugar and cinnamon (Alentejo)
–salgado *–sahlgahdo* salt-cured bacon
trança *trangsuh* pastry topped with coconut mixture and chopped nuts
Transmontana, à *ah trangzhmongtuhnuh* Trás-os-Montes style; a rich and hearty dish usually flavoured with sausages and other meat, along with lots of garlic and onion
travessa *truhvehsuh* serving platter
tremoços *trmohsoosh* salted, preserved yellow beans eaten as a snack
trinchar *tringshahr* to slice
tripas *treepuhzh* tripe
–à moda do Porto *–ah mohduh doo portoo* slow-cooked dish of dried beans, trotters, tripe, chicken, vegetables, sausages and cumin (Porto)
trouxas de ovos *troshuh d ohvoozh* poached thin layers of beaten egg yolk rolled into little bundles and soaked in sugar syrup (Caldas da Rainha)
truta *trootuh* trout
–de escabeche *–d shkuhbbehsh* trout is prepared as **escabeche**, then fried and a garlic, onion and parsley dressing is poured over. Served cold with boiled potatoes (Beiras)
túberas com ovos *toobruhzh kong ohvoozh* sliced tubers fried with onion, bay leaf and eggs (Alentejo)
túberas de fricassé *toobruhzh d freekuhseh* (*see* **túberas com ovos**)

U

untar *oongtahr* to baste
uvas *oovuhzh* grapes

V

vapor à *ah vuhpor* steamed
veado *veeahdoo* venison
velhoses *vlyohzezh* orange and brandy flavoured pumpkin fritters (Ribatejo)
verde *verd* unripe (fruit)
vinagre *veenahgr* vinegar
–de vinho *–d veenyoo* wine vinegar
vinha d'alhos *veenyuh d ahlyoozh* meat marinated in wine or vinegar, olive oil, garlic and bay leaf
vinho *veenyoo* wine
–a copo *–uh kohpoo* wine by the glass
–branco *–brangkoo* white wine
–da casa *–duh kahzuh* house wine
–da Madeira *–duh muhdayruh* Madeira wine
–da região *–duh rrezheeõw* local wine
–de maduro *–d muhdooroo* mature
–de reserva *–d rrzehrvuh* reserve or high quality wine
–do porto *–doo portoo* port: fortified wine produced in the Demarcated Region of the Douro under special conditions. Port has an alcohol content of 19–22%.
–do porto branco *–doo portoo brangkoo* dry white port, often consumed as an aperitif
–do porto crusted *–doo portoo kruhsteed* port aged in wood casks for two or three years; should be consumed three or four years after being bottled

–do porto ruby *–doo portoo rroobee* ruby port; blend of old and young wines; tends to be sweeter than tawny port

–do porto tawny *–doo portoo tohnee* amber-coloured port aged in wood casks for 10, 20 or 30 years; has a velvety consistency

–jarra pequena/grande *–zhahrruh pkenuh/grangd* small/large wine jug

–quente *–kengt* mulled wine

–rosé *–rroze* rosé wine

–tinto *–tingtoo* red wine

–verde *–verd* 'green wine'; light sparkling red, white or rosé wine

vintage porto *vangtahzh portoo* port of superior quality produced in a declared vintage year; best consumed immediately upon opening

Vitela (assada) *veetehluh (uhsahduh)* (roast) veal

vodka laranja *vohdkuh luhrangzhuh* vodka and orange

X

xerém *shrãy* cornmeal porridge; can be served with shellfish, **chouriço**, pork or other meat

Recommended Reading

Anderson, Jean *The Food of Portugal* Hearst Books (1994)

Feibleman, Peter, et al *The Cooking of Spain and Portugal* Time-Life International (1976)

Goldstein, Joyce *Savouring Spain and Portugal* Five Mile Press (2000)

Instituto da Vinha e do Vinho *Vinhos e Aguardentes de Portugal*

de Lourdes Modesto, Maria *Traditional Portuguese Cooking* Verbo (1989)

Saramago, Alfredo *Para uma Historia da Alimentação no Alentejo* Assírio & Alvim (1997)

Vieira, Edite *The Taste of Portugal* Grub Street (1995)

Photo Credits

Paul Bernhardt	p63 top right, p99 top left, p106, p129, p147, p205 top left, p205 bottom right.
Carlos Costa	p95, p99 top right, p100, p105, p113 left, p136, p193, p210.
Greg Elms	p42, p48, p60, p109, p111, p118, p130, p144, p205 bottom left, p198.
Mason Florence	p94.
John S King	p1, p185 left.
Gerry Reilly	p113 top right.
Oliver Strewe	p23 top right, p39, p58-59, p82-83, p195 bottom left.
Brenda Turnidge	p13.
Vitor Vieira	p205 top right.
Julia Wilkinson	p99 bottom left, p160.

A

B

C

INDEX

H

I

K

L

M

INDEX

Q

R

S

Boxed Text

Maps

Recipes

MORE WORLD FOOD TITLES

Brimming with cultural insight, the World Food series takes the guesswork out of new cuisines and provides the ideal guide to your own culinary adventures. These books cover the full spectrum of food and drink in each country – the history and evolution of the cuisine, its staples & specialities, and the kitchen philosophy of the people. You'll find definitive two way dictionaries, menu readers, useful phrases for shopping, drunken apologies, and much more.

The World Food series is the essential guide for travelling and non-travelling food lovers across the globe.

The Lonely Planet Story

Lonely Planet published its first book in 1973 in response to the numerous 'How did you do it?' questions Maureen and Tony Wheeler were asked after driving, bussing, hitching, sailing and railing their way from England to Australia. Written at a kitchen table and hand collated, trimmed and stapled, Across Asia on the Cheap became an instant local bestseller.

Eighteen months in South-East Asia resulted in their second guide, South-East Asia on a Shoestring, which they put together in a backstreet Chinese hotel in Singapore in 1975. The 'yellow bible', as it quickly became known to backpackers around the world, soon became the guide to the region. It has sold well over 3/4 million copies and is now in its 10th edition, still retaining its familiar yellow cover.

Today there are over 400 titles, including travel guides, walking guides, language kits & phrasebooks, travel atlases & maps, diving guides, first time travel guides, condensed guides, illustrated pictorials and travel literature. The company is the largest independent travel publisher in the world.

The emphasis continues to be on travel for independent travellers. Tony and Maureen still travel for several months of each year and play an active part in the writing, updating and quality control of Lonely Planet's guides.

They have been joined by over 120 authors and over 400 staff at our offices in Melbourne (Australia), Oakland (USA), London (UK) and Paris (France). Travellers themselves also make a valuable contribution to the guides through the feedback we receive in thousands of letters each year and on our web site.

The people at Lonely Planet strongly believe that travellers can make a positive contribution to the countries they visit, both through their appreciation of the countries' culture, wildlife and natural features, and through the money they spend. In addition, the company makes a direct contribution to the countries and regions it covers. Since 1986 a percentage of the income from each book has been donated to ventures such as famine relief in Africa; aid projects in India; agricultural projects in Central America; Greenpeace's efforts to halt French nuclear testing in the Pacific.

Lonely Planet Offices

Australia
90 Maribyrnong St, Footscray, Victoria, 3011
☎ 03 8379 8000
fax 03 8379 8111
email: talk2us@lonelyplanet.com.au

USA
150 Linden St, Oakland, CA 94607
☎ 510 893 8555 TOLL FREE: 800 275 8555
fax 510 893 8572
email: info@lonelyplanet.com

UK
10a Spring Place, London NW5 3BH
☎ 020 7428 4800
fax 020 7428 4828
email: go@lonelyplanet.co.uk

France
1 rue du Dahomey, 75011 Paris
☎ 01 55 25 33 00
fax 01 55 25 33 01
email: bip@lonelyplanet.fr